ISLANDS Contemporary architecture on water

Zeitgenössische Architektur am Wasser INSELN

ÎLES Architecture contemporaine sur l'eau

Mark Fletcher

ISLANDS Contemporary architecture on water

Zeitgenössische Architektur am Wasser INSELN

ÎLES Architecture contemporaine sur l'eau

h.f.ullmann

previous page Mur Island in Graz, Austria—a restaurant and theater space designed by Vito Acconci.

Vorherige Seite Die Insel in der Mur in Graz, Österreich – ein Restaurant und eine Theaterfläche nach einem Entwurf von Vito Acconci.

page précédente Île de Mur à Graz, Autriche. Un restaurant et un théâtre conçus par Vito Acconci.

right Foster + Partners' design for Crystal Island in Moscow, Russia.

rechts Foster + Partners Entwurf für die Kristallinsel in Moskau, Russland.

droite Conception de Foster + Partners' pour l'Île de Cristal à Moscou, Russie.

Contents/Inhaltsverzeichnis/Sommaire

Introduction
Einleitung
Introduction

left Museum of Islamic Art, Doha, Qatar, by I. M. Pei.

links Museum für Islamische Kunst, Doha, Katar, entworfen von I.M. Pei.

gauche Musée d'art islamique, Doha, Qatar, d'I.M. Pei.

Introduction

Throughout history people have existed near water. In the past, the primary reasons for building on water were to do with defense (naval bases, fortresses, prisons), economics (ports, dockyards), and religion (temples, shrines). Ease of access to water would aid trade and communications, encourage irrigation, and facilitate drainage. Not surprisingly, nearly all the great cities were built near the sea or on rivers and many of those were on islands.

One of the most impressive early examples of a man-made island city is Tenochtitlan in Mexico. The Aztec seat, which was founded in the 14th century, used the *chinampa* system to expand an original small, swampy island in the middle of Lake Texcoco into a city for 200,000 people. These were artificial islands consisting of wattle-fenced rectangles filled with mud and sediment and secured by willow trees grown in the corners. Causeways with wooden drawbridges linked the island to the lake's shore.

In Europe, Venice was a great maritime power from the 13th to the 17th centuries. The "City of Water" is situated in the middle of a saltwater lagoon. Where once there was just marshland, new islands were built and existing ones were extended, turning waterways into canals and building foundations by driving closely spaced wooden piles into the mud. The Netherlands, too, has a long tradition of building over water. During the Golden Age of Amsterdam in the 17th century, a complex system of canals and dikes was constructed to protect buildings from flooding and allow ships direct access to the city. In the same period, fortified ports with city walls, canals, and moats were constructed along the rivers and coasts of Europe, in Livorno, Antwerp, Gothenburg, and elsewhere. Here the "island city" was an effective means of defense.

Island buildings were also used in this way. A common type was the moated fort, castle, or manor house, popular in the Middle Ages. Water was an effective defensive mechanism, preventing attackers from digging tunnels, or bringing siege weapons close to the walls. Leeds Castle in Kent, England, is a spectacular example, sitting on two islands surrounded by the waters of River Len. Like most castles, the only access was by a wooden drawbridge. Moated castles were also common in Asia. The two most famous examples were the Japanese Imperial Palace in Tokyo and the Forbidden City in Beijing.

On the other hand, island buildings were often spiritual places. A very early example was at Hadrian's Villa in Tivoli. Created as a retreat for the Roman Emperor in the 2nd Century AD, it included a circular *nymphaeum* complete with surrounding canal and two wooden swing bridges. This personal architectural complex, with fountain, dining rooms, bathroom, and library, was a place where Hadrian could isolate himself from the outside world.

In Japanese culture there is a reverence for seascapes so shrines are often designed around a water landscape. The Itsukushima shinto shrine in Japan, dating back to the 6th century, is built on a sacred island. Its dramatic wooden gate, or *torii*, is one of Japan's most popular sites—at high tide it appears to be floating. Similarly, Mont-Saint-Michel, in Normandy, France, became home to a monastery in the 8th century. At high tides, the steep rocky island became completely enclosed by the sea. The Golden Temple at Amritsar, in northern India, built in 1604 is the principal Sikh place of worship. It sits in the middle of a man-made sacred lake, its gleaming spires reflected in the waters.

By the 20th century the reasons for building on water had changed. Many leading modern architects now saw water as a design device. By surrounding buildings with a man-made shallow pond, it was possible to use the reflective power of water to enhance the iconic aspect of a museum, opera house, or parliament building. Water could be used symbolically, linking a building to its environment. Or it might simply be a device to isolate a structure from the surrounding landscape, a way to make it stand out from the crowd—a sort of metaphorical island.

Frank Lloyd Wright's famous house in Pennsylvania, Fallingwater (1935), sits above a waterfall. Its cantilevered stone and concrete terraces are set off against the drama of the cascading water. In the 1950s in Brazil, Oscar Niemeyer constructed pools around many of his government buildings in Brasília. Itamaraty Palace, the Foreign Office, is almost completely encircled by water and ornamental tropical plants serve to soften the effect of its great arches. Louis I. Kahn was also a pioneer in this respect, most notably in Bangladesh where he built the National Assembly Building in Dhaka (1982). A created lake on three sides of the Bhaban not only refers to the natural beauty of Bangladesh with its networks of rivers, but also serves to enhance the striking

brick and concrete façades. Later, the Japanese architect Tadao Ando would acknowledge Kahn when he built the Modern Art Museum of Fort Worth (2002) next to his Kimbell Art Museum (1972). Ando designed concrete and glass pavilions set within reflecting ponds.

The World Expos of the 20th century have had a considerable influence on ideas about designing on water. These large public national exhibitions have allowed architects the freedom to try out new ideas ever since the Chicago World's Fair in 1893 combined classical architecture, lagoons, and canals. At Expo '67 in Montreal, the existing Ile Ste-Hélène was enlarged while a new artificial island, the Ile Notre-Dame, was created alongside. In 1970 at Osaka, the Japanese artist Fujiko Nakaya exhibited a fog sculpture, which was later to influence Diller Scofidio + Renfro's island design, Blur Building, for the Swiss Expo.02 in Yverdon-les-Bains, Switzerland. Kiyonori Kikutake designed a floating future city called "Aquapolis" for the Okinawa Expo in 1975, and in Vancouver in 1986 the Canadian Pavilion, built on an existing pier with its Teflon roofing fabric, resembled a giant ocean liner. All these experiments helped develop ideas of what to build on water.

Today, the trend for island architecture is also a reflection of changes in the world's economy and environment. Rich Gulf states are investing billions in new islands in an attempt to build a future economy based on tourism and culture. Japan, a mountainous country with heavily built up coastal areas, is pioneering the realization of artificial islands. New York and San Francisco are two major cities among many planning to redevelop abandoned islands off their shores. And low-lying countries, in particular the Netherlands, are constantly investigating solutions to combating rising sea levels and consequent flooding.

Now more than ever water is featuring in the most advanced and challenging architectural designs. We no longer think of ports, rivers, and canals as purely functional places, but see them as desirable places to live and visit. Rivers that before had served to clear sewage are now clean, old warehouses once used to store goods are now apartments, abandoned power plants have become museums. People are drawn more and more to coexisting with water.

This book looks at the architecture of built and yet-to-be-realized island structures and shows how water has become the new frontier. Many different types of island are featured and each of the nearly 50 projects, many by leading architects, represents some of the most innovative contemporary architecture in the world. Seven thematic chapters look at all aspects of the subject, from modest villas to ambitious masterplans. Some of the projects are islands themselves, others are on islands, a few have islands within them, and many are simply perched at the water's edge. Some are good examples of sustainable design, for others water simply acts as a dramatic feature. They offer a glimpse into the future of architecture, engineering, and urban development, and show the infinite possibilities of island living.

Einleitung

Seit jeher haben Menschen neben Wasser gelebt. In der Vergangenheit wurden Bauten am oder auf dem Wasser hauptsächlich aus Gründen der Verteidigung (Flottenstützpunkte, Festungen, Gefängnisse), der Wirtschaft (Häfen, Werften) und der Religion (Tempel, Schreine) errichtet. Der einfache Zugang zum Wasser förderte Handel und Kommunikation, half bei der Bewässerung und vereinfachte die Entwässerung. Es überrascht daher nicht, dass fast alle großen Städte in der Nähe des Meeres oder an Flüssen erbaut wurden und viele davon sich auf Inseln befanden.

Eines der beeindruckendsten frühen Beispiele einer künstlich angelegten Insel ist Tenochtitlán in Mexiko. Der Regierungssitz der Azteken, der im 14. Jahrhundert gegründet wurde, machte sich das System der *chinampa* zu Nutze, um eine ursprünglich kleine, morastige Insel in der Mitte des Texcoco-Sees in eine Stadt für 200.000 Einwohner auszubauen. Diese *chinampa* waren künstliche Inseln aus mit Flechtwerk eingezäunten Rechtecken, die mit Schlamm und Sedimenten aufgefüllt wurden und mit in den Ecken angepflanzten Weidenbäumen befestigt wurden. Die Inseln waren über Dammstraßen mit hölzernen Zugbrücken mit dem Ufer des Sees verbunden.

In Europa war Venedig vom 13. bis zum 17. Jahrhundert die bedeutende Seemacht. Die „Wasserstadt" liegt in der Mitte einer Salzwasserlagune. Wo sich einst nur Marschland befand, wurden neue Inseln angelegt und bestehende erweitert, Wasserwege in Kanäle umgewandelt und Fundamente aus eng beieinander liegenden Holzpfosten angelegt, die in den Schlamm gerammt wurden. Auch die Niederlande haben eine lange Tradition des Bauens über Wasser. Während des Goldenen Zeitalters von Amsterdam im 17. Jahrhundert wurde ein komplexes System von Kanälen und Deichen angelegt, um Gebäude vor Überflutung zu schützen und Schiffen unmittelbaren Zugang zur Stadt zu gewähren. Zur gleichen Zeit wurden entlang der Flüsse und Küsten Europas befestigte Häfen mit Stadtmauern, Kanälen und Wassergräben erbaut, so etwa in Livorno, Antwerpen oder Göteborg. Hier diente die „Inselstadt" als wirksames Mittel zur Verteidigung.

Inselgebäude wurden auf dieselbe Weise genutzt. Von Wassergräben umgebene Festungen, Burgen oder Herrenhäuser waren vor allem im Mittelalter beliebte, häufig auftretende Gebäudetypen. Wasser diente als wirksamer Verteidigungsmechanismus, der Angreifer davon abhielt, Tunnel zu graben oder Belagerungswaffen nahe an die Mauern zu schaffen. Leeds Castle in Kent, England, das auf zwei Inseln erbaut wurde und vom Wasser des Flusses Len umgeben ist, ist ein spektakuläres Beispiel dafür. Wie bei den meisten Burgen bot eine hölzerne Zugbrücke den einzigen Zugang. Burgen mit Wassergräben fanden sich gewöhnlich auch in Asien. Die beiden berühmtesten Beispiele waren der japanische Kaiserpalast in Tokio und die Verbotene Stadt in Peking.

Andererseits waren Inselgebäude häufig auch religiöse Orte. Ein sehr frühes Beispiel ist die Hadriansvilla in Tivoli. Die im 2. Jahrhundert n.Chr. als Zufluchtsort für den römischen Kaiser erbaute Villa schloss auch ein kreisförmiges *Nymphaeum* mit einem umgebenden Kanal und zwei hölzernen Schwingbrücken mit ein. Dieser private architektonische Komplex mit Springbrunnen, Speisezimmern, Badezimmer und Bibliothek war ein Ort, an dem Hadrian sich vor der äußerlichen Welt zurückziehen konnte.

In der japanischen Kultur werden Seenlandschaften verehrt, so dass Schreine oft um eine Wasserlandschaft herum gestaltet werden. Der Itsukushima-Schinto-Schrein in Japan aus dem 6. Jahrhundert ist auf einer heiligen Insel erbaut. Sein beeindruckend dramatisches hölzernes Tor oder *torii* ist eines der beliebtesten Sehenswürdigkeiten Japans - bei Flut scheint es auf dem Wasser zu schwimmen. Auf ähnliche Weise wurde auf dem Mont Saint-Michel in der französischen Normandie im 8. Jahrhundert ein Kloster errichtet. Bei Flut war die steil aufragende, felsige Insel ganz vom Meer umschlossen. Der Goldene Tempel von Amritsar in Nordindien, der 1604 erbaut wurde, ist das wichtigste Heiligtum der Sikh. Er befindet sich in der Mitte eines künstlich angelegten heiligen Sees, wobei sich seine glänzenden Türme im Wasser spiegeln.

Bis zum 20. Jahrhundert hatten sich die Gründe für den Bau von Gebäuden auf dem Wasser verändert. Viele führende moderne Architekten verstanden Wasser jetzt als Mittel der Kunst. Indem sie Gebäude mit einem künstlich angelegten, flachen See umgaben, konnten sie die spiegelnde Eigenschaft des Wassers zur Verstärkung der symbolhaften Wirkung eines Museums, Opernhauses oder Parlamentsgebäudes nutzen. Wasser konnte symbolisch verwendet werden, um

ein Gebäude mit seiner Umgebung zu verbinden. Oder es konnte ganz einfach ein Mittel sein, um ein Bauwerk von der umgebenden Landschaft zu isolieren, es aus der Masse hervorzuheben – eine Art metaphorische Insel.

Frank Lloyd Wrights berühmtes Haus in Pennsylvania, Fallingwater (1935), liegt über einem Wasserfall. Seine auskragenden Stein- und Betonterrassen heben sich von der dramatischen Wirkung des fallenden Wassers ab. Oscar Niemeyer legte in den Fünfziger Jahren in Brasilien Becken um viele Regierungsgebäude in der Hauptstadt Brasilia an. Der Itamaraty-Palast, in dem sich das Auswärtige Amt befindet, ist nahezu vollkommen von Wasser umgeben und tropische Zierpflanzen mildern die Wirkung der großen Bögen. Louis I. Kahn war in dieser Hinsicht ebenfalls ein Vorreiter, insbesondere in Bangladesh, wo er das Gebäude der Nationalversammlung in Dhaka (1982) erbaute. Ein künstlicher See auf drei Seiten der Bhaban verweist nicht nur auf die natürliche Schönheit Bangladeshs mit seinem Netz aus Flüssen, sondern soll auch die Wirkung der auffallenden Fassaden aus Ziegeln und Beton verstärken. Später sollte der japanische Architekt Tadao Ando Kahn Anerkennung zollen, als er das Modern Art Museum in Fort Worth (2002) neben seinem Kimbell Art Museum (1972) erbaute. Ando entwarf Pavillons aus Beton und Glas inmitten spiegelnder Seen.

Die Weltausstellungen des 20. Jahrhunderts hatten einen maßgeblichen Einfluss auf Ideen für Bauwerke auf dem Wasser. Seit die Weltausstellung in Chicago im Jahre 1893 klassische Architektur mit Lagunen und Kanälen verband, boten diese großen öffentlichen National-ausstellungen Architekten die Freiheit, neue Ideen auszuprobieren. Bei der Expo '67 in Montréal wurde die bestehende Île Ste-Hélène vergrößert, während unmittelbar daneben eine neue künstliche Insel, die Île Notre-Dame, angelegt wurde. 1970 stellte der japanische Künstler Fujiko Nakaya in Osaka eine Nebelskulptur aus, die später Diller Scofidio + Renfros Inseldesign Blur Building auf der schweizerischen Expo.02 in Yverdon-les-Bains beeinflussen sollte. Kiyonori Kikutake entwarf für die Expo 1975 in Okinawa eine schwimmende Zukunftsstadt namens „Aquapolis", und der kanadische Pavillon auf der Expo 1986 in Vancouver, der auf mit seinem Dachbezug aus Teflon auf einem vorhandenen Pier errichtet wurde, glich einem gigantischen Ozeandampfer. All diese Experimente trugen zur Entwicklung von Ideen bei, wie auf Wasser gebaut werden könnte.

Heute spiegelt der Trend zur Inselarchitektur auch die wirtschaftlichen und umweltbezogenen Veränderungen der Welt wider. In einem Versuch, die Wirtschaft der Zukunft auf der Grundlage von Tourismus und Kultur aufzubauen, investieren reiche Golfstaaten Milliarden in neue Inseln. Japan, ein bergiges Land mit stark bebauten Küstenregionen, ist Vorreiter bei der Anlage künstlicher Inseln. New York und San Francisco sind zwei wichtige große Städte unter vielen, die verlassene Inseln vor ihren Küsten umbauen und nutzen werden. Und niedrig liegende Länder, insbesondere die Niederlande, suchen stetig nach Lösungen, um gegen den steigenden Meeresspiegel und die daraus folgenden Überflutungen anzukämpfen.

Wasser spielt daher mehr denn je zuvor eine Rolle in den fortgeschrittensten und ehrgeizigsten architektonischen Entwürfen. Wir verstehen Häfen, Flüsse und Kanäle nicht mehr nur als rein funktionale Orte, sondern als begehrte Wohnorte und Sehenswürdigkeiten. Flüsse, die zuvor zur Abwasserentsorgung dienten, sind jetzt sauber, alte Speicher-häuser, die einst zur Lagerung von Waren genutzt wurden, werden als Apartments genutzt und verlassene Kraftwerke werden in Museen umgewandelt. Menschen fühlen sich mehr und mehr zum Leben am und mit Wasser hingezogen.

Dieses Buch beschäftigt sich mit der Architektur bereits gebauter und noch umzusetzender Inselstrukturen und zeigt, inwiefern Wasser zu einer neuen Grenze geworden ist. Es beschreibt viele verschiedene Arten von Inseln, und jedes der nahezu 50 Projekte - viele davon Entwürfe führender Architekten - repräsentiert eine der innovativsten zeitgenössischen architektonischen Projekte der Welt. Sieben thematische Kapitel befassen sich mit allen Aspekten des Themas, von bescheidenen Villen bis hin zu anspruchsvollen Masterplänen. Einige der Projekte sind selbst Inseln, andere befinden sich auf Inseln, wieder andere haben Inseln in ihnen und viele wurden einfach am Rand des Wassers erbaut. Einige sind gute Beispiele für nachhaltiges Design, bei anderen dient Wasser einfach als dramatisches Element. Sie bieten Einblick in die Zukunft der Architektur, des Ingenieurwesens und der Städteplanung, und zeigen die unendlichen Möglichkeiten des Insellebens.

Introduction

De tout temps, les hommes ont vécu à proximité de l'eau. Auparavant, les principales raisons qui poussaient à construire sur l'eau étaient liées à la défense (bases navales, forteresses, prisons), à l'économie (ports, quais) et à la religion (temples, sanctuaires). La facilité d'accès favorisait le commerce et les communications, encourageait l'irrigation et simplifiait le drainage. Il n'est donc pas surprenant que la majorité des grandes villes aient été construites à proximité de la mer ou de fleuves. La plupart se trouvaient même sur des îles.

Un des premiers exemples, mais non le moindre, de ville flottante artificielle est Tenochtitlan, au Mexique. Le siège aztèque, fondé au XIVe siècle, s'est servi de la technique des chinampas pour étendre une petite île originale, dans les marais, au milieu du lac de Texcoco, en une ville de 200.000 habitants. Ces petites îles artificielles consistaient en des rectangles clôturés de bois, remplis de boue et de sédiment et sécurisés par des saules plantés aux quatre coins. Des passerelles avec des ponts-levis en bois reliaient l'île à la rive du lac.

Du XIIIe au XVIIe siècle en Europe, Venise était une grande puissance maritime. La « ville d'eau » se trouve au milieu d'un lagon d'eau salée. Il n'y avait à l'époque que des marais mais de nouvelles îles furent construites. Les îles existantes furent étendues, transformant les voies navigables en canaux. Les fondations furent réalisées avec des tas de bois peu espacés posés dans la boue. À l'Âge d'Or d'Amsterdam, au XVIIe siècle, un système complexe de canaux et de digues fut mis en place pour protéger les bâtiments des inondations et laisser aux navires un accès direct à la ville. Durant la même période, des ports fortifiés de remparts, de canaux et de fossés furent construits le long des fleuves et des côtes d'Europe, à Livourne, Anvers, Göteborg et d'autres villes. Ici, la « ville flottante » était un moyen de défense efficace.

Les bâtiments flottants jouaient également le rôle de défense. Les forts, châteaux et manoirs entourés de fossés étaient relativement fréquents et populaires au Moyen-âge. L'eau était un mécanisme de défense naturel qui empêchait les assaillants de creuser des tunnels ou d'apporter leurs armes à proximité des murs. Le château de Leeds, à Kent, en Angleterre, est un exemple exceptionnel, posé sur deux îles entourées du fleuve Len. Comme la plupart des châteaux, le seul accès se fait par un pont-levis en bois. Les châteaux entourés de fossés étaient également fréquents en Asie. Les deux exemples les plus célèbres sont le Palais impérial japonais à Tokyo et la Ville interdite de Pékin.

Souvent, les constructions flottantes étaient également des lieux spirituels. Un des premiers exemples est la Villa d'Hadrien, à Tivoli. Créée comme retraite de l'Empereur romain au IIe siècle avant J.-C., elle se caractérise par un numphaion entouré d'un canal et deux ponts tournants en bois. Ce complexe architectural personnel, avec sa fontaine, ses salles à manger, sa salle de bain et sa bibliothèque, permettait à Hadrien de s'isoler du monde extérieur.

Dans la culture japonaise, les paysages marins sont très respectés et les sanctuaires sont souvent érigés à proximité de l'eau. Le sanctuaire shinto d'Itsukushima au Japon, datant du VIe siècle, est bâti une île sacrée. Son imposante porte en bois, ou torii, est l'un des sites japonais les plus populaires. Il semble flotter à marée haute. De la même manière, le Mont-Saint-Michel, situé dans la région de Normandie, en France, a accueilli un monastère au VIIIe siècle. À marée haute, l'île raide et rocailleuse est entièrement entourée par la mer. Le Temple d'Or, construit en 1604 à Amritsar au nord de l'Inde, est le lieu principal lieu de culte sikh. Situé au milieu d'un lac sacré artificiel, ses pointes brillantes se reflètent dans l'eau.

Au XXe siècle, les raisons qui incitent à construire sur l'eau ont changé. De nombreux architectes modernes de renommée internationale considèrent à présent l'eau comme un outil de conception. En entourant les bâtiments d'un bassin artificiel peu profond, le pouvoir réfléchissant de l'eau peut être utilisé pour améliorer l'aspect iconique d'un musée, d'un opéra ou d'un parlement. L'eau pourrait être employée de manière symbolique, reliant un bâtiment à son environnement. Elle pourrait aussi simplement être un outil permettant d'isoler une structure de son paysage environnant, un moyen de le distinguer de la foule, une sorte d'île métaphorique.

La célèbre maison de Fallinwater (1935) de Frank Lloyd Wright, en Pennsylvanie, siège au dessus d'une chute d'eau. Ses terrasses de pierre et de béton en porte-à-faux contrastent face aux cascades. Dans les années 1950 au Brésil, Oscar Niemeyer bâtit des piscines autour de plusieurs

de ses bâtiments gouvernementaux à Brasilia. Le Palais d'Itamaraty, siège de la diplomatie brésilienne, est presque entièrement entouré d'eau et les plantes tropicales ornementales adoucissent l'effet de ses arches imposantes. Louis I. Kahn était également un pionnier en la matière, particulièrement au Bangladesh où il construisit le bâtiment de l'Assemblée nationale à Dhaka (1982). Le Bhaban est entouré d'un lac artificiel sur trois côtés, ce qui ne fait pas uniquement référence à la beauté naturelle du Bangladesh avec ses réseaux de fleuves, mais permet également d'améliorer les façades frappantes de brique et de béton. Plus tard, l'architecte japonais Tadao Ando remerciait Louis I. Kahn lorsqu'il construisit le Musée d'art moderne de Fort Worth (2002), à côté de son Kimbell Art Museum (1972). Tadao Ando a conçu des pavillons de verre et de béton au milieu de bassins réfléchissants.

Les expositions universelles du XXe siècle ont considérablement influencé les idées de construction sur l'eau. Ces grandes expositions publiques nationales ont permis aux architectes de tenter de nouvelles idées depuis l'exposition universelle de Chicago en 1893, qui combinait architecture classique, lagons et canaux. Lors de l'exposition universelle de Montréal en 1970, l'Île Sainte-Hélène existante fut élargie tandis qu'une nouvelle île artificielle, l'Île Notre-Dame, était créée à côté. En 1970 à Osaka, l'artiste japonais Fujiko Nakaya a exposé une sculpture de brume qui allait plus tard influencer la conception de l'île de Diller Scofidio + Renfro, le Bâtiment Blur, pour l'exposition universelle de Suisse en 2002 à Yverdon-les-Bains. Kiyonori Kikutake a conçu une ville flottante future dénommée « Aquapolis » pour l'exposition d'Okinawa en 1975, et le Pavillon canadien à Vancouver en 1986, conçu sur un embarcadère existant avec une toiture en Téflon, ressemblant à un paquebot géant. Toutes ces expérimentations ont permis de développer des idées de construction sur l'eau.

Aujourd'hui, la tendance de l'architecture flottante est également un reflet des changements de l'économie mondiale et de l'environnement. Les riches États du Golfe investissent des milliards dans de nouvelles îles afin de bâtir une économie future basée sur le tourisme et la culture. Le Japon, pays montagneux aux zones côtières lourdement construites, est le premier à réaliser des îles artificielles. New York et San Francisco sont deux grandes villes parmi

d'autres à redévelopper des îles abandonnées de leurs côtes. Et les pays à basse latitude, notamment les Pays-Bas, recherchent continuellement des solutions pour affronter la montée du niveau de l'eau et les inondations qui en résultent.

Aujourd'hui plus que jamais l'eau apparaît dans la plupart des conceptions architecturales ambitieuses et avancées. Nous ne considérons plus les ports, les fleuves et les canaux uniquement comme des lieux fonctionnels mais comme des endroits pour vivre et à visiter. Les fleuves qui servaient auparavant à évacuer les eaux usées sont désormais propres, les vieux entrepôts qui servaient autrefois au stockage sont aujourd'hui des appartements, et les centrales abandonnées sont transformées en musées. L'homme est de plus en plus attiré par l'eau.

Cet ouvrage étudie l'architecture des structures existantes et futures et présente la manière dont l'eau s'est transformée en nouvelle frontière. De nombreux types d'îles sont présentés ici et chacun des projets, sur les près de 50, la plupart conçus par des architectes renommés, représentent une architecture contemporaine des plus innovantes au monde. Divisé en sept chapitres thématiques, ce livre analyse tous les aspects du sujet, d'une villa modeste à un plan directeur ambitieux. Certains projets sont des îles, d'autres se trouvent sur des îles ; certains sont composés d'îles et un grand nombre sont simplement perchés au bord de l'eau. Certains sont de parfaits exemples de design durable ; pour d'autres, l'eau est simplement une caractéristique fondamentale. Ces projets offrent un aperçu de l'avenir de l'architecture, de l'ingénierie et du développement urbain, et montrent les possibilités infinies d'habitat sur l'eau.

Island Buildings
Inselgebäude
Bâtiments flottants

Aluminium Centrum I Octospider I Mur Island I Kastrup Sea Bath
Prayer and Meditation Pavilion I wNw Bar I Wave Tower

The reasons architects choose to build on or near water are complex and many. The examples presented in this chapter show solutions for specific requirements, all in different locations around the world—the sea in Denmark, a lake in Thailand, a shallow pool in Sudan. In some cases, the prime factor is temperature and water is used for cooling; in others, it is religion and water is employed for symbolic reasons; while in others, water is the only reason for the building, as in the case of a sea bath. The structures, too, range widely, from linear white boxes, to a dome made of bamboo, and include a metal box on stilts and a circular wooden swimming platform. However, these highly original designs all have one thing in common—they are completely surrounded by water. They are island buildings.

previous page Entrance to wNw Bar in South Vietnam.

vorherige Seite Eingang der wNw Bar in Südvietnam.

page précédente Entrée du bar WnW au sud du Vietnam.

left Detail of Octospider restaurant in Thailand.

links Detail des Octospider-Restaurants in Thailand.

gauche Restaurant de l'Octospider, en Thaïlande.

Les raisons pour lesquelles les architectes choisissent de bâtir sur l'eau ou à proximité sont nombreuses et variées. Les exemples de ce chapitre présentent les réponses à de nombreuses demandes, dans le monde entier, sur la mer au Danemark, sur un lac en Thaïlande ou un bassin au Soudan. La raison principale est souvent la température, lorsque l'eau rafraîchit les hommes; il s'agit parfois de la religion, lorsque l'eau est symbolique; dans d'autres cas, l'eau est la seule et unique raison, comme pour un bain de mer. Les structures varient également, allant de carrés blancs linéaires à un dôme de bambou, en passant par une boîte métallique et une plate-forme en bois circulaire. Ces conceptions très originales ont cependant un point commun: elles sont entourées d'eau. Ce sont des bâtiments flottants.

Die Gründe, aus denen Architekten beschließen, auf oder nahe am Wasser zu bauen, sind komplex und vielfältig. Die in diesem Kapitel vorgestellten Beispiele zeigen Lösungen für bestimmte Anforderungen, alle an unterschiedlichen Orten rund um die Welt: das Meer in Dänemark, ein See in Thailand, ein niedriges Becken im Sudan. In einigen Fällen ist der ausschlaggebende Faktor die Temperatur, wenn Wasser zur Kühlung dienen soll, in anderen die Religion, wenn es aus symbolischen Gründen verwendet wird, während es in weiteren Fällen zum alleinigen Grund für das Bauwerk wird, wie etwa in dem beschriebenen Seebad. Auch die Baustile der Gebäude selbst sind vielfältig, von linearen weißen Kästen bis zu einer Kuppel aus Bambus, von einem Metallkasten auf Stelzen bis zu einer kreisförmigen hölzernen Badeplattform. Diese höchst originellen Entwürfe haben jedoch alle eine Gemeinsamkeit – sie alle sind vollkommen von Wasser umgeben. Sie sind Inselgebäude.

Aluminium Centrum

Houten, the Netherlands

Abbink x De Haas Architectures

2001

left The idea for the building came from a matchbox balanced on pins.

links Die Idee für das Gebäude stammt von einer auf Stecknadeln aufgespießten Streichholzschachtel.

gauche Le bâtiment a vu le jour en imaginant une boîte d'allumettes en équilibre sur une pelote.

right Site plan showing the square building with water on three sides.

rechts Lageplan mit einer Ansicht des quadratischen Gebäudes, das von drei Seiten mit Wasser umgeben ist.

droite Plan du site avec l'édifice carré et l'eau sur trois côtés.

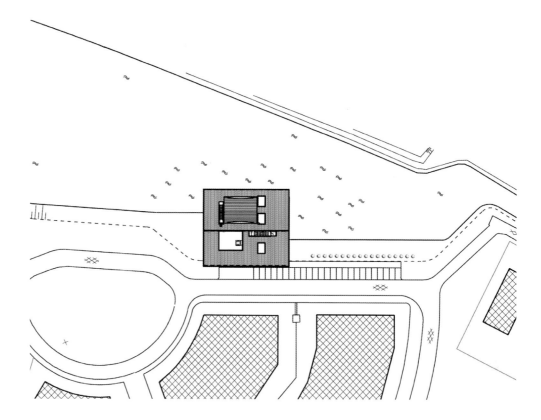

The Aluminium Centrum in Houten, just outside Utrecht in the Netherlands, could be described as a flying island. In 1997, a young, then unknown, architect from Amsterdam, Micha de Haas, won a competition to build a new aluminum knowledge and technology center. His design was revolutionary—a 10,764 square feet metal box balanced on a forest of thin aluminum columns. De Haas took much of his inspiration from the Dutch countryside, in particular the typical square arrangements of poplar trees whose tops merge to create a canopy of leaves.

The first model was a matchbox balanced on a pincushion. De Haas's original objective was to try to work with the smallest span possible for the columns—1,200 were first envisaged. In the end 368 tubular columns approximately 20 feet high were used, ranging from 3.5 to 8.26 in. in diameter. Like a forest, the columns are not all upright, some of them are raked. Used not only to support the structure, they also act as drainpipes and service conduits for the building above.

The structure was designed to show off the versatility of aluminum and act as a showcase of aluminum products. All the components are made of aluminum: stairs, columns, window frames, cladding, floor beams. Even the gravel outside is lumps of pink bauxite, the raw

Das Aluminium Centrum in Houten, nahe bei Utrecht in den Niederlanden gelegen, könnte als fliegende Insel beschrieben werden. 1997 gewann ein junger, zu dieser Zeit noch völlig unbekannter Architekt aus Amsterdam namens Micha de Haas einen Wettbewerb zum Bau eines neuen Wissens- und Technologiezentrums für Aluminium. Sein Entwurf war revolutionär: ein 1.000 Quadratmeter großer Kasten aus Metall, der auf einem Wald aus dünnen Aluminiumsäulen balancierte. De Haas ließ sich weitgehend von der niederländischen Landschaft inspirieren, insbesondere von der typisch quadratischen Anordnung von Pappeln, deren Wipfel sich zu einem Baldachin aus Blättern vereinigen.

Sein erstes Modell bestand aus einer Streichholzschachtel, die auf einem Nadelkissen ruhte. Ursprünglich bemühte er sich darum, mit dem kleinstmöglichen Abstand zwischen den Säulen zu arbeiten – zunächst plante er 1.200. Am Ende wurden 368 röhrenförmige Säulen von etwa 6 Meter Höhe und einem Durchmesser zwischen 90 mm und 210 mm errichtet. Wie Bäume in einem Wald stehen nicht alle Säulen völlig aufrecht, sondern einige neigen sich leicht zur Seite. Sie stützen nicht nur das Bauwerk, sondern dienen auch als Abfluss- und Wartungsrohre für das Gebäude über ihnen.

On pourrait décrire l'Aluminium Centrum de Houten, proche d'Utrecht aux Pays-Bas, comme une île volante. En 1997, un jeune architecte d'Amsterdam jusqu'alors inconnu, Micha de Haas, a remporté un concours qui consistait à créer un nouveau centre de connaissances et de technologies en aluminium. Sa conception fut révolutionnaire: une boîte métallique de 1000 mètres carrés en équilibre sur une forêt de fines colonnes en aluminium. Micha de Haas s'est fortement inspiré de la campagne néerlandaise, en particulier des carrés de peupliers dont les cimes fusionnent pour former un ciel de feuilles.

Son idée a vu le jour avec une boîte d'allumettes en équilibre sur une pelote. À l'origine, Micha de Haas essayait de travailler avec la plus petite envergure possible de colonnes. Il en envisageait 1200. Finalement, il a utilisé 368 colonnes tubulaires d'environ 6 mètres de haut et d'un diamètre compris entre 90mm et 210mm. Tout comme une forêt, les colonnes ne sont pas parfaitement droites et certaines sont même regroupées. Soutenant la structure, elles jouent aussi le rôle de conduits d'écoulement et de service pour le bâtiment qu'elles supportent.

La structure a été conçue pour montrer la souplesse de l'aluminium et permet de présenter les produits issus de cette matière. Tous les

material from which aluminum is smelted. Because of the complexity of the construction, sophisticated engineering techniques were employed. For example, the triangular roof trusses in the main exhibition hall are held together using glue, rather than bolted or welded, a technique developed by the aerospace industry. It was also important that the building be sustainable so all the components can be replaced separately, to be reused or recycled.

Set partly above an artifical lake, the structure can be reached either by a glass elevator or retractable metal stairs. The interior, in contrast to the busy exterior, is devoid of any columns and has as few walls as possible. Volume and light were the priorities here. Glimpses of the columns as well as the surrounding lake and countryside are visible from the various conference and meeting rooms. Thin horizontal window slits give the silver colored box an

Der Entwurf sollte die Vielseitigkeit des Aluminiums als Baumaterial hervorheben und als Vorzeigeprojekt für Aluminiumprodukte dienen. Alle Bestandteile sind aus Aluminium hergestellt: Treppen, Säulen, Fensterrahmen, Verkleidung und Deckenträger. Selbst bei dem Kies außerhalb des Gebäudes handelt es sich um Klumpen aus rosafarbenem Bauxit – dem Rohmaterial, aus dem Aluminium geschmolzen wird. Aufgrund der Komplexität des Bauwerks wurden anspruchsvolle Ingenieurtechniken verwendet. Die dreieckigen Dachbinder in der Hauptausstellungshalle beispielsweise werden mit Klebstoff zusammengehalten, anstatt angeschraubt oder geschweißt zu werden – eine Technik, die von der Luftfahrtindustrie entwickelt wurde. Außerdem war bei der Erbauung des Gebäudes Nachhaltigkeit wichtig, so dass alle Bestandteile getrennt voneinander ersetzt werden können, um

composants sont en aluminium: escaliers, colonnes, châssis de fenêtres, parement et poutres de plancher. À l'extérieur, le gravier est constitué de bauxite rose, matière première à partir de laquelle est fondu l'aluminium. En raison de la complexité de la construction, des techniques d'ingénierie sophistiquées ont dû être employées. Par exemple, les fermes triangulaires du hall d'exposition principal ne sont pas soudées ni fixées mais collées, une technique développée dans l'industrie aérospatiale. Le bâtiment devait également être durable et tous les composants devraient donc pouvoir être remplacés séparément, réutilisés ou recyclés.

Installée en partie sur un lac artificiel, on accède à la structure par un ascenseur en verre ou des escaliers métalliques escamotables. L'intérieur, contrairement à l'extérieur chargé, est dépourvu de colonnes et compte très peu de

left Virtually everything on the building is made of aluminum.

links Nahezu alle Bestandteile des Gebäudes sind aus Aluminium hergestellt.

gauche Le bâtiment est presque entièrement construit en aluminium.

above The block-like box contrasts with the slim pillars beneath.

oben Der blockförmige Kasten hebt sich von den schlanken Pfeilern ab, auf denen er ruht.

ci-dessus Le bloc contraste avec les piliers filiformes situés en dessous.

impression of mass which contrasts with the spindly looking stilts underneath.

As Haas says, "The project was not only about exhibiting the strength of the material but also about stretching the imagination." It won the European Architecture and Technology Award in 2003.

wiederverwendet oder wiederaufbereitet zu werden.

Das teilweise über einem künstlichen See angelegte Gebäude kann entweder über einen gläsernen Aufzug oder einziehbare Metalltreppen erreicht werden. Im Gegensatz zu seinem geschäftig wirkenden Äußeren ist das Gebäude im Inneren frei von Säulen und verfügt über so wenige Wände wie nur möglich. Hier bildeten Raum und Licht die Prioritäten. Aus den verschiedenen Konferenz- und Besprechungsräumen kann der Betrachter Blicke auf die Säulen, den umgebenden See und die Landschaft erhaschen. Dünne, waagerechte Fensterschlitze verleihen dem silberfarbenen Kasten einen Anschein von Masse, der sich von den spindeldürren Stelzen darunter abhebt.

Wie Haas sagt: „Bei diesem Projekt ging es nicht nur darum, die Stärke des Materials zur Schau zu stellen, sondern auch die Fantasie anzuregen." Der Entwurf gewann im Jahr 2003 den European Architecture and Technology Award.

parois. Le volume et la lumière étaient à l'origine les priorités. Les colonnes, le lac et la campagne environnante sont visibles depuis les nombreuses salles de conférence et de réunion. D'étroites fenêtres horizontales donnent à ce pavé argenté une impression de lourdeur contrastant avec les piliers iliformes situés en dessous.

Comme l'affirme Micha de Haas, « le projet n'entendait pas seulement démontrer la force de cette matière mais également ouvrir des perspectives. » Il a remporté le Prix européen de l'architecture et de la technologie en 2003.

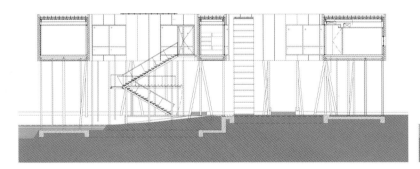 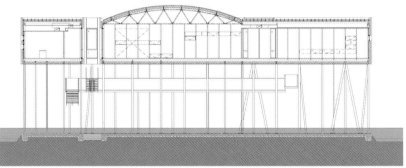

left Looking from the interior toward the inner courtyard.

links Blick aus dem Inneren in Richtung des Innenhofs.

gauche Vue de l'intérieur sur la cour intérieure.

above Section of inner courtyards (left) and cross section through the lake (right).

oben Querschnitt des Innenhofes (links) und Querschnitt durch den See (rechts).

ci-dessus Section des cours intérieures (gauche) et coupe à travers le lac (droite).

right Elevator tower encased in glass.

rechts Von Glas ummantelter Aufzugsturm.

droite Tour d'ascenseur dans une enceinte de verre.

below Access staircase with pillars glimpsed below.

unten Zugangstreppe mit Ansicht der darunterliegenden Pfeiler.

ci-dessous Escaliers d'accès avec aperçu des piliers.

right The gravel used for the foundations is made of bauxite, the raw material from which aluminum is made.

rechts Der Kies, der für das Fundament verwendet wurde, besteht aus Bauxit, dem Rohmaterial, aus dem Aluminium hergestellt wird.

droite Le gravier utilisé pour les fondations est constitué de bauxite, matière première à partir de laquelle est fabriqué l'aluminium.

Octospider

Klongsarn, Bangkok, Thailand
Exposure Architects
2003

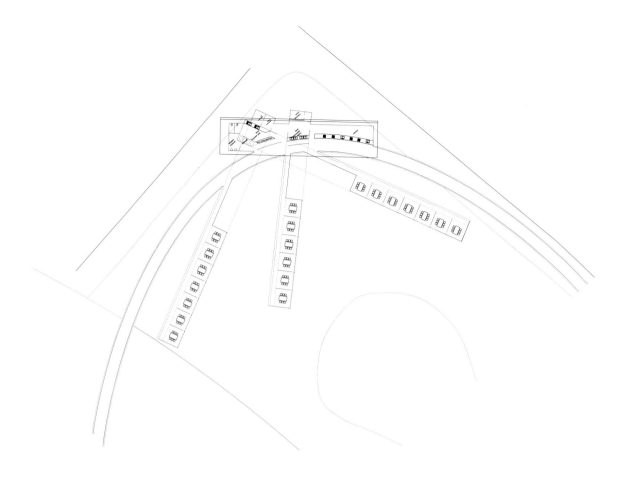

Exposure is an architecture studio based in Bergamo, in northern Italy, whose principal members are Dorit Mizrahi (Israel) and Oliviero Godi (Italy). In 2000, they began work on designing a cafeteria/restaurant for the staff of a textile manufacturer in Bangkok and Octospider was the dramatic result. As their own name implies, they want people to be"exposed" to their buildings to trigger reactions, so that users become actors rather than mere spectators.

This spectacular building rises out of water like some sort of multi-legged water insect—an island spider. The structure is made of up several elements that collide at a central point and then extend over the artificial lake: a curved element—the walkway into and out of the restaurant linking the weaving factory with the textiles finishing buildings—a central narrow building used for the kitchen and cafeteria, and three rectangular platforms that radiate out from the center—the actual dining areas. Rising to 26 feet above the water, the structure allows its visitors many benefits: it gives them views over the surrounding landscape, it allows them a spacious isolation from their workplace, and it acts as a transition between work and rest. But perhaps most important of all, it brings back "some nobility to the moment of eating."

The main materials are concrete, steel, and

Exposure ist ein im norditalienischen Bergamo ansässiges Architekturstudio, das von Dorit Mizrahi (Israel) und Oliviero Godi (Italien) geleitet wird. Im Jahr 2000 begannen sie am Entwurf einer Cafeteria/eines Restaurants für die Mitarbeiter eines Textilherstellers in Bangkok zu arbeiten – und der Octospider war das außergewöhnliche Ergebnis. Wie der Name des Architekturstudios bereits andeutet, möchten dessen Mitglieder den Betrachter der Wirkung ihrer Gebäude aussetzen, um Reaktionen auszulösen, durch die sie zu Handelnden anstatt zu bloßen Betrachtern werden.

Dieses spektakuläre Gebäude erhebt sich aus dem Wasser wie eine Art vielbeiniges Wasserinsekt – eine Inselspinne. Das Bauwerk besteht aus mehreren Elementen, die an einem zentralen Punkt zusammenstoßen und sich dann über den künstlichen See erstrecken: ein gebogenes Element – der Steg in das und aus dem Restaurant, der die Weberei mit den Gebäuden verbindet, in denen die Endfertigung der Stoffe erfolgt –, ein schmales Zentralgebäude, das die Küche und die Cafeteria beherbergt, und drei rechteckige Plattformen, die sich strahlenförmig vom Mittelpunkt aus ausbreiten – die eigentlichen Essbereiche. Das Gebäude erhebt sich bis zu acht Meter über das Wasser

Exposure est un cabinet d'architectes situé à Bergame au nord de l'Italie, dont les principaux membres sont Dorit Mizrahi (Israël) et Oliviero Godi (Italie). En 2000, ils ont commencé à travailler sur une cafétéria pour le personnel d'une entreprise textile de Bangkok. C'est ainsi qu'est né l'Octospider. Comme le nom du cabinet l'implique, les architectes veulent que les personnes soient exposées à leurs bâtiments pour déclencher des réactions. Les utilisateurs deviennent ainsi des acteurs et ne sont plus de simples spectateurs.

Cet édifice spectaculaire surgit hors de l'eau tel un insecte aquatique, une araignée flottante. La structure est composée de plusieurs éléments qui se rejoignent en un point central puis s'étendent sur le lac artificiel: une courbe (la passerelle d'entrée et de sortie du restaurant reliant l'usine de tissage aux bâtiments de finition des textiles), un bâtiment central étroit hébergeant la cuisine, la cafétéria et trois plates-formes rectangulaires rayonnant à partir du centre (les espaces de restauration). S'élevant à huit mètres au-dessus de l'eau, la structure offre à ses visiteurs de nombreux avantages: une vue sur le paysage environnant, un espace isolé de leur lieu de travail et une transition entre le travail et le repos. Mais il redonne par-dessus tout « une certaine noblesse au repas ».

glass. The legs of the walkway are thin steel pipes densely spaced to blend with the surrounding vegetation, while the main three eating areas are supported by reinforced-concrete columns. Temperatures are controlled by way of a double roofing system using overhanging light insulated panels that allow wind to pass in between to cool the lower roof, a louver system along the side wall, and a wall on the dining side with panels that can be moved to protect the interior from sun and rain. In addition, the water under the piers acts as a natural cooling system for the dining area.

und bietet seinen Besuchern so manchen Vorteil: Es verschafft ihnen Aussichten auf die umgebende Landschaft sowie eine weiträumige Trennung von ihrem Arbeitsplatz und fungiert so als Übergang zwischen Arbeit und Ruhezeit. Aber das Wichtigste von allem ist womöglich, dass es „dem Moment des Essens wieder etwas Edles verleiht".

Die Hauptmaterialien sind Beton, Stahl und Glas. Der Laufsteg ruht auf Pfeilern aus dünnen Stahlrohren, die in kurzen Abständen voneinander errichtet wurden, um mit der sie umgebenden Vegetation zu verschmelzen, während die drei Hauptessbereiche sich auf Säulen aus Stahlbeton stützen. Die Temperatur wird mit Hilfe eines doppelten Dachsystems kontrolliert, bei dem vorspringende lichtisolierte Platten verwendet wurden, durch die der Wind hindurchströmen kann, um das darunterliegende Dach zu kühlen, des Weiteren mit einem System von Lüftungsschlitzen entlang der Seitenmauer und des Mittelgangs sowie einer Wand mit beweglichen Platten auf der Seite des Essbereichs, um das Innere vor Sonnenein-strahlung und Regen zu schützen. Außerdem fungiert das Wasser unter den Stegen als natürliches Kühlsystem für den Essbereich.

Le bâtiment est principalement constitué de béton, d'acier et de verre. Les pieds de la passerelle sont de fins conduits en acier suffisamment espacés pour se mêler à la végétation, tandis que les trois espaces de restauration sont soutenus par des colonnes en béton armé. La température est contrôlée par un système de double toiture et de panneaux isolants qui laissent le vent s'infiltrer pour rafraîchir la toiture inférieure et un système de persiennes sur les murs de l'aile latérale. Un mur de l'espace de restauration est constitué de panneaux pouvant être déplacés pour protéger l'intérieur du soleil et de la pluie. L'eau qui passe sous la plate-forme rafraîchit naturellement l'espace de restauration.

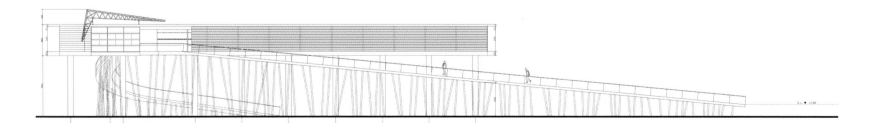

left South elevation with the dining rooms at the top.

links unten Südliche Ansicht mit den Essräumen im oberen Teil.

ci-dessus à gauche Élévation niveau sud avec les salles de restauration en haut.

below Steel columns (left) support the walkway, while concrete pillars (right) are used for the dining rooms.

unten Stahlsäulen (links) stützen den Steg, während für den Essbereich Betonpfeiler (rechts) verwendet wurden.

ci-dessous Colonnes en acier (à gauche) soutenant la passerelle, et piliers en béton (à droite) pour les espaces de restauration.

above The lake not only provides a beautiful setting, but it also helps cool the building. Louvers running down the side of the dining areas offer protection from the sun.

oben Der See bildet nicht nur einen schönen landschaftlichen Hintergrund, sondern spielt auch bei der Kühlung des Gebäudes eine wichtige Rolle. Lüftungsschlitze verlaufen entlang der Seiten der Essbereiche und bieten Schutz vor Sonneneinstrahlung.

ci-dessus Le lac offre une vue magnifique mais permet également de garder la fraîcheur dans le bâtiment. Les persiennes sur le côté des espaces de restauration protègent l'intérieur du soleil.

right Detail shot clearly showing the louvers, steel columns, and thicker concrete pillars.

rechts Detailansicht der Lüftungsschlitze, Stahlsäulen und der dickeren Betonpfeiler.

droite Prise de vue détaillée présentant clairement les persiennes, les colonnes en acier et les piliers en bétons plus épais.

above Inclined walkways offer the workers dramatic views over the surrounding water landscape.

oben Schräg angelegte Fußgängerwege bieten den Arbeitern spektakuläre Ausblicke über die umgebende Wasserlandschaft.

ci-dessus Les passerelles inclinées offrent aux travailleurs une vue spectaculaire sur le paysage environnant.

right The isolated canteen gives the workers an opportunity to be in a quiet environment away from their workplace.

rechts Die isoliert gelegene Kantine bietet den Arbeitern Gelegenheit, sich abseits ihres Arbeitsplatzes in einer ruhigen Umgebung aufzuhalten.

droite La cantine isolée permet aux travailleurs de profiter d'un environnement calme, éloigné de leur lieu de travail.

below right The building's appearance is dramatically altered from day to night.

unten rechts Das Aussehen des Gebäudes unterscheidet sich tagsüber dramatisch von seinem Anblick bei Nacht.

ci-dessous à droite L'apparence du bâtiment se transforme la nuit.

above Workers making their way up the sloping walkway.

oben Arbeiter gehen über die ansteigende Fußgängerbrücke.

ci-dessus Employés remontant la pente.

Mur Island

Graz, Austria
Acconci Studio
2003

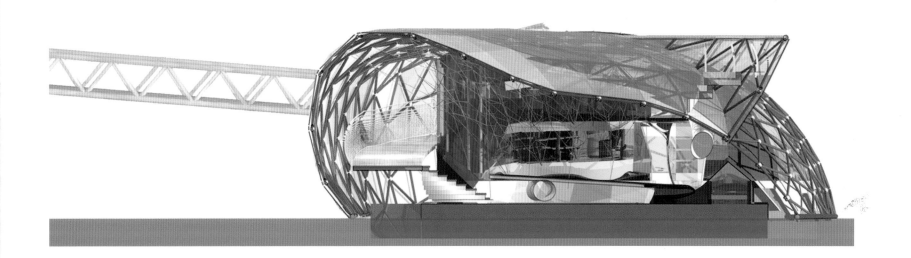

In 2003, as part of Graz becoming European Capital of Culture, the New York artist and designer Vito Acconci was commissioned to design an exceptional project in the middle of the River Mur. Acconci began his career as a poet and performance artist in the 1960s, before moving on to video and performance art. Today, he is primarily known for his landscape design and architecture. For Graz, he came up with an object that is both art and architecture—an isolated microcosm of urban life, a floating island.

Measuring 164 by 65.6 feet, this giant snail floats on the water, linked to the river banks by two hinged footbridges. Part theater, part meeting place, it sits on large pontoons, rising and falling with the tides. The structure, a geodesic diagrid form, is made of a glass skin and stainless steel mesh. Two public spaces meet in the middle, rather like the interconnecting yin and yang symbols. As Acconci puts it, "We wanted to design a space that is divided into two specific zones, and these zones should gradually merge."

An external courtyard functions as a theater, meeting place, plaza, and children's playground. It is lined with transparent bleachers made of

Als Graz 2003 zur Kulturhauptstadt Europas erklärt wurde, erhielt der New Yorker Künstler und Designer Vito Acconci als Teil der Planungen den Auftrag für den Entwurf eines außergewöhnlichen Projektes in der Mitte der Mur. Acconci begann seine Laufbahn in den Sechziger Jahren als Dichter und Performance-Künstler, bevor er sich mit Video- und Performancekunst beschäftigte. Heute ist er vor allem für seine Landschaftsgestaltung und Architektur bekannt. Für Graz entwarf er ein Objekt, das sowohl Kunst als auch Architektur ist – einen isolierten Mikrokosmos städtischen Lebens, eine schwimmende Insel.

Mit ihrer Ausdehnung von 50 x 20 Metern treibt diese Riesenschnecke auf dem Wasser und ist über zwei schwenkbare Laufstege mit beiden Seiten des Ufers verbunden. Teils Theater, teils Treffpunkt, ruht die Insel auf weiträumigen Plattformen, die sich mit Ebbe und Flut im Wasser auf- und abbewegen. Das Bauwerk, eine geodätische Form aus Gitterrosten, besteht aus einer gläsernen Haut und einem Netz aus rostfreiem Edelstahl. In der Mitte treffen zwei öffentliche Räume wie die miteinander verbundenen Yin- und Yang-Symbole zusammen. Acconci beschreibt es so:

En 2003, Graz accédant au titre de capitale européenne de la culture, l'artiste et designer new-yorkais Vito Acconci fut chargé d'un projet exceptionnel placé au milieu de la rivière Mur. Vito Acconci a débuté sa carrière dans les années 1960, en se consacrant à la poésie et à la scène, avant de passer au cinéma. Il est aujourd'hui principalement connu pour ses travaux d'architecture. Pour le projet de Graz, il a proposé un microcosme de vie urbaine, à la fois artistique et architectural: une île flottante.

Cet escargot géant de 50mx20m flotte sur l'eau, relié à la rive par deux passerelles mobiles. À la fois théâtre et lieu de réunion, il repose sur de larges pontons épousant le rythme des flots. La structure géodésique, aux formes triangulaires, est constituée d'une couche de verre et de grille d'acier inoxydable. Deux espaces publics se rencontrent au centre, rappelant le yin et le yang. Comme l'affirme Vito Acconci, « Nous voulions concevoir un espace divisé en deux zones spécifiques qui entrent progressivement en fusion. »

Une cour extérieure fait office de théâtre, de lieu de réunion, de place et de terrain de jeux pour les enfants. Elle est bordée de gradins en métal perforé dont les ondulations permettent

below Wave-shaped benches are positioned so as to encourage people to interact with each other.

unten Wellenförmige Sitzbänke sind so aufgestellt, dass sie Menschen zur Interaktion miteinander ermuntern.

ci-dessous Les bancs courbés invitent à la communication.

right One half is an open theater space with seating, the other half is an enclosed café/bar.

rechts Eine Hälfte bildet einen offenen Theaterraum mit Sitzen, die andere Hälfte ein überdachtes Café/eine Bar.

droite Un module accueille un théâtre ouvert avec des sièges, l'autre un café/bar intérieur.

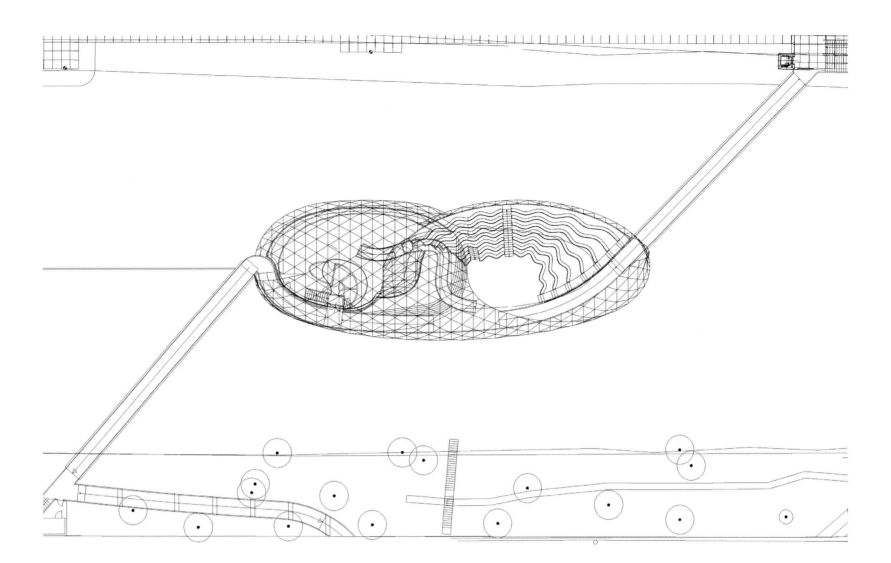

perforated metal that wave in and out and are designed for people to sit face to face. A landscape for children has been created where the external and internal spaces meet.

The internal space, under a glass dome, functions as café and bar. A spiralling rising ramp wraps around the inside of the dome to form a terrace above the bar. Along the edge of the terrace, there are tables and seats for socializing. Below, in the bar itself, specially designed furniture continues the curving biomorphic theme. Curved triangular white tables and blue seats can be joined together to make tables for four or six people.

People are key to this project—how they interact, look, communicate, play, or daydream. "If people sit in the theater, they see the playground in the back; if they sit in the café, they are protected by the playground forming part of the café's roof. These different functions should not be separated radically: water flows around the island, and we wanted to construct an object that is also flowing and changeable."

Acconci also used light and views to cleverly offer new perspectives along the river, thereby linking the urban and the natural. During the day, the surrounding hills are reflected in the

„Wir wollten etwas entwerfen, das sich markant in zwei Zonen teilt, und diese sollten flüssig ineinander laufen."

Ein äußerer Hof fungiert als Theater, Treffpunkt, Plaza und Kinderspielplatz. Er ist von Reihen durchsichtiger Sitzbänke aus perforiertem Metall gesäumt, die wellenförmig angelegt sind, damit die Menschen einander gegenüber sitzen können. An der Stelle, an der die äußeren und inneren Räume zusammentreffen, wurde eine Landschaft für Kinder geschaffen.

Der unter einer gläsernen Kuppel gelegene Innenraum fungiert als Café und Bar. Eine spiralförmig aufsteigende Rampe windet sich um die Innenseite der Kuppel und bildet eine Terrasse über der Bar. Am Rand der Terrasse befinden sich Tische und Sitzgelegenheiten, auf denen sich Besucher gemütlich niederlassen können. In der darunter gelegenen, eigentlichen Bar setzt sich das wellenförmige biomorphische Thema in dem eigens entworfenen Mobiliar fort. Gebogene, dreieckige Tische in Weiß und Sitzgelegenheiten in Blau können zu Tischen für vier oder sechs Personen zusammengestellt werden.

Menschen sind für dieses Projekt wesentlich – wie sie interagieren, aussehen, kommunizieren, spielen oder ihren Tagträumen nachgehen. „Wenn

aux visiteurs de s'asseoir face à face. Un espace a été créé pour les enfants, à la rencontre des modules intérieur et extérieur.

La partie intérieure, sous un dôme de verre, héberge un café et un bar. Une passerelle en spirale s'élève à l'intérieur du dôme pour atteindre une terrasse juste au-dessus, entourée de tables et de chaises qui invitent à la communication. Dans le bar situé plus bas, le mobilier a été spécialement conçu selon un thème biophormique et arrondi. Les tables blanches triangulaires et les sièges bleus peuvent être regroupés pour former des tables de quatre ou six personnes.

Les personnes, la manière dont elles agissent, se regardent, communiquent, jouent ou rêvent, sont essentielles à ce projet. « Si les visiteurs s'assoient au théâtre, ils aperçoivent l'aire de jeu au fond; s'ils s'assoient au café, ils sont protégés par le terrain de jeu qui forme une partie du toit. Ces différentes fonctions ne doivent pas être radicalement séparées. Nous voulions construire un objet à la fois fluide et changeant. »

Vito Acconci a également joué sur les lumières et la vue pour offrir de nouvelles perspectives intelligentes le long de la rivière, liant ainsi l'urbain au naturel. La journée, les

glass and stainless steel, while people inside can look out at the landscape through glass and steel lattice peepholes. At night the "artificial joint" is lit up with blue lights making it look like a space craft.

Leute im Theater sitzen, sehen sie den Spielplatz als Hintergrundelement, wenn sie sich im Café befinden, schützt sie der Spielplatz als Teil des Daches des Cafés. Diese verschiedenen Funktionen dürfen nicht radikal voneinander getrennt sein: denn das Wasser rund um diese Insel fließt und bewegt sich ständig, und wir wollten etwas konstruieren, das ebenfalls flüssig und veränderlich ist."

Acconci arbeitete außerdem geschickt mit Licht und verschiedenen Aussichten, um den Menschen entlang des Flusses neue Perspektiven zu bieten, und verband damit das Städtische mit dem Natürlichen. Tagsüber spiegeln sich die umgebenden Hügel in der Glas- und Edelstahlkonstruktion, während sich den Menschen im Inneren durch das Glas und durch Gucklöcher aus Stahlgittern Ausblicke auf die Landschaft bieten. Bei Nacht ist das „künstliche Gelenk" mit blauen Lichtern hell erleuchtet und gleicht einem Raumschiff.

collines environnantes se reflètent dans le verre et l'acier inoxydable et l'on peut profiter du paysage depuis l'intérieur à travers les interstices du verre et de l'acier. La nuit, « le lieu artificiel » est éclairé de bleu tel un vaisseau spatial.

left The bar area is enclosed in a geodesic dome of a steel frame and glass panels.

links Der Barbereich wird von einer geodätischen Kuppel aus einem Stahlrahmen und Glasscheiben umschlossen.

gauche L'espace bar est enfermé dans un dôme géodésique en panneaux de verre et d'acier.

below Specially designed curving white tables and blue seats in the bar.

unten Eigens für die Bar entworfene kurvenförmige weiße Tische und blaue Sitzgelegenheiten.

ci-dessous Au bar, les tables blanches courbées et les sièges bleus ont été spécialement conçus pour le bâtiment.

Kastrup Sea Bath

Kastrup, Denmark

White Arkitekter

2004

The Kastrup Sea Bath in Denmark is a special kind of island architecture—a water island. A circular wooden structure out at sea surrounds a small area of water to create a natural bathing area. Although a very simple idea, the design is effective thanks to careful planning by the Swedish architects, White. Kastrup is an industrial area not far from Copenhagen and the architects were given the job of regenerating the area as a seaside destination. White designed the main building on the water, a new beach, and new changing rooms on the shore. As Fredrik Pettersson of White puts it, "My idea was to achieve a sculptural, dynamic form that can be seen from the land, from the sea and from the air. The silhouette changes as the spectator moves around it."

A 328-feet long pier leads out to a wooden circular platform. The Sea Bath stands on thin legs 3 feet above the water. A circular screen, rising from 5 feet to 26 feet at its highest point, offers bathers and visitors shelter from winds from all directions and acts as a sun trap. Swimmers can lounge and sunbathe on a continuous bench that runs around the inside of the screen. Series of steps, ramps, and platforms lead down into the sea. Rather like an amphitheater, the structure welcomes people in—in winter, it can be used as a promenade,

Das Seebad im dänischen Kastrup ist eine besondere Art von Inselarchitektur – eine Wasserinsel. Eine runde hölzerne Struktur im Meer umgibt eine kleine Wasserfläche und bildet so einen natürlichen Badebereich. Obgleich eine sehr schlichte Idee, erzielt der Entwurf dank der sorgfältigen Planung des schwedischen Architektenbüros White effektiv seine Wirkung. Kastrup ist ein Gewerbegebiet unweit von Kopenhagen, und die Architekten erhielten den Auftrag, die Gegend zu einem Seebad umzugestalten. White entwarf das Hauptgebäude auf dem Wasser, einen neuen Strand und neue Umkleideräume am Ufer. Fredrik Pettersson von White beschreibt den Entwurf: „Meine Idee war es, eine bildhauerische, dynamische Form zu erzielen, die vom Land, von der See und von der Luft aus sichtbar ist. Die Silhouette verändert sich, wenn der Betrachter sie aus einem anderen Blickwinkel betrachtet."

Ein 100 Meter langer Steg führt hinaus zu einer runden, hölzernen Plattform. Das Seebad steht auf dünnen Pfeilern einen Meter über dem Wasser. Eine runde Abschirmung, die sich von 1,5 Metern auf 8 Meter an ihrem höchsten Punkt erhebt, bietet Badenden wie Besuchern Schutz vor Wind aus allen Richtungen und fungiert als Plätzchen für Sonnenanbeter. Die Schwimmer können sich auf einer Bank räkeln und sonnen-

Au Danemark, le bain de mer de Kastrup est une architecture flottante particulière – une île dans l'eau. Une structure circulaire en bois, sur la mer, entoure une petite surface d'eau pour créer un bain naturel. Même si l'idée est très simple, la conception est efficace grâce à la planification attentionnée du cabinet d'architectes suédois, White. Kastrup est une zone industrielle à proximité de Copenhague et les architectes ont été chargés de modifier cette zone en centre touristique. White a conçu le bâtiment principal sur l'eau, une nouvelle plage et de nouveaux vestiaires. Comme l'affirme Fredrik Pettersson du cabinet White, « Je voulais créer une forme sculpturale et dynamique visible depuis la terre, depuis la mer et depuis les airs. La silhouette change à mesure que le spectateur en fait le tour. »

Un embarcadère de 100 mètres de long mène à la plate-forme en bois circulaire. Le bain de mer repose un mètre au-dessus de la mer sur des piliers filiformes. Une paroi circulaire s'élevant de 1,5 à 8 mètres de haut, à son point le plus élevé, offre aux baigneurs et aux visiteurs une protection contre le vent mais aussi du soleil. Les nageurs peuvent se prélasser au soleil, sur le banc continu courant le long de cette paroi. Des escaliers, des rampes et des plates-formes descendent jusqu'à la mer. La

previous page Looking from the beach out toward the sea bath.

vorherige Seite Blick vom Strand zum Seebad.

page précédente Vue du bain de mer depuis la plage.

left Details of the azobe planking. Azobe is particularly resilient to sea water.

links Detailansicht der Verschalung aus Azobé. Azobé ist besonders widerstandsfähig gegen Meerwasser.

gauche Détails du ponton en azobé, un bois particulièrement résistant à l'eau de mer.

below left Site plan showing the pier and sea bath out at sea. The changing rooms are located on the shore.

unter links Lageplan mit Ansicht des Stegs und des Seebads draußen im Meer. Die Umkleideräume befinden sich am Ufer.

ci-dessous à gauche Plan du site montrant l'embarcadère et le bain depuis la mer. Les vestiaires se trouvent sur la plage.

right Elevation showing the inclined outer wooden wall.

rechts Ansicht der leicht geneigten äußeren Holzwand.

droite Élévation présentant le mur extérieur asymétrique en bois.

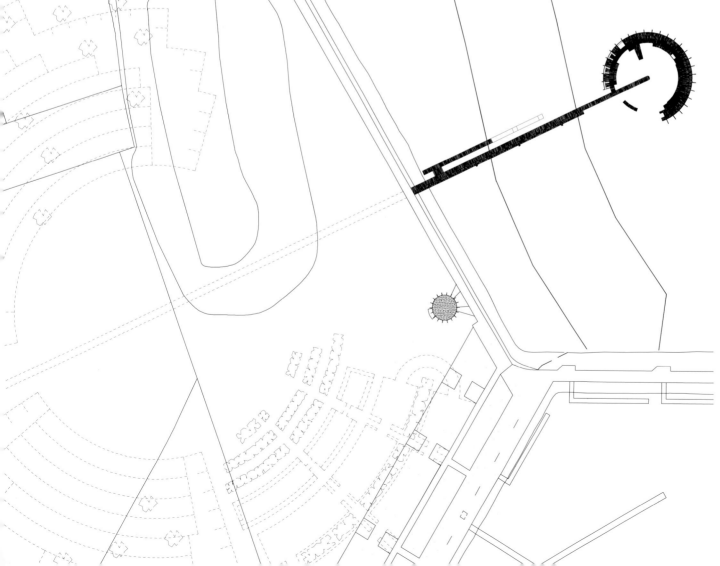

in summer, as a place to swim. Designed as a place for both young and old, to be neither private nor exclusive, it is open to everyone.

What makes the design work so well—it won endless architectural awards when it was completed in 2004—is the attention to detail. Strips of timber, made of azobe, a particularly robust wood that is very durable in sea water, vary in thickness, both on the walls and floors, and are positioned randomly. This gives the building a very organic look (in the same way that trees vary in size), something that wouldn't have been achieved if the planks had been uniform in size and alignment. Lighting, supplied by Erco, is also key to the overall effect. LED spotlights along the bridge lead visitors out to sea where upward facing spotlights illuminate the inside of the structure. A contrasting blue light from behind the diving platforms adds further drama. The Sea Bath is a carved installation for people to walk on and dive from.

baden, die entlang der gesamten Innenseite der Abschirmung verläuft. Treppenstufen, Rampen und Plattformen führen hinab ins Meer. Das Bauwerk heißt Menschen wie ein Amphitheater willkommen – im Winter kann es als Promenade für Spaziergänge dienen, im Sommer als Seebad. Als Treffpunkt für Alt und Jung entworfen und weder privat noch bestimmten Personen-gruppen vorbehalten, steht der Zugang zum Seebad allen frei.

Der Entwurf funktioniert vor allem dank seiner Liebe zum Detail – er gewann nach seiner Fertigstellung im Jahre 2004 zahlreiche Architekturpreise. An den Wänden wie auf dem Boden variieren Holzleisten aus Azobé, einer besonders robusten Holzart, die in Meerwasser sehr widerstandfähig ist, in ihrer Dicke und sind zufällig angeordnet. Dies verleiht dem Gebäude ein sehr organisches Aussehen (wie auch Bäume sich in ihrer Größe unterscheiden); dies hätte nicht funktioniert, falls ihre Größe und Anordnung einheitlich gewesen wären. Die von Erco gelieferte Beleuchtung spielt für die Gesamtwirkung ebenfalls eine wichtige Rolle. Entlang der Brücke angebrachte LED-Strahler führen Besucher auf das Meer hinaus, wo aufwärts leuchtende Strahler das Innere des Baus beleuchten. Kontrastierendes blaues Licht, das hinter den Sprungtürmen aufsteigt, sorgt für einen noch dramatischeren Effekt. Das Seebad ist eine bildhauerische Installation, die Menschen zum Spaziergang und zum Tauchen einlädt.

structure accueille les visiteurs à la manière d'un amphithéâtre. Elle est un lieu de promenade en hiver et de baignade en été. Ce lieu ni privé ni exclusif est ouvert aux plus jeunes comme aux plus âgés.

L'attention aux détails fait le succès de cette conception, qui a remporté de nombreux prix architecturaux depuis son achèvement en 2004. Des lattes d'azobé, un bois particulièrement résistant à l'eau de mer et durable, dont l'épaisseur varie, recouvrent à la fois les parois et le sol. Cela donne au bâtiment un aspect très organique (de la même manière que la taille des arbres varie) qui n'aurait pas été perçu si les bandes avaient été alignées et uniformes. Les éclairages, fournis par Erco, jouent également un rôle important. Des spots à LED longent le pont et conduisent les visiteurs vers la mer, où des spots dirigés vers le ciel illuminent l'intérieur de la structure. Une lumière bleue à l'arrière des plates-formes ajoute une touche théâtrale supplémentaire. Le bain de mer est une installation sculptée pour la promenade et la baignade.

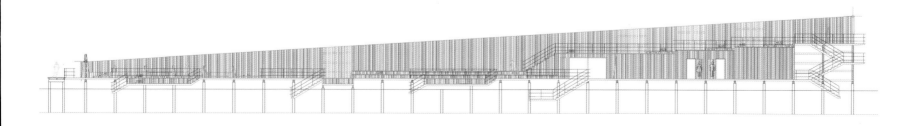

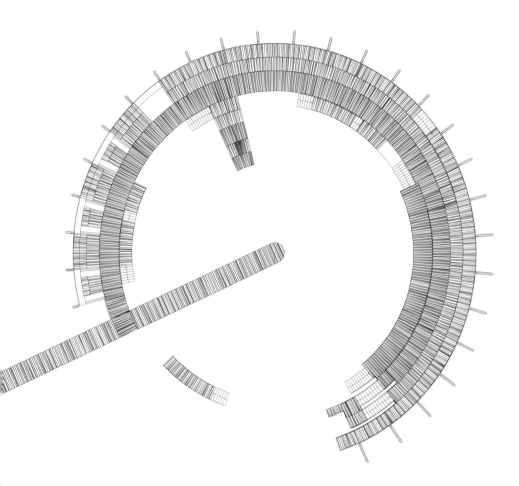

left Plan showing the wooden planks. They vary in thickness and are positioned randomly to give the structure an organic look.

links Plan mit Ansicht der hölzernen Planken. Sie unterscheiden sich in ihrer Dicke und sind zufällig angeordnet, um dem Bau ein organisches Aussehen zu verleihen.

gauche Plan présentant les planches de bois, posées de manière aléatoire et variant en épaisseur, pour donner à la structure un aspect naturel.

below left A dynamic interplay of piers, benches, platforms, and steps.

unten links Ein dynamisches Zusammenspiel von Stegen, Bänken, Plattformen und Stufen.

ci-dessous à gauche Le contraste des éclairages blancs et bleus crée une ambiance théâtrale.

right The sea bath was designed as a sculptural, dynamic form to be seen from land, air, and sea.

rechts Das Seebad wurde als bildhauerische, dynamische Form geschaffen, die vom Land, von der See und aus der Luft sichtbar sein sollte.

droite Interaction dynamique des embarcadères, plates-formes et escaliers.

Prayer and
Meditation Pavilion

Khartoum, Sudan
Studio Tamassociati
2007

This island of interconnected boxes is the most simple of structures, and yet it is also a very clever solution to a difficult problem. Designed as a prayer and meditation pavilion, it is an integral part of a cardiac surgery center in Sudan, built by an Italian humanitarian organization. The center provides free health care to patients within a radius of 10 million square kilometers, a total of three million people. Sudan has a long history of inter-ethnic and religious conflict—39 percent of the population are Arab ethnic, 61 percent African; 70 percent are Muslim and 30 percent Christian or other faiths—so it was important to make the pavilion a place all people could use for prayer.

The architects, a Venice-based studio, chose a single space that can accommodate all religions. Two white cubes are surrounded by a pool of low water. Thin footbridges over the water lead into the spaces. Inside, the decoration is minimal and natural. Roof covers of loosely woven bamboo create calming shadows. Small vertical window slits add to the intimacy and allow diffused light in. The two cubes each contain a small tree, natural elements within artificial spaces. Reed mats cover the floors.

The surrounding water is highly symbolic in this sub-Saharan location. "The pool creates a

Diese Insel aus miteinander verbundenen Kästen ist die einfachste aller Strukturen und dennoch eine äußerst intelligente Lösung für ein schwieriges Problem. Das als Gebets- und Meditationspavillon entworfene Gebäude ist wesentlicher Bestandteil einer herzchirurgischen Klinik im Sudan, die von einer italienischen humanitären Organisation erbaut wurde. Die Klinik bietet drei Millionen Patienten in einem Umkreis von 10 Millionen Quadratkilometern kostenlose medizinische Versorgung. Der Sudan weist eine lange Geschichte von Konflikten zwischen verschiedenen Volksgruppen und Religionen auf: 39 Prozent der Bevölkerung sind Araber, 61 Prozent Afrikaner; 70 Prozent sind Muslime und 30 Prozent Christen oder Anhänger anderer Glaubensrichtungen. Daher war es wichtig, den Pavillon zu einem Ort zu machen, an dem alle diese Gruppen beten können.

Das Architekturstudio aus Venedig entschied sich für einen einzigen Raum, der alle Religionen aufnehmen kann. Zwei weiße Würfel sind von einem niedrigen Becken mit Wasser umgeben. Schlanke, über das Wasser verlaufende Stege führen in die Räumlichkeiten. Im Inneren ist die Ausstattung minimal und natürlich gehalten. Dachbedeckungen aus lose gewobenem Bambus sorgen für beruhigende Schatten. Kleine senkrechte Fensterschlitze ergänzen die

Cette île de boîtes interconnectées est la plus simple des structures, mais une solution très intelligente à un problème complexe. Conçue comme un centre de prière et de méditation, cette construction fait partie du centre de chirurgie cardiaque du Soudan, construit par une organisation humanitaire italienne. Le centre offre des soins gratuits aux patients dans un rayon de 10 millions de kilomètres carrés, couvrant trois millions de personnes. Le Soudan possède une longue histoire de conflits religieux et interethniques (la population est à 39% arabe, 61% africaine, 70% musulmane et à 30% chrétienne ou autre). Il était donc important de créer un centre de prière pour tous.

Les architectes, un cabinet basé à Venise, ont choisi un espace unique pouvant accueillir toutes les religions. Deux cubes blancs sont entourés d'un bassin peu profond et de fines passerelles au-dessus de l'eau conduisent à l'intérieur. La décoration intérieure est minimale et naturelle. Le toit recouvert de canisses de bambou crée des ombres apaisantes. De petites fenêtres verticales ajoutent une certaine intimité et laissent entrer une lumière diffuse. Les cubes accueillent tous deux un petit arbre et des éléments naturels dans des espaces artificiels. Des tapis de roseaux recouvrent le sol.

previous page Water is used to create an artificial lake, but it also has symbolic meaning.

vorherige Seite Wasser wird zur Schaffung eines künstlichen Sees verwendet, hat jedoch auch eine symbolische Bedeutung.

page précédente L'eau permet de créer un lac articficiel mais a également une signification symbolique.

below left Two interlocking square boxes with two narrow foot bridges either side.

unten links Zwei miteinander verschachtelte quadratische Kästen mit zwei engen Stegen auf jeder Seite.

ci-dessous à gauche Deux boîtes cubiques imbriquées et leurs fines passerelles de chaque côté.

below Clean lines and white walls create a striking contrast with the dark water.

unten Klare Linien und weiße Wände schaffen einen auffallenden Kontrast zu dem dunklen Wasser.

ci-dessous Les lignes épurées et les murs blancs créent un contraste frappant avec l'eau plus sombre.

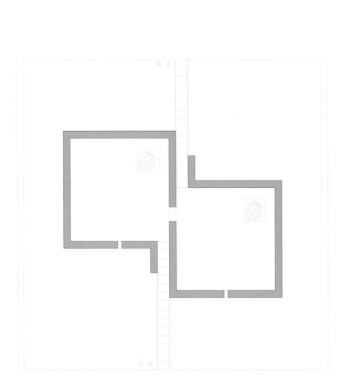

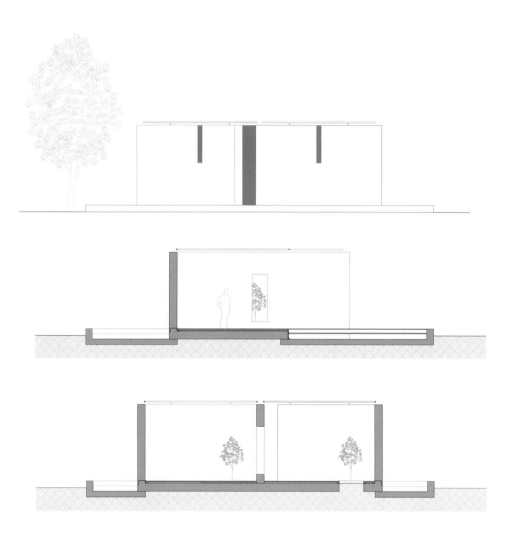

spiritual separation between the external macrocosm of the hospital/world and the central microcosm of the building formed by two unaligned white cubes." All religious symbols and elements have been concealed. For example, the high water spray which is an element of the water pool also acts as the ablution area for Muslims. This is a place of calm for all faiths.

Intimität und lassen diffuses Licht hinein. In jedem der beiden Würfel steht ein kleiner Baum – ein natürliches Element innerhalb eines künstlichen Raums. Die Böden sind von Schilfmatten bedeckt.

Das umgebende Wasser ist an diesem südlich der Sahara gelegenen Ort von großer symbolischer Bedeutung. „Das Becken schafft eine spirituelle Trennung zwischen dem äußeren Makrokosmos der Klinik/Welt und dem ventralen Mikrokosmos des aus zwei versetzt angeordneten weißen Würfeln bestehenden Gebäudes." Jegliche religiösen Symbole und Elemente wurden verborgen. Beispielsweise dient der Sprühregen des Wassers, der ein Element des Beckens ist, gleichzeitig auch als Bereich für die rituelle Waschung der Muslime. Es ist ein Platz der Ruhe für alle Glaubensrichtungen.

L'eau est très symbolique dans ce lieu sub-saharien. « La piscine crée une séparation spirituelle entre le macrocosme externe du monde/de l'hôpital et le microcosme ventral du bâtiment formé par deux cubes blancs non alignés. » Tous les symboles et les éléments religieux ont été dissimulés. La fontaine d'eau dans la piscine est par exemple également l'espace d'ablution des musulmans. C'est un lieu de calme pour toutes les croyances.

left The bamboo roof creates calming shadows along the walls, while narrow slits form windows.

links Das Bambusdach schafft beruhigende Schatten entlang der Wände, während schmale Schlitze als Fenster dienen.

gauche Le toit en bambous crée des ombres relaxantes le long des murs, tandis que les fentes étroites forment les fenêtres.

right Two small trees are the only elements inside the two meditation boxes.

rechts Zwei kleine Bäume sind die einzigen beiden Elemente innerhalb der beiden Meditationsräume.

droite Les petits arbres sont les deux seuls éléments présents dans les salles de méditation.

wNw Bar

Vo Trong Nghia
Thu Dau Mot, Vietnam
2008

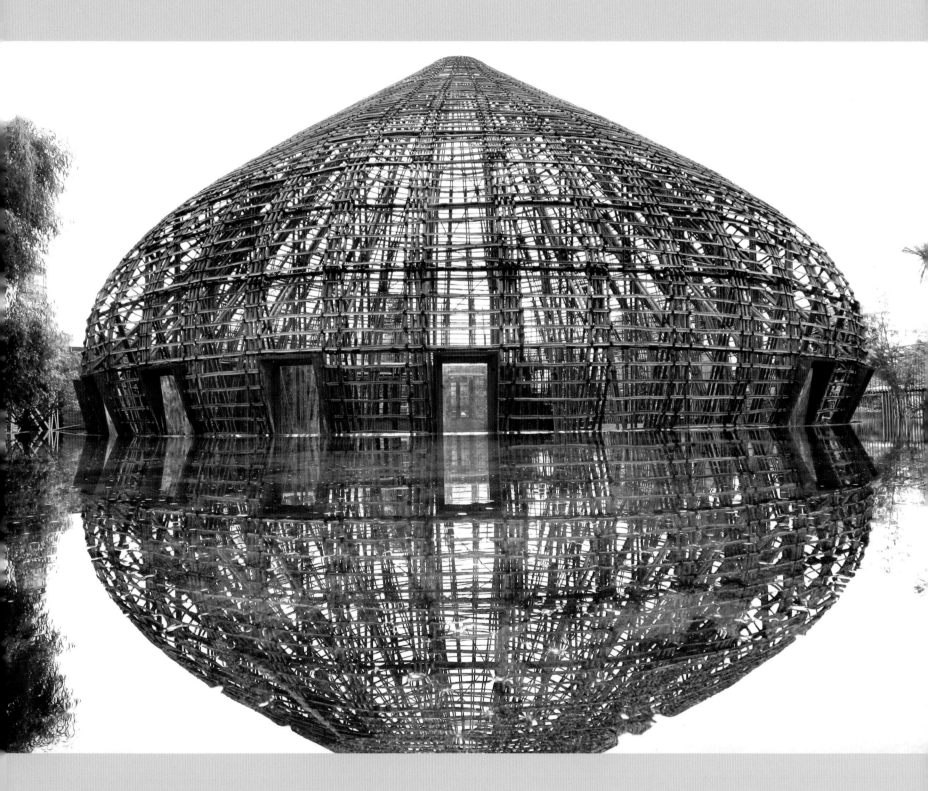

left and below The bamboo dome structure before and after the thatch roof was put on. The floor level of the bar is below the water line.

links und unten Die Bambuskuppelstruktur vor und nach der Anbringung des Reetdachs. Der Boden der Bar befindet sich unter der Wasseroberfläche.

ci-dessous et gauche Structure de bambou du dôme, avant et après la pose du toit en chaume. Le rez-de-chaussée du bar se trouve sous le niveau de l'eau.

left Stepping stones lead into the dome across the artificial lake.

links Trittsteine führen über den künstlichen See in den Kuppelbau.

gauche Sur le lac artificiel, les marches en pierre mènent à l'intérieur du dôme.

right All elements, including the platform, furniture, and stairs are made of bamboo.

rechts Alle Elemente, einschließlich der Treppen, der Plattform und des Mobiliars, sind aus Bambus angefertigt.

droite Tous les éléments, dont les escaliers, la plate-forme et le mobilier, sont fabriqués en bambou.

far right Interior view showing the dome during construction.

ganz rechts Innenansicht der Kuppel während ihrer Erbauung.

au loin à droite Vue intérieure présentant le dôme en cours de construction.

Vietnam has witnessed a boom in new design and architecture since the early 2000s as its economy has grown. One architect who is becoming increasingly well-known for his work outside Vietnam is Vo Trong Nghia. He has developed a reputation for designing buildings that combine traditional elements and innovative, modernist design.

The wNw Bar was opened to the public in 2008 and took only three months to build. It sits in the middle of an artificial lake and can be reached by a series of stepping stones perched above the water line. The building itself is an experiment in creating a cheap, sustainable space that can easily be dismantled and reassembled elsewhere. As the Mekong Delta area is prone to flooding, this sort of structure, which can be constructed quickly using local materials and workers, is an ideal solution. The architect imagines that such structures will be used either as prefabricated housing or for business purposes, such as bars, cafés, or hotel resorts.

Almost the entire building is made of bamboo (only the base is not). It uses a structural arch system 32.8 feet in height with a span of 49 feet. A main frame is made of 48 units of bamboo elements—traditionally bamboo is soaked in mud and then smoked to

Mit zunehmendem Wirtschaftswachstum hat Vietnam seit dem Beginn des 21. Jahrhunderts einen Boom in neuem Design und neuer Architektur erlebt. Ein Architekt, der für seine Arbeiten außerhalb Vietnams zunehmende Bekanntheit erlangt hat, ist Vo Trong Nghia, der sich einen Ruf für den Entwurf von Gebäuden erworben hat, die traditionelle Elemente mit innovativem, modernistischen Design verbinden.

Die wNw Bar wurde der Öffentlichkeit im Jahr 2008 nach nur drei Monaten Bauzeit zugänglich gemacht. Sie befindet sich inmitten eines künstlichen Sees und kann über eine Reihe von Trittsteinen erreicht werden, die knapp über der Wasseroberfläche liegen. Das Gebäude selbst ist ein Experiment zur Schaffung eines günstigen, nachhaltigen Raums, dessen Bestandteile auf einfache Weise auseinandergebaut und an einem anderen Ort wieder aufgebaut werden können. In dem für Überflutungen anfälligen Mekong-Delta ist diese Art Bauwerk, das mit heimischen Materialien und Arbeitern schnell erbaut werden kann, die ideale Lösung. Der Architekt stellt sich vor, dass solche Bauwerke entweder als vorgefertigte Wohnbauten oder für gewerbliche Zwecke wie etwa als Bars, Cafés oder Hotelanlagen Verwendung finden.

Depuis le début des années 2000, la croissance économique vietnamienne est accompagnée d'un essor du design et de l'architecture. L'architecte Vo Trong Nghia est de plus en plus connu pour ses travaux à l'étranger et s'est établi une réputation pour ses bâtiments qui associent des éléments traditionnels à un design innovant et moderniste.

Le wNw Bar a ouvert ses portes au public en 2008. Sa construction n'a pris que trois mois. S'élevant au milieu d'un lac artificiel, on y accède par un cordon de marches de pierre situées à la surface de l'eau. Le bâtiment en lui-même tente de créer un espace durable avec peu de moyens, pouvant facilement être démonté et recréé ailleurs. Comme le delta du Mekong est enclin aux inondations, ce type de structure, pouvant être rapidement construite avec des matériaux et des travailleurs locaux, est une solution idéale. Selon l'architecte, une telle structure sera utilisée pour construire des maisons préfabriquées ou des bars, des cafés et des hôtels.

La totalité du bâtiment, à l'exception de la base, est conçue en bambou, avec un système d'arc de 10 mètres de haut et de 15 mètres de diamètre. Le cadre principal compte 48 éléments de bambou; ce végétal est traditionnellement trempé dans la boue puis fumé pour lui conférer

above A 5-foot wide oculus allows light to enter and hot air to escape.

oben Ein 1,5 Meter breites Rundfenster lässt Licht herein und heiße Luft heraus.

ci-dessus Un oculus de 1,5 mètre de diamètre laisse entrer la lumière et s'échapper l'air.

right Although massive, this island building took only three months to construct.

rechts Obgleich es aus massiven Bestandteilen besteht, betrug die Bauzeit für dieses Inselgebäude nur drei Monate.

droite Bien que massive, la construction de la structure flottante n'a nécessité que trois mois.

make it as durable as possible. The entire frame is covered in bamboo thatch. An oculus in the ceiling, 5 feet in diameter, allows for light to enter and for hot air to escape.

Ventilation is an important part of the design. Vietnam has a very humid and hot climate. Typically outside temperatures in South Vietnam, where this café is situated, can be as much as 95 degrees Fahrenheit throughout the year. Therefore, in order to maintain a cooler interior temperature of 77 degrees, a natural air-conditioning system using water and wind is employed. The surrounding water cools the natural winds before they enter the structure and then rise to the top of the dome.

Das gesamte Gebäude besteht beinahe ausschließlich aus Bambus (mit Ausnahme des Fundaments). Es beruht auf einem strukturellen, 10 Meter hohen Gewölbesystem mit einer Spannweite von 15 Metern. Das Hauptgerüst besteht aus 48 Einheiten Bambuselement – traditionell wird Bambus in Schlamm eingeweicht und dann geräuchert, um ihn so widerstandsfähig wie möglich zu machen. Das gesamte Gerüst wird mit Bambusreet bedeckt. Ein Rundfenster in der Decke, 1,5 Meter im Durchmesser, lässt Licht herein und heiße Luft heraus.

Die Belüftung ist wesentlicher Bestandteil des Entwurfs. Vietnam hat ein sehr feuchtes, heißes Klima. Die Außentemperaturen in Südvietnam, wo sich dieses Café befindet, können während des gesamten Jahres 35° Celsius erreichen. Um eine kühlere Innentemperatur von 25° Celsius aufrechtzuerhalten, wird deshalb ein natürliches Belüftungssystem auf der Grundlage von Wasser und Wind verwendet. Das umgebende Wasser kühlt die natürlichen Winde, bevor sie das Bauwerk erreichen und dann in die Kuppel aufsteigen.

une durabilité maximale. Le cadre est totalement recouvert de chaume de bambou. Au plafond, un oculus de 1,5 mètre de diamètre laisse entrer la lumière et s'échapper l'air chaud.

La ventilation est une part importante de la conception car le climat vietnamien est chaud et très humide. Les températures extérieures au Sud du Vietnam, où se trouve ce bar, avoisinent généralement les 35°C toute l'année. La température intérieure est maintenue à environ 25°C par un système naturel de climatisation utilisant l'eau et l'air. L'eau du lac refroidit le vent s'infiltrant dans la structure et monte ensuite dans le dôme.

Wave Tower

A-cero Studio and Joaquín Torres & Rafael Llamazares architects
Dubai, UAE
2012

A-cero Studio and Joaquín Torres & Rafael Llamazares architects is a Madrid-based studio that was founded by architect Joaquín Torres Vérez in 1996. Considered one of the most exciting Spanish architecture and urban design studios they are best known for their residential projects, including a number of spectacular modern minimalist stone and glass villas in Spain. Torres has said, "We try to communicate simplicity, purity and the absence of superfluous ornaments."

The Wave Tower is a proposed 92-story iconic skyscraper that will be built on its own artificial island in the Madinat Al Arab District on Dubai's coastline. A light, thin bridge will link the island to the shore. When finished it will be 1,215 feet tall and for mixed-use—a commercial complex in the lower levels and offices, luxury residences and a hotel in the tower. Elevators will be located in the central core, and interior gardens will be present on all levels, improving the air quality and working as natural temperature regulators.

A number of energy-saving design devices have been incorporated into the design. A double-skin façade made of silk-screened glass will be designed to reflect radiation and reduce energy consumption. At night it will be transparent, during the day opaque. In an effort

A-cero Studio and Joaquín Torres & Rafael Llamazares architects ist ein in Madrid ansässiges Architekturstudio, das 1996 von Joaquín Torres Vérez gegründet wurde. Heute gilt es als eines der aufregendsten spanischen Studios für Architektur und Städteplanung und ist am besten für seine Wohngebäude bekannt, darunter einer Anzahl spektakulärer moderner, minimalistischer Stein- und Glasvillen in Spanien. Torres sagt: „Wir versuchen Einfachheit, Reinheit und die Abwesenheit überflüssiger Ornamente zu vermitteln."

Der Wave Tower ist ein derzeit in Planung befindlicher 92-stöckiger ikonischer Wolkenkratzer, der auf einer eigens dafür angelegten künstlichen Insel im Bezirk Madinat Al Arab an der Küste Dubais gebaut werden wird. Die Insel wird über eine leichte, schlanke Brücke mit dem Ufer verbunden sein. Nach seiner Fertigstellung soll das Gebäude 370 Meter hoch sein und verschiedenen Zwecken dienen – so sollen in den unteren Stockwerken Geschäfte und im darüberliegenden Turm Büros, Luxuswohnungen und ein Hotel entstehen. Im Kern des Gebäudes werden Aufzüge eingebaut, und auf allen Stockwerken werden Innenhöfe mit Gärten angelegt, die die Luftqualität verbessern und zur natürlichen Temperaturregulierung dienen sollen.

A-cero Studio and Joaquín Torres & Rafael Llamazares architects est un cabinet d'architectes basé à Madrid, fondé en 1996 par Joaquín Torres Vérez. Aujourd'hui considéré comme l'un des cabinets espagnols offrant une architecture et une conception urbaine des plus excitantes, il est plus connu pour ses projets résidentiels, dont un certain nombre de villas réalisées en Espagne, en pierre et en verre, spectaculaires, modernes et minimalistes. « Nous essayons de communiquer la simplicité, la pureté et l'absence d'ornements superflus », affirme Joaquín Torres.

La Wave Tower sera un gratte-ciel de 92 étages construit sur une île artificielle dans le disctrict de Madinat Al Arab sur la côte de Dubaï. Une passerelle légère et étroite reliera l'île à la côte. Le bâtiment mesurera 370 mètres de haut et accueillera un centre commercial aux niveaux inférieurs et des bureaux, des appartements de luxe et un hôtel dans la tour. Les ascenseurs seront installés au cœur de la tour, des jardins intérieurs seront présents à tous les étages, améliorant la qualité de l'air et jouant le rôle de régulateurs naturels de température.

Divers appareils modernes seront intégrés à la tour pour réaliser des économies d'énergie, comme une double façade de verre sérigraphié qui permettra de réfléchir les rayons du soleil.

previous page A thin, light bridge links the island tower to the mainland.

vorherige Seite Eine leichte, schlanke Brücke verbindet die Insel mit dem Festland.

page précédente Une passerelle étroite relie la tour flottante à la terre.

above Elevations illustrate the tower's dynamic, twisting form.

oben Die Ansichten veranschaulichen die dynamische, gewundene Form des Turms.

ci-dessus Le plan longitudinal montre la forme torsadée et dynamique de la tour.

right A double-skin silk-screen glass façade is designed to reduce heat by reflecting radiation.

rechts Zur Verringerung der Hitze durch die Reflektion der Sonneneinstrahlung wurde eine Fassade mit einer doppelten Haut aus Siebdruckglas entworfen.

droite La double façade en verre sérigraphié permet de réduire la chaleur en réfléchissant les rayons du soleil.

right Plan showing the tower's structure of V-shaped forms that radiate from the middle.

rechts Der Plan zeigt die Struktur des Turms aus V-förmigen Elementen, die strahlenförmig von der Mitte ausgehen.

droite Plan présentant la structure de la tour en plusieurs V rayonnant à partir du centre.

to control water consumption, the architects plan to incorporate a water purification plant inside the building. This plant will desalinate and purify the surrounding sea water which will then be filtered for drinking, sewage, and landscape irrigation.

The tower's structure is made up of various V-shaped forms that radiate out from a central core. It rises and flows up like a plant, a thin stem about to bloom. Torres explains, "A-cero's design is based on the concept of the intervention between sea and land. The tower 'grows' gently inland to create the forceful sight of a tall building that mimics the waves of the Gulf Sea." The firm's philosophy revolves around capturing the connection between landscape and the physical environment in sculptured form. Torres and his partner Llamazares owe their architectural inspiration to the renowned British sculptor David Nash, who is best known for his "land art" in which large pieces of wood are transformed with chainsaw, axe, and torch. According to Torres, the Wave Tower is, "a clear reference to the work of David Nash, which conjugates form and function."

Eine Anzahl energiesparender Designelemente wurde ebenfalls in den Entwurf mit einbezogen. Zur Reflektion der Sonneneinstrahlung und zur Verringerung des Energieverbrauchs wird eine Fassade mit einer doppelten Haut aus Siebdruckglas entwickelt. Das Glas wird in der Nacht durchsichtig und am Tag undurchsichtig sein. Im Bestreben, den Wasserverbrauch zu kontrollieren, haben die Architekten die Einbeziehung einer Wasseraufbereitungsanlage in das Gebäude vorgesehen. Diese Anlage wird das umgebende Meerwasser entsalzen und reinigen, das dann gefiltert wird, um als Trinkwasser, Abwasser und zur Bewässerung weiter verwendet zu werden.

Die Struktur des Hochhauses setzt sich aus verschiedenen V-förmigen Elementen zusammen, die von einem zentralen Kern ausgehen. Wave Tower erhebt sich dynamisch wie eine Pflanze aus dem Boden, entfaltet sich wie ein dünner Stängel kurz vor der Blüte. Torres erklärt: „A-ceros Entwurf beruht auf dem Konzept der Vermittlung zwischen Land und Meer. Der Turm „wächst" sanft landeinwärts und schafft dort den kraftvollen Anblick eines Hochhauses, das die Wellen des Golfs nachahmt." Laut Unternehmensphilosophie von A-cero sollen Bauwerke die Verbindung zwischen Landschaft und physischer Umgebung in bildhauerisch gestalteter Form erfassen. Torres und sein Partner Llamazares verdanken ihre architektonische Inspiration dem britischen Bildhauer David Nash, der am besten für seine „land art" (Landschaftskunst) bekannt ist. Laut Torres ist der Wave Tower „ein deutlicher Bezug zum Werk David Nashs, in dem Form und Funktion vereint sind."

Le bâtiment sera transparent de nuit, opaque de jour. Afin de contrôler la consommation d'eau, les architectes prévoient d'ajouter un système de purification à l'intérieur du bâtiment. Celui-ci dessalera et purifiera l'eau de mer qui sera alors filtrée pour la consommation, les installations sanitaires et l'irrigation.

La partie inférieure de la structure sera composée de plusieurs V rayonnant à partir d'un point central. La tour s'élévera telle une plante, tige filiforme sur le point de fleurir. Joaquín Torres explique que « la conception d'A-cero utilise le concept d'interaction entre terre et mer. La tour pousse doucement vers l'intérieur des terres pour créer la vue incomparable d'un bâtiment imitant les vagues du Golfe persique. » La philosophie des architectes est axée sur la connexion entre le paysage et l'environnement physique, sous une forme sculptée. Joaquín Torres et son partenaire Llamazares doivent leur inspiration architecturale au sculpteur anglais David Nash, davantage connu pour son « land art ». Selon Joaquín Torres, « la Wave Tower fait clairement référence au travail de David Nash, qui conjugue formes et fonctions. »

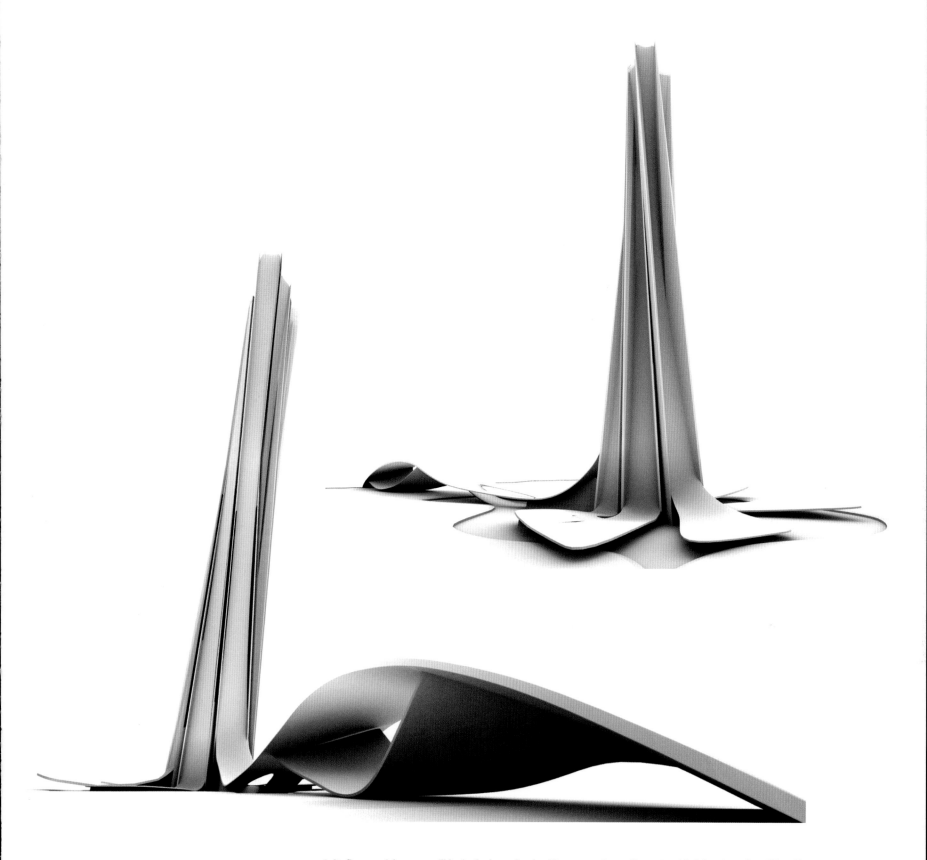

left Commercial spaces will be in the lower level, with offices, luxury residences, and a hotel in the tower itself.

links Auf der unteren Ebene werden Gewerbeflächen eingerichtet, während im Turm selbst Büros, Luxuswohnungen und ein Hotel Platz finden werden.

gauche La partie inférieure accueillera des locaux commerciaux tandis que la tour hébergera bureaux, appartements de luxe et un hôtel.

above Computer-aided drawings show Wave Tower rising up from the ground like a living organism.

oben Computergestützte Zeichnungen stellen den Wave Tower dar, der sich wie ein lebendiger Organismus aus dem Boden erhebt.

ci-dessus Dessin assisté par ordinateur présentant la Wave Tower s'élevant tel un organisme vivant.

Cultural Islands
Kulturinseln
Îles de culture

Benesse House Museum and Oval I National Center for the Performing Arts
Museum of Islamic Art I Royal Danish Playhouse
Liangzhu Culture Museum I Oslo Opera House
Elbphilharmonie I Louvre Abu Dhabi I Performing Arts Center
Maritime Museum I Guggenheim Abu Dhabi Museum

Modern museums, theaters, and concert halls have become the new cathedrals. Designed as iconic symbols to represent their cities, they aim to impress and attract as many visitors as possible. There can be no more imposing setting for an ambitious design than at the water's edge, and even more so when that building is almost or completely surrounded by water. For port cities, such as Hamburg, Copenhagen, and Oslo, the riverside is the logical place for their new symbols of culture. Meanwhile, new wealthy nations, like China, Abu Dhabi, and Qatar, have created islands for their cultural centers. Inevitably great architects are attracted to great projects and the examples here are no exception, from Tadao Ando's deceptively modest contemporary art museum on Naoshima Island to Paul Andreu's vast opera house in the middle of an artificial lake in Beijing. All are grand statements, made yet grander by being on islands.

Les musées modernes, théâtres et salles de concert sont aujourd'hui les nouvelles églises. Conçus comme les symboles des villes auxquelles ils appartiennent, ils visent à époustoufler et à attirer le plus grand nombre de visiteurs. Il n'y a pas d'emplacement plus grandiose pour une construction ambitieuse que le bord de mer, surtout lorsque celle-ci est en partie ou en totalité entourée d'eau. Pour les villes portuaires telles que Hambourg, Copenhague et Oslo, les rives sont idéales pour les nouveaux symboles de culture. Parallèlement, les nouvelles nations qui s'enrichissent, comme la Chine, Abu Dhabi et le Qatar, créent directement des îles pour leurs centres culturels. Inévitablement, les grands architectes sont attirés par les grands projets et les exemples ici ne font pas exception, du musée d'art contemporain trompeusement modeste de Tadao Andi sur l'île de Naoshima à l'immense opéra de Paul Andreu situé au milieu d'un lac artificiel à Pékin, toutes ces constructions sont exceptionnelles en elles-mêmes, mais le sont davantage parce qu'elles sont flottantes.

Moderne Museen, Theater und Konzertsäle sind die Kathedralen der Gegenwart. Als ikonische Wahrzeichen für ihre Stadt entworfen, sollen sie beeindrucken und so viele Besucher wie möglich anlocken. Für einen anspruchsvollen Entwurf kann es keinen imposanteren Standort geben als am Rande des Wassers und dies gilt erst recht, wenn das Gebäude fast vollkommen oder sogar zur Gänze von Wasser umgeben ist. Im Falle von Hafenstädten wie Hamburg, Kopenhagen und Oslo ist das Flussufer der naheliegendste Ort für die neuen Kultursymbole. Neu zu Wohlstand gekommene Länder wie China, Abu Dhabi und Katar haben hingegen eigens Inseln für ihre Kulturzentren geschaffen. Große Architekten werden unweigerlich von großen Projekten angezogen, und die hier aufgeführten Beispiele sind keine Ausnahmen: von Tadao Andos täuschend schlichtem Museum für Zeitgenössische Kunst auf der Insel Naoshima bis hin zu Paul Andreus gigantischem Opernhaus in der Mitte eines künstlichen Sees in Peking. Jedes von ihnen will eine wichtige Botschaft vermitteln, deren Bedeutung durch den Inselstandort noch mehr Gewicht erhält.

Benesse House Museum and Oval

Naoshima, Japan
Tadao Ando Architect & Associates
1992/1995

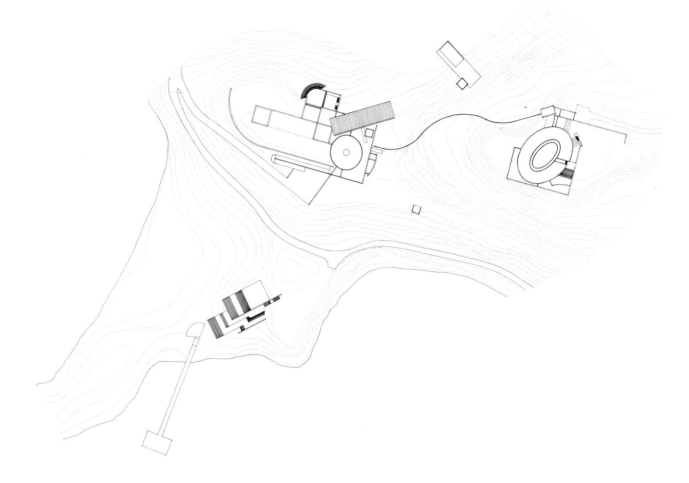

left View of the peninsula with the Benesse House Museum (top) and the Benesse House Oval below it.

links Ansicht der Insel mit dem Benesse House Museum (oben) und dem Benesse House Oval darunter.

gauche Vue de la péninsule, Benesse House Museum (en haut) et Benesse House Oval en dessous.

right Site plan. Visitors must arrive on the island by boat, docking at the pier, before walking up to the museum.

rechts Lageplan. Der einzig mögliche Zugang zur Insel erfolgt per Boot. Über den Landesteg gelangen Besucher auf die Insel, bevor sie zum Museum hinaufsteigen.

droite Plan du site. Les visiteurs arrivent sur l'île en bateau avant de monter jusqu'au musée.

In the second half of the 1980s, the small island of Naoshima, which lies 8 miles north of Takamatsu in the Seto Inland Sea, became the focus of a new regeneration project to create an "island of nature filled with art." The architect Tadao Ando was commissioned to make a series of buildings over the following 20 years. His first was the Benesse House Museum in 1992, followed by the Benesse House Oval three years later. This entire project is still ongoing—an experiment in organic architecture, something unplanned and unexpected.

The museum is reached from the sea by boat. On arriving at a pier, visitors make their way up a wide stepped plaza from which the rough stone wall of the museum and the roof cone can just be seen above a wildflower plateau. The plaza is designed not only as a dramatic entrance, but also as a space for outdoor performances. Since the museum is located within a national park, Ando decided to build half of the volume underground to impose on the environment as little as possible. This underground theme is common in much of his work and is repeated in other buildings across the island, including the Benesse House Oval and the Chichu Art Museum which was built much later. As the architect puts it, "I have an almost unconscious inclination towards underground spaces."

So the museum sits on the hilltop blending in with nature. Interlocking simple geometric shapes—a circle and two rectangles—are

In der zweiten Hälfte der Achtziger Jahre wurde die kleine Insel Naoshima, 13 km nördlich von Takamatsu in der Seto-Inlandsee gelegen, zum Zentrum eines Erneuerungsprojekts, bei dem eine „mit Kunst angefüllte Insel der Natur" entstehen sollte. Über die folgenden 20 Jahre wurde der Architekt Tadao Ando beauftragt, eine Reihe von Gebäuden zu entwerfen. Sein erster Entwurf war das Benesse House Museum im Jahre 1992, drei Jahre später gefolgt vom Benesse House Oval. Das gesamte Projekt befindet sich nach wie vor in der Entwicklung – ein Experiment mit organischer Architektur, vollkommen ungeplant und unerwartet.

Das Museum wird vom Meer aus mit Booten erreicht. Nach ihrer Ankunft am Landesteg nähern Besucher sich dem Gebäude über einen breiten, mit Stufen versehenen Platz, von dem aus die raue Steinwand und der Dachkegel des Museums über einem Plateau mit Wildblumen gerade soeben sichtbar sind. Der Platz bildet nicht nur einen dramatisch wirkenden Aufgang zum Museum, sondern dient gleichzeitig als Ort für Aufführungen im Freien. Da das Museum sich in einem Nationalpark befindet, beschloss Ando, die Hälfte des Gebäudeinhalts unterirdisch zu bauen, um störende Einflüsse auf die natürliche Umgebung so gering wie möglich zu halten. Dieses unterirdische Thema tritt bei vielen seiner Bauwerke auf und wiederholt sich auch bei anderen Gebäuden auf der Insel, einschließlich des Benesse House Ovals und des viel später erbauten Chichu Kunstmuseums. Der

Durant la seconde moitié des années 1980, la petite île de Naoshima, à 13 km au nord de Tamamatsu dans la mer intérieure de Seto, est devenue le centre d'attention d'un nouveau projet de régénération visant à créer une « île naturelle réservée à l'art ». Les 20 années suivantes, l'architecte Tadao Ando a été chargé de créer plusieurs bâtiments. Le premier fut le Benesse House Museum en 1992, suivi du Benesse House Oval trois ans plus tard. Le projet est toujours en cours – une expérience dans l'architecture organique, inattendue et non planifiée.

Le musée n'est accessible que par bateau: une fois à quai, les visiteurs atteignent une grande place aux larges marches, depuis laquelle on aperçoit le mur de pierres du musée et le toit conique surplombant un plateau de fleurs sauvages. La place joue le rôle d'entrée principale mais également de scène de plein air. Le musée étant situé à l'intérieur d'un parc national, Tadao Ando a décidé de construire la moitié de son volume sous terre afin d'affecter le moins possible l'environnement. Ce thème souterrain est récurrent chez l'architecte, notamment sur d'autres bâtiments de l'île, dont le Benesse House Oval et le Chichu Art Museum, construit beaucoup plus tard. Comme l'affirme l'architecte, « J'ai presque un penchant inconscient pour les espaces souterrains. »

Le musée se trouve au sommet d'une colline et se fond dans la nature. Des formes géométriques simples sont emboîtées (un cercle

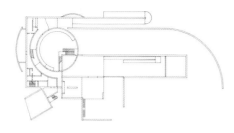

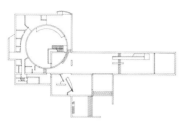

above Floor plans of the museum showing the circular gallery with surrounding spaces where there is a hotel and restaurant.

oben Grundrisse des Museums zeigen die kreisförmige Galerie mit den umgebenden Räumen, in denen sich ein Hotel und ein Restaurant befinden.

ci-dessus Espace incliné de la galerie dans le musée. La lumière est une composante clé de tous les travaux de Tadao Ando.

right The roof cone of the museum can just be glimpsed above a wild flower meadow. Most of the building is situated below ground.

rechts Der Dachkegel des Museums ist über einer Wiese mit Wildblumen gerade soeben sichtbar. Der größte Teil des Gebäudes befindet sich unter der Erde.

droite Le toit conique du musée surgit au-dessus d'un champ de fleurs sauvages. Une grande partie du bâtiment se trouve sous terre.

right Ando typically uses exposed concrete for his buildings. Here, on a terrace at the museum, the walls are used to frame views of the island.

rechts Ando verwendet für seine Gebäude üblicherweise Sichtbeton. Hier auf einer Terrasse des Museums dienen die Wände als Rahmen für verschiedene Ansichten der Insel.

droite Tadao Ando travaille généralement avec du béton apparent. Ici, sur une terrasse du musée, les murs servent de cadres aux différentes vues de l'île.

far right The main circular underground exhibition hall in the museum. Massive concrete walls offer shelter for the visitor.

ganz rechts Der kreisförmige unterirdische Hauptausstellungssaal im Museum. Massive Betonmauern bieten dem Besucher Schutz.

au loin à gauche Plans d'étage du musée présentant la galerie circulaire et ses espaces environnants, dont un hôtel et un restaurant.

placed at angles to each other to offer visitors varying views over the surrounding seascape. These house the art galleries, hotel rooms, and restaurant. Here the predominant material is concrete, the beautifully crafted thick walls acting as protective spiritual shelter. A vast double-height exhibition space is crowned by a pyramidal glass skylight.

The second phase was to build an annex, the Benesse House Oval, further up the slope. Consisting of 10 guest rooms, gallery, library, shop, and cafeteria, it can be reached either by cable car or a footpath. Again much of the building is buried into the cliffs making only part of it visible above ground. Water is the predominant theme, with a cascade near the entrance and an oval pond filling the center of the building. The building is composed of a square in the middle of which is an ellipse at an offset axis. Within the ellipse is the inner pool, conceived as a contemplative water sculpture. A patio surrounds the pool and is used as an outdoor gallery and entrance to the guest rooms.

Water and light are key to Ando's work. The oval house is like an inverted island, with the sea surrounded by land, the blue sky reflected in its waters. As the architect has said, "The use of water in my architecture is an attempt to bear a spiritual dimension which is directly related to Japanese thought and tradition."

Architekt drückt es so aus: „Ich habe einen fast unbewussten Hang zu unterirdischen Räumen."

Das Museum befindet sich daher auf der Bergkuppe, wo es mit der Natur verschmilzt. Drei ineinander greifende schlichte geometrische Formen – ein Kreis und zwei Rechtecke – wurden schräg zueinander erbaut, um Besuchern verschiedene Blickwinkel auf das Meerespanorama zu bieten. Diese Gebäude beherbergen die Kunstgalerien, Hotelzimmer und ein Restaurant. Beton ist das hier vorherrschende Material, wobei die wunderschön verarbeiteten dicken Wände als schützende geistige Zuflucht dienen sollen. Ein weitläufiger Ausstellungsraum von doppelter Höhe wird von einem pyramidenförmigen gläsernen Oberlicht gekrönt.

In der zweiten Bauphase wurde weiter oben am Abhang ein Anbau errichtet, das Benesse House Oval. Das aus 10 Gästezimmern, einer Galerie, einer Bibliothek, einem Laden und einer Cafeteria bestehende Gebäude kann entweder mit einer Seilbahn oder über einen Fußweg erreicht werden. Ein Großteil des Gebäudes ist wiederum in die Klippen eingelagert, so dass nur ein Teil überirdisch sichtbar ist. Ein Wasserfall nahe beim Eingang und ein ovaler Teich, der den Mittelpunkt des Baus ausfüllt, machen Wasser zum vorherrschenden Thema. Das Gebäude besteht aus einem Quadrat mit einer Ellipse in der Mitte, die auf einer versetzten Achse angelegt wurde. Innerhalb der Ellipse befindet sich das innere Becken, das als kontemplative Wasserskulptur entworfen wurde. Das Becken ist von einem Patio umgeben, der als Freiluftgalerie und Eingang zu den Gästezimmern dient.

Wasser und Licht sind Schlüsselelemente in Andos Werk. Das ovale Haus gleicht einer seitenverkehrten Insel, bei der das Meer von Land umgeben ist und der blaue Himmel sich in den Wassern spiegelt. Der Architekt sagt: „Die Verwendung von Wasser in meiner Architektur ist ein Versuch, eine spirituelle Dimension zu schaffen, die unmittelbar mit japanischem Denken und japanischer Tradition verbunden ist."

et deux rectangles) et placées côte à côte pour offrir aux visiteurs une vue variée sur le paysage marin. Ces constructions hébergent des galeries d'art, des chambres d'hôtels et un restaurant. Le matériau prédominant est le béton; les murs épais, magnifiquement travaillés, offrent un abri spirituel protecteur. Un espace d'exposition à double hauteur est couronné d'un ciel pyramidal en verre.

La deuxième étape consistait à construire une annexe plus en hauteur, le Benesse House Oval. Composé de 10 chambres, d'une galerie, d'une bibliothèque, de boutiques et d'une cafétéria, on y accède par télécabine ou à pied. Ici encore, une grande partie du bâtiment est enterrée dans les falaises dont une seule partie reste visible au-dessus du sol. L'eau y est le thème prédominant: une cascade se trouve à proximité de l'entrée et un bassin ovale occupe le centre du bâtiment. Cette construction carrée enserre une ellipse dont l'axe est décalé. En son sein se trouve la piscine intérieure, une sorte de sculpture aquatique contemplative. Une cour entoure la piscine servant de galerie extérieure et d'entrée aux chambres.

Dans le travail de Tadao Ando, l'eau et la lumière sont essentielles. La maison ovale est une île inversée, où l'eau reflétant le ciel est entourée de terre. Comme l'affirme l'architecte, « En intégrant l'eau à mon architecture, j'essaie de donner une dimension spirituelle directement liée à la pensée et à la tradition japonaises. »

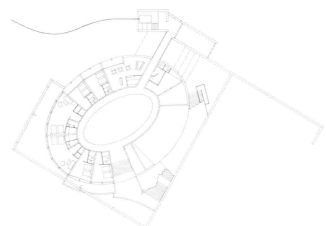

left An enormous pool dominates the internal space of the House Oval, designed as a contemplative sculpture—an inverted island on an island.

links Ein gewaltiges, als kontemplative Skulptur entworfenes Becken dominiert den Innenraum des House Oval – eine seitenverkehrte Insel auf einer Insel.

gauche Une immense piscine domine l'intérieur du House Oval, conçue comme une sculpture contemplative. Une île inversée sur une île.

above Plan of the Benesse House Oval. The oval pool is offset the axis of the surrounding square building.

oben Grundriss des Benesse House Oval. Das ovale Becken ist von der Achse des umgebenden quadratischen Gebäudes abgesetzt.

ci-dessus Plan du Benesse House Oval. La piscine ovale compense l'axe du bâtiment carré.

National Center for the Performing Arts

Paul Andreu
Beijing, China
2007

Variously described by critics as an egg, a pearl, and a spaceship, the National Center for the Performing Arts in Beijing faced a great deal of controversy during its construction. Designed by French architect Paul Andreu—best known for his Charles de Gaulle Airport, Roissy—the project was criticized for being too costly, too hard to clean, and not "Chinese" enough in its design. However, since its opening in December 2007 this "cultural island" has silenced many of its doubters. What cannot be doubted is the sheer ambition of the project. It is one of the largest performing arts centers in the world. It encases an opera house, a concert hall, and a theater all sunk beneath a massive ellipsoid dome. Set in massive water-resistant concrete foundations 107 feet deep, a 24,250-ton titanium-clad shell sits within a square artificial lake. The dome itself is constructed out of 148 radial steel trusses to allow it to be as large and transparent as possible. It has an east-west span of 699 feet, a north-south span of 472 feet, and is 150 feet at its highest–the exact height of the neighboring Great Hall of the People. The titanium dome is cut in two by a glass droplet 328 feet at the base that tapers to a strip over the roof. The curving glass structure allows light in during the day and is lit up at night. In order to emphasize the idea of a cultural

Von Kritikern abwechselnd als Ei, als Perle und Raumschiff beschrieben, war das Chinesische Staatstheater in Peking während seiner Erbauung vielerlei Kontroversen ausgesetzt. Das von dem französischen Architekten Paul Andreu – am besten bekannt für den Flughafen Charles de Gaulle in Paris – entworfene Projekt wurde als zu teuer, als zu schwer zu reinigen und als in seinem Entwurf nicht „chinesisch" genug kritisiert. Seit ihrer Eröffnung im Dezember 2007 hat diese „Kulturinsel" jedoch viele Zweifler zum Schweigen gebracht.

Kein Zweifel besteht an dem extrem außerordentlichen Ehrgeiz des Projekts. Es ist eines der größten Zentren für darstellende Kunst in der Welt und umfasst ein Opernhaus, einen Konzertsaal und ein Theater, die alle unter einer massiven ellipsenförmigen Kuppel versenkt sind. Eine 22.000 Tonnen schwere, mit Titan verkleidete Muschel ruht auf massiven wasserbeständigen Betonfundamenten in einem quadratischen künstlichen See. Die Kuppel selbst besteht aus 148 strahlenförmig angelegten Stahlträgern, um sie so groß und transparent wie möglich erscheinen zu lassen. Die Spannweite der Kuppel beträgt von Osten nach Westen 213 Meter und von Norden nach Süden 144 Meter. An ihrem höchsten Punkt erreicht sie 46 Meter – exakt die Höhe der unmittelbar benachbarten

Décrit à diverses reprises comme un œuf, une perle ou encore un vaisseau spatial, le Centre national des arts scéniques de Pékin a dû faire face à une grande controverse durant sa construction. Conçu par l'architecte français Paul Andreu, plus connu pour son Aéroport Charles de Gaulle à Paris, le projet a été critiqué pour son prix démesuré, sa difficulté d'entretien et son style trop peu « chinois ». Cependant, depuis son ouverture en 2007, cette « île culturelle » a fait taire de nombreux sceptiques.

L'ambition pure du projet ne fait en revanche aucun doute. C'est l'un des centres d'arts scéniques les plus grands au monde; il comprend un opéra, une salle de concert et un théâtre, le tout sous un imposant dôme ellipsoïdal. Installée sur des fondations en béton étanche de 32,5 mètres de profondeur, une coquille de 22 000 tonnes recouverte de titane repose sur un lac artificiel carré. Le dôme est construit sur 148 poutres radiales métalliques qui lui permettent d'être aussi large et transparent que possible. D'un diamètre est-ouest de 213 mètres, nord-sud de 144 mètres, et d'une hauteur de 46 mètres à son sommet (exactement la même hauteur que l'Assemblée du peuple située à côté), le dôme en titane est traversé par une goutte de verre d'une largeur de 100 mètres à la base mais plus étroite à

far left The glass façade, in the shape of a water droplet, sweeps up from the artificial lake to the top of the dome.

ganz links Die Glasfassade in Form eines Wassertropfens erhebt sich aus dem künstlichen See bis zum obersten Punkt der Kuppel.

au loin à gauche La façade de verre, en forme de goutte d'eau, surgit du lac artificiel et s'étend jusqu'au sommet du dôme.

left Computer rendering showing the curved red entrance that leads to an underground passage running under the lake.

links Computergrafik mit Ansicht des gebogenen roten Eingangs, der in eine unterirdische Passage unter dem See mündet

gauche Modélisation présentant l'entrée incurvée de couleur rouge conduisant à un passage souterrain sous le lac.

above During the day the titanium façade reflects the light back, while the glass front sits back. The effect is reversed at night.

oben Tagsüber reflektiert die Titanfassade das Licht, während die Glasfront wenig auffällig erscheint. Bei Nacht tritt der umgekehrte Effekt ein.

ci-dessus La nuit, l'extérieur sombre habillé de titane est éclairé par de petites lumières semblables à des étoiles. La façade de verre se distingue, par sa transparence et sa brillance.

above At night the dark, titanium-clad exterior is lit up with tiny star-like lights. In contrast, the glass façade is transparent and glowing.

oben Nachts wird das dunkle, mit Titan verkleidete Äußere mit kleinen sternartigen Lichtern erleuchtet. Im Gegensatz dazu ist die Glasfassade transparent und scheint zu glühen.

ci-dessus En soirée, la façade en titane s'illumine comme de petites étoiles. Par contraste, la façade de verre est brillante et transparente.

island, it is reached by an underground passage so that it appears that there is no visible means of access. Visitors enter through a curved red wall, designed to echo the masonry of the Forbidden City (situated opposite), and walk along a 197-foot long transparent underpass beneath the artifical lake. The lobby is clad in warm, dark Brazilian mahogany panels, and the floors are made of 22 different types of marble from all over China—white, cream, and gray. The theater spaces are equally luxurious: the calm, white concert hall contrasting with the rich, red opera house.

The National Center is not the first cultural center to be designed next to an artificial lake, earlier examples include Louis Kahn's Kimbell Art Museum (1972) and Tadao Ando's Modern Art Museum (2002), both at Fort Worth, Texas. However, this is arguably the most impressive example of its type in the world.

Großen Halle des Volkes. Die Titankuppel wird von einem gläsernen, an der Basis hundert Meter breiten Tropfen in zwei Hälften geteilt, der sich auf dem Dach des Gebäudes zu einem schmalen Streifen verjüngt. Die gebogene Glasstruktur lässt tagsüber Licht in das Bauwerk und wird bei Nacht erleuchtet.

Um die Idee einer Kulturinsel zu betonen, kann das Gebäude nur über einen unterirdischen Gang erreicht werden, so dass es den Anschein hat, es gebe keinen sichtbaren Zugang. Besucher betreten das Gebäude durch eine gebogene rote Mauer, deren Gestaltung das Mauerwerk der gegenüber gelegenen Verbotenen Stadt widerspiegeln soll, und gehen anschließend durch eine 60 Meter lange, durchsichtige Unterführung unter dem künstlichen See. Die Lobby ist mit warmen, dunklen Mahagoniplatten aus Brasilien verkleidet und die Böden bestehen aus 22 verschiedenen Marmorarten aus ganz China – weiß, cremefarben und grau. Die Theaterräume sind ebenso luxuriös: Der ruhige, weiße Konzertsaal bildet einen Kontrast zu dem üppig ausgestatteten roten Opernhaus.

Das Staatstheater ist nicht das erste Kulturzentrum in Verbindung mit einem künstlichen See – frühere Beispiele sind das von Louis Kahn entworfene Kimbell Art Museum in Fort Worth, USA (1972), und Tadao Andos Museum of Art in Fort Worth (2002). Es ist jedoch wahrscheinlich das eindrucksvollste Beispiel seiner Art in der Welt.

mesure qu'elle remonte. Cette structure de verre courbée laisse entrer la lumière en journée et s'éclaire en soirée.

Afin d'accentuer l'idée d'îlot culturel, on y accède par un passage souterrain, donc invisible. Les visiteurs pénètrent une paroi rouge incurvée qui rappelle la Cité interdite (située à l'opposé), pour atteindre un passage souterrain de 60 mètres de long, transparent, situé sous le lac artificiel. Le hall est habillé de panneaux sombres en acajou brésilien et le sol est constitué de 22 types de marbres en provenance de Chine (blanc, crème et gris). Le théâtre est tout aussi luxueux: la salle de concert, blanche et calme, contraste avec l'opéra rouge, chaud et riche.

Le Centre national n'est pas le premier centre culturel posé sur un lac artificiel, il a notamment été précédé par le Musée d'Art Kimbell de Louis Kahn situé aux États-Unis (1972) et le Musée d'Art de Tadao Ando, à Fort Worth (2002). Il est cependant sans aucun doute l'exemple le plus impressionnant de ce type d'architecture.

left Plan showing the arts center sitting in the middle of the shallow artificial lake.

links Grundriss mit Ansicht des Kunstzentrums in der Mitte des flachen künstlichen Sees

gauche Plan du centre des arts au milieu du lac artificiel peu profond.

above Marble is one of the predominant building materials, seen here on the floor of the entrance hall at ground level.

oben Marmor ist eines der vorherrschenden Baumaterialien. Hier ist er auf dem Boden der Eingangshalle im Erdgeschoss zu sehen.

ci-dessus Le marbre est l'un des matériaux prédominants. On peut le voir ici au sol dans le hall d'entrée.

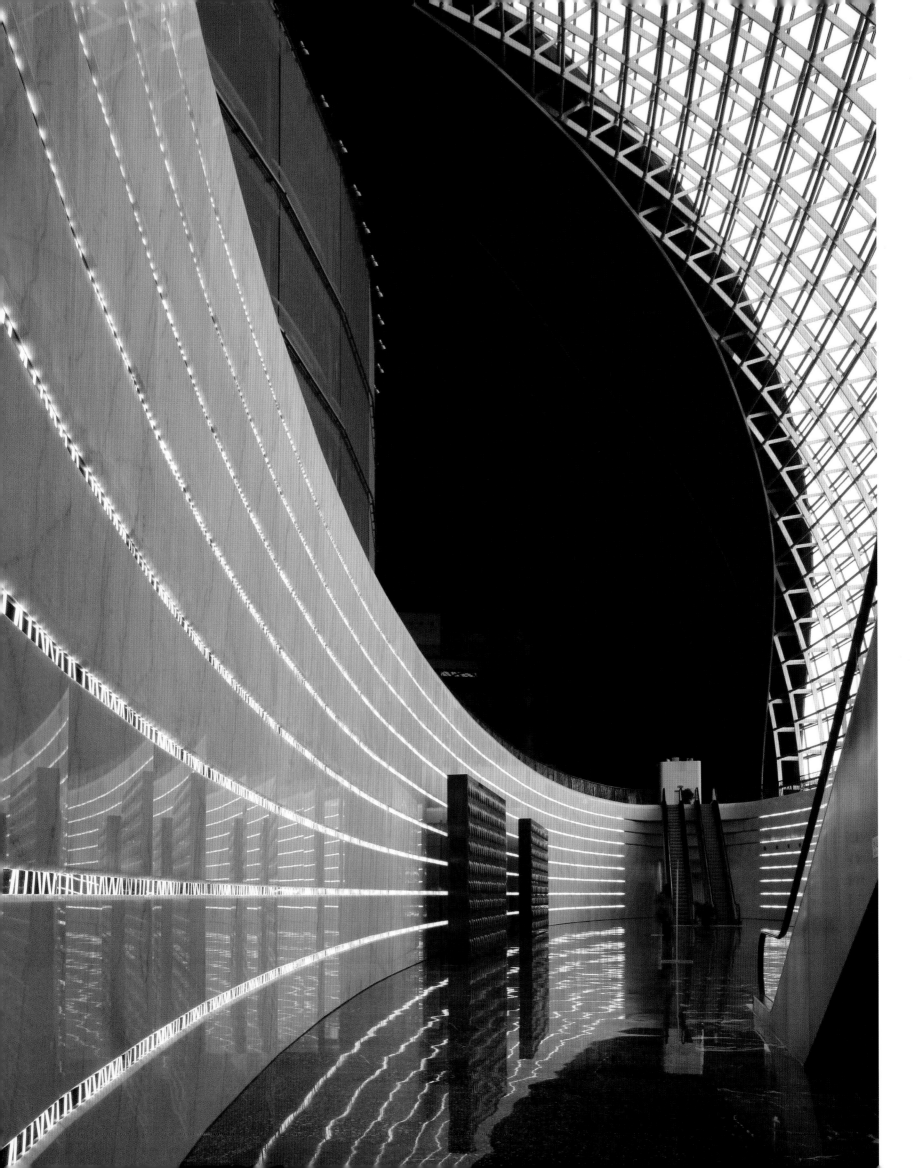

left The enormous entrance hall, below ground level, from where visitors reach the main building via escalators.

links Die gewaltige Eingangshalle im Untergeschoss, aus der Besucher das Hauptgebäude mit Rolltreppen erreichen

gauche L'immense hall d'entrée, au sous-sol, où les visiteurs empruntent des escalators pour atteindre le bâtiment principal.

below Within the concert hall the effect is one of calm restraint—white and light brown are the dominant colors.

unten Die Wirkung innerhalb des Konzertsaals ist ruhige Zurückhaltung – weiß und hellbraun sind die vorherrschenden Farben.

ci-dessous La salle de concert se caractérise par son calme. Les couleurs prédominantes sont le blanc et le marron clair.

Museum of Islamic Art

Doha, Qatar

I.M. Pei, Wilmotte et Associés

2008

above The exterior is clad in French limestone with gray granite running around the windows and along the base of the building.

oben Die Außenseite des Museums ist mit französischem Kalkstein verkleidet, und die Fenster und das Fundament des Gebäudes sind von grauem Granit umrahmt.

ci-dessus L'extérieur est revêtu de calcaire blanc français. Les fenêtres et la base du bâtiment sont entourés de granit gris.

Celebrated Chinese-born American architect, I. M. Pei, who is best known for designing the metal-and-glass pyramid for the Musée du Louvre, Paris (1993), officially retired from his firm, Pei Cobb Freed & Partners, in 1990. However, he has continued to work on projects outside the United States. Now in his nineties, he has designed a new museum for the Emirate state of Qatar to house the country's collection of Islamic art.

Pei only agreed to build the museum on the condition that the Emir of Qatar reclaimed an island in the Persian Gulf. He wanted to make sure the city's skyscrapers didn't overshadow the museum and for other buildings to not encroach. It was designed as a cultural island to stand on its own and become a symbol for this relatively new and very prosperous country.

Because Qatar does not have a long history, Pei took his inspiration from outside the country. He traveled to Spain, India, Egypt, Syria, and the Middle East, keen to learn as much as possible about the Islamic faith and architecture. In the end, the museum was more influenced by the Mosque of Ibn Tulun in Cairo, Egypt, than any other building. The 13th-century mosque has an enclosed *sabil*, or ablution fountain, whose refined geometry is both austere and beautiful— a series of cubic shapes set one on top of

Der gefeierte chinesischstämmige Architekt aus den USA, I. M Pei, der für seinen Entwurf der Pyramide aus Metall und Glas für den Louvre in Paris (1993) wohl am berühmtesten ist, zog sich bereits 1990 offiziell aus seinem Unternehmen, Pei Cobb Freed & Partners, zurück. Dennoch arbeitete er seitdem weiterhin an verschiedenen Projekten außerhalb der Vereinigten Staaten mit. So hat der mittlerweile über neunzig Jahre alte Architekt auch ein neues Museum für das Emirat Katar entworfen, das dessen Sammlung islamischer Kunst beherbergen soll.

Pei stimmte dem Bau des Museums nur unter der Voraussetzung zu, dass der Emir von Katar eine Insel im Persischen Golf zur Verfügung stellen würde. Er wollte vermeiden, dass das Museum unter den Wolkenkratzern der Stadt untergehen und seine Wirkung durch andere Bauten geschmälert würde. Das Bauwerk wurde als Kulturinsel entworfen, die für sich allein stehen und Symbol dieses verhältnismäßig neuen und sehr wohlhabenden Landes werden sollte.

Da das Emirat Katar nicht über eine lange Geschichte verfügt, holte sich Pei seine Inspiration von außerhalb. Er unternahm Reisen durch Spanien, Indien, Ägypten, Syrien und den Mittleren Osten, um sich so viel Wissen wie möglich über Glauben und Architektur des Islam anzueignen. Schließlich zeigte sich sein Entwurf

Célèbre architecte américain d'origine chinoise, I.M. Pei, plus connu pour sa pyramide de métal et de verre au Musée du Louvre à Paris (1993), a officiellement pris sa retraite de son cabinet Pei Cobb Freed & Partners en 1990. Il a cependant continué à travailler sur des projets à l'extérieur des États-Unis. Aujourd'hui, à plus de quatre-vingt-dix ans, il conçoit un nouveau musée pour l'émirat du Qatar, qui accueillera la collection nationale d'art islamique.

I.M. Pei a accepté de concevoir le musée à la seule et unique condition que l'Émir du Qatar crée une île dans le Golfe persique. Il voulait éviter que les tours d'immeubles de la ville ne le surplombent et que d'autres bâtiments n'empiètent dessus. Le musée fut ainsi conçu comme une île culturelle et est devenu un symbole pour ce nouveau pays très prospère.

L'histoire du Qatar étant relativement récente, I.M. Pei s'est inspiré d'autres pays. Il a voyagé en Espagne, en Inde, en Égypte, en Syrie et au Moyen-Orient, désireux d'apprendre tout ce qui a trait à la foi et à l'architecture islamique. Il a finalement été plus influencé par la Mosquée d'Ibn Tulun située au Caire, en Égypte. Cette mosquée du XIIe siècle comporte un *sabil* fermé, ou une fontaine d'ablution, dont la géométrie raffinée est à la fois magnifique et austère. Plusieurs formes cubiques sont posées

below Looking north, the colossal museum rises from the sea. A glass curtain wall, 150 feet high, dominates the façade.

unten Das nach Norden ausgerichtete, gewaltige Museum erhebt sich aus dem Meer. Eine 45 Meter hohe vorgehängte Wand aus Glas dominiert die Fassade.

ci-dessous En direction du nord, le musée colossal semble s'élever de la mer. Un mur de verre de 45 mètres de haut domine la façade.

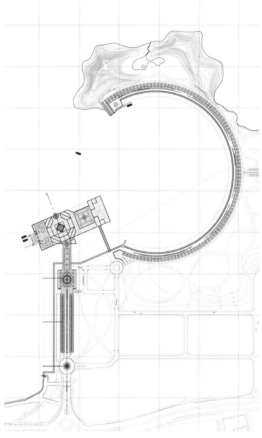

above Site plan. The entire building is surrounded by water, linked to the shore by a footbridge.

oben Lageplan. Das gesamte Gebäude ist von Wasser umgeben und über eine Fußgängerbrücke mit dem Ufer verbunden.

ci-dessus Plan du site. Le bâtiment est entièrement entouré d'eau et relié à la terre par une passerelle.

left An inclined walkway lined by palm trees leads to the footbridge linking the shore to the museum island. The museum itself is a series of cubic shapes, one on top of the other.

links Ein schräg angelegter, von Palmen gesäumter Fußgängerweg führt zu der Brücke, die die Museumsinsel mit dem Ufer verbindet. Das Museum selbst besteht aus einer Reihe würfelförmiger, aufeinander gesetzter Elemente.

gauche Une allée bordée de palmiers conduit à une passerelle reliant la côte au musée flottant. Le musée est une série de formes cubiques empilées les unes sur les autres.

another with a dome on top. As the architect puts it, "an almost Cubist expression of geometric progression." For his museum in Qatar, he developed the same theme.

Located 200 feet from the Corniche of Doha harbor, the museum has a total area of 484,000 square feet. An inclined causeway lined with palm trees with a waterway running down the middle leads to a footbridge. On the island itself is the stand-alone structure: the five-story museum, a two-story education wing, and a central courtyard separating the two. The exterior is clad in a French white limestone, used for its combination of softness and strength, the ideal material for the rigors of the sun, heat, and sea salt. Gray granite is used around the windows and the base of the building.

The design of the main building is based on a series of tiered geometric shapes: the circle turns in the square, the square into the octagon. Like a ziggurat it rises out of the water, its white façade reflected in the surrounding blue waters. Its sharp angles respond to the bright sunlight by creating shapes and shadows.

On entering the museum, there is a sweeping double staircase under a 213-foot polyhedral dome. At the top of the dome, an oculus allows light to be reflected on the surface of the

für das Museum von der ägyptischen Ibn-Tulun-Moschee in Kairo mehr als von irgendeinem anderen Bauwerk beeinflusst. Die im 13. Jahrhundert errichtete Moschee verfügt über einen umschlossenen Sabil oder Waschungsbrunnen, dessen verfeinerte Geometrie streng und schön zugleich wirkt – eine Reihe würfelförmiger, aufeinander gesetzter Formen, die von einer Kuppel bedeckt sind. Der Architekt beschreibt sie als „nahezu kubistischen Ausdruck einer geometrischen Abfolge". Für sein Museum in Katar entwickelte er dasselbe Thema.

Das 60 Meter vom Hafen in der Corniche von Doha entfernt gelegene Museum verfügt über eine Gesamtfläche von 45.000 Quadratmetern. Ein schräg angelegter, mit Palmen gesäumter Damm mit einem Kanal in der Mitte führt zu einer Fußgängerbrücke. Das freistehende Bauwerk befindet sich auf der Insel selbst: ein fünfstöckiges Museum, ein zweistöckiger Flügel für Bildungsarbeit und ein zentraler Hof, der beide trennt. Die Außenseite ist mit einem weißen französischen Kalkstein verkleidet, eine Verbindung aus Weichheit und Stärke – das ideale Material, um den Angriffen der Sonne, der Hitze und des Meeressalzes zu trotzen. Um die Fenster und das Fundament des Gebäudes herum wurde grauer Granit verwendet.

les unes sur les autres et couronnées d'un dôme. Comme le décrit l'architecte, c'est « une expression presque cubiste de progression géométrique ». Il a développé le même thème pour le musée du Qatar.

Situé à 60 mètres de la Corniche du port de Doha, le musée fait 45 000 mètres carrés. Une allée bordée de palmiers au milieu de laquelle s'écoule l'eau conduit à une passerelle. La structure se trouve sur l'île. Les cinq étages du musée et les deux étages de l'aile consacrée à l'éducation sont séparés par une cour centrale. L'extérieur de calcaire blanc, choisi pour sa douceur et sa solidité, est le matériau idéal pour affronter le soleil, la chaleur et le sel de mer. Le contour des fenêtres et la base du bâtiment sont en granit gris.

Le design du bâtiment principal utilise différentes formes géométriques superposées sur plusieurs étages: le cercle fait partie du carré, lui-même inséré dans l'octogone. À la manière d'une ziggourat, la structure s'élève hors de l'eau, réfléchissant sa façade blanche dans les eaux bleues. Les nombreuses arêtes répondent à la lumière vive du pays en créant formes et ombres.

En entrant dans le musée, le visiteur est accueilli par un double escalier situé sous un dôme polyédrique de 65 mètres de haut. Au

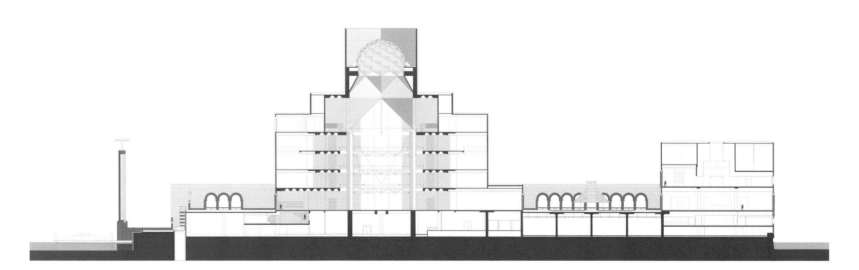

above Cross section showing the museum to the left, the central courtyard in the middle, and the education center to the right.

oben Querschnitt mit Ansicht des Museums auf der linken Seite, des zentralen Hofes in der Mitte und des Bildungszentrums auf der rechten Seite.

ci-dessus Coupe présentant le musée à gauche, la cour centrale et le centre d'éducation à droite.

left At the top of the polyhedral silver dome an oculus captures the light and reflects it back off the angled walls.

links An der Spitze der vielflächigen Silberkuppel fängt ein Rundfenster das Licht ein, das von den gewinkelten Wänden reflektiert wird.

gauche Au sommet du dôme argenté polyédrique, un oculus capture la lumière et la réfléchit sur les murs inclinés.

left Interior of the Education Wing Library designed by Jean-Michel Wilmotte et Associés.

links Innenraum der Bibliothek im Bildungszentrum, der von Jean-Michel Wilmotte et Associés entworfen wurde.

gauche Intérieur de la bibliothèque dans la partie consacrée à l'éducation, conçue par Jean-Michel Wilmotte et Associés.

above The sweeping double staircase in the main entrance directly beneath the 50-meter atrium dome.

oben Der weitläufige doppelte Treppenaufgang im Hauptein-gangsbereich befindet sich unmittelbar unter der 50 Meter hohen Kuppel des Atriums.

ci-dessus Le double escalier dans l'entrée principale se trouve directement sous le dôme de l'atrium de 50 mètres de haut.

interior. Galleries for textiles, ceramics, calligraphy, and other arts, lead off in all directions. Islamic influences can be seen in the traditional arched windows and geometric patterning. On the north side, facing out to sea, the atrium is illuminated by a 150-foot high glass curtain wall that rises over all five floors.

Pei wanted his building to draw on the tradition of Islamic architecture for using the sun. "I noticed that the sun is always there in Islamic architecture. It is animated by the sun. My design is just a humble interpretation of Islamic architecture."

Der Entwurf des Hauptgebäudes beruht auf einer Reihe abgestufter geometrischer Formen: Der Kreis geht in ein Quadrat über, das Quadrat in ein Achteck. Es erhebt sich aus dem Wasser wie eine Zikkurat, wobei seine weiße Fassade sich im blauen Meer spiegelt. Seine scharfen Winkel begegnen dem hellen Sonnenlicht, indem sie Formen und Schatten bilden.

Beim Eintreten in das Museum findet sich der Besucher vor einem weitläufigen doppelten Treppenaufgang unter einer 65 Meter hohen, vielflächigen Kuppel wieder. An der höchsten Stelle der Kuppel lässt ein Rundfenster Licht hineinfluten, das sich auf der Oberfläche des Innenraums spiegelt. Von hier aus führen Galerien für Stoffe, Keramik, Kalligrafie und andere Künste in alle Richtungen. Islamische Einflüsse werden in den traditionellen gewölbten Fenstern und den geometrischen Mustern erkennbar. Auf der Nordseite, zum Meer hin, lässt eine 45 Meter hohe vorgehängte Fassade aus Glas, die sich über alle fünf Stockwerke erhebt, Licht in das Atrium fließen.

Peis Absicht war es, sein Gebäude nach dem Vorbild islamischer Architektur zu gestalten, die sich die Sonne zu Nutze macht: „Ich stellte fest, dass die Sonne in der islamischen Architektur immer vorhanden ist. Sie wird von der Sonne belebt. Mein Entwurf ist nur eine bescheidene Interpretation der islamischen Architektur."

sommet, un oculus laisse la lumière entrer et se réfléchir sur les surfaces intérieures. Les galeries présentant tissus, céramique, calligraphie et autres arts, partent dans toutes les directions. On retrouve l'influence islamique dans les fenêtres voûtées et les motifs géométriques. Du côté nord, face à la mer, l'atrium est illuminé par un mur de verre de 45 mètres de haut qui s'élève sur les cinq niveaux.

I.M. Pei a voulu perpétuer la tradition architecturale islamique exploitant au maximum le soleil. « J'ai remarqué l'omniprésence du soleil l'architecture islamique. Elle est animée par l'astre. Ma conception n'est qu'une humble représentation de l'architecture islamique. »

right The enormous glass curtain wall on the north side of the building throws light into the atrium.

rechts Die riesige vorgehängte Glasfassade auf der Nordseite des Gebäudes lässt Licht in das Atrium fließen.

droite L'immense panneau de verre du côté nord du bâtiment projette la lumière à l'intérieur.

Royal Danish Playhouse

Copenhagen, Denmark

Lundgaard & Tranberg Arkitekter

2008

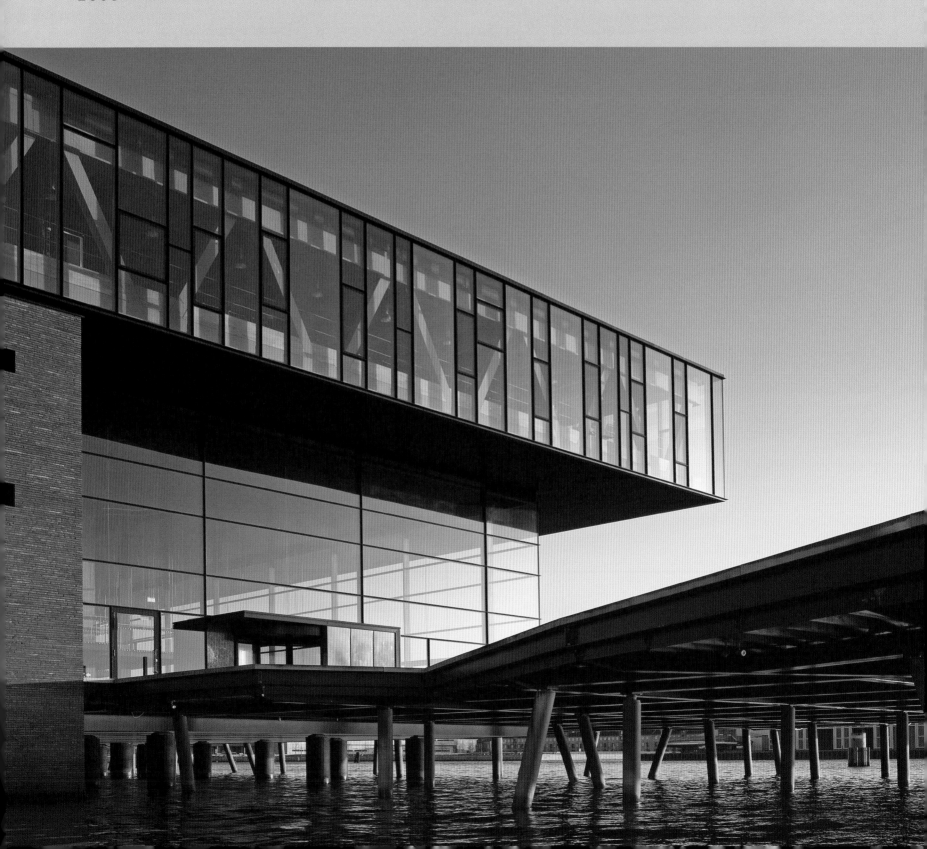

left Slender pillars under the wooden walkway are deliberately tilted—an inspiration from Venice.

links Die schlanken Pfeiler unter dem hölzernen Fußgängerweg sind bewusst schräg angelegt – inspiriert von Venedig.

gauche Les piliers filiformes sous l'allée en bois sont volontairement inclinés; une inspiration vénitienne.

above The Playhouse lit up at night. Its principal materials—glass and copper—show up against the night sky.

oben Bei Nacht ist das Schauspielhaus erleuchtet. Die wichtigsten Baumaterialien – Glas und Kupfer – heben sich gegen den Nachthimmel ab.

ci-dessus Le Théâtre s'illumine la nuit. Ses matériaux principaux, le verre et le cuivre, ressortent dans le ciel nocturne.

In 2002, the Danish architects Boje Lundgaard and Lene Tranberg won a competition to build the new Playhouse for the Danish Theater. The competition called for three theaters, a large one and two small stages, a restaurant, café, and service areas. For their design the architects turned to neighboring warehouse architecture for inspiration, creating a square plan that looks out from the city toward the harbor.

The Playhouse is perched on the edge of a long promenade that runs along the edge of the Copenhagen waterfront. Surrounded by water on three sides, the main entrance is on the harbor side. Like a ship, it embraces the water that surrounds it, an "anchor for this meeting of the city and sea." A steel and oak walkway wraps around the front of the building acting as both promenade—an inviting walkway that dances over the water—and support for the glass foyer. Slender, tilted steel columns, beneath the platform were inspired by Venetian piers. By varying the angles of the columns the deck is given a visual lightness. Thicker columns are used beneath the foyer to support the three-story structure above. In addition to the promenade, there are two other compositional elements: the scene building on the first floor that houses the foyer and auditoria; and the expansive, cantilevered upper

Im Jahr 2002 gewannen die dänischen Architekten Boje Lundgaard und Lene Tranberg einen Wettbewerb um den Bau des neuen Schauspielhauses des Dänischen Theaters. Die Ausschreibung sah den Entwurf von drei Theatern, eines mit einer großen und zwei mit kleinen Bühnen, eines Restaurants, eines Cafés und Dienstleistungsbereichen vor. Die Architekten ließen sich bei ihrem Entwurf von der Architektur der benachbarten Lagerhallen inspirieren und schufen ein Gebäude mit einem quadratischen Grundriss, das von der Stadt zum Hafen hin ausgerichtet ist.

Das Schauspielhaus steht am Rand einer langen Promenade, die entlang des Kopenhagener Hafenviertels verläuft. Der Haupteingang des auf drei Seiten von Wasser umgebenen Gebäudes befindet sich auf der Hafenseite. Wie ein Schiff ist es vom Wasser umfangen, ein „Anker für das Zusammentreffen von Stadt und Meer". Ein Fußgängerweg aus Stahl und Eichenholz verläuft um die Vorderseite des Gebäudes und dient wie ein Laufsteg, der zum Flanieren einlädt und über dem Wasser tanzt, als Promenade und als Stütze für das gläserne Foyer zugleich. Die schlanken, schrägen Säulen aus Stahl unter der Plattform wurden von venezianischen Bootsstegen inspiriert. Die unterschiedlich großen Neigungswinkel der

En 2002, les architectes néerlandais Boje Lundgaard et Lene Tranberg ont remporté un concours pour la construction du nouveau Théâtre royal danois. Il fallait concevoir trois théâtres, un grand, deux petites scènes, un restaurant, un café et des espaces de services. Les architectes se sont inspirés de l'architecture des entrepôts voisins, créant ainsi un plan carré tournant le dos à la ville pour faire face au le port.

Le théâtre est perché sur une promenade bordant le front de mer de Copenhague. Entourée d'eau sur trois côtés, l'entrée principale se fait du côté du port. Tel un navire, le Théâtre embrasse l'eau qui l'entoure; c'est une « ancre pour la rencontre de la ville et de la mer ». Une allée en acier et chêne entoure l'avant de la construction, jouant à la fois le rôle de promenade, d'allée attrayante en mouvement sur l'eau, et de support à l'atrium de verre. Les fines colonnes d'acier inclinées sous la plate-forme rappellent les embarcadères vénitiens. Leurs différents angles d'inclinaison confèrent à la plate-forme une certaine légèreté visuelle. Des colonnes plus épaisses situées sous l'entrée supportent la structure de trois niveaux. En plus de l'allée, la structure est composée de deux autres éléments: le rez-de-chaussée, qui accueille le foyer et la salle de théâtre, et le premier étage, en porte-à-faux, qui héberge les

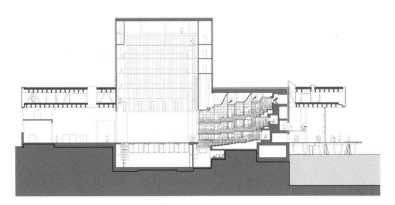

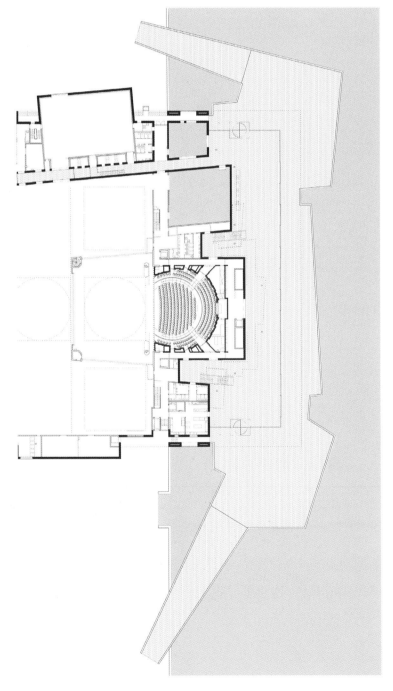

right The vertical lines on the second floor glass façade contrast with the horizontal panels of the copper cladding above.

rechts Die senkrechten Linien in der Glasfassade des zweiten Stocks heben sich von den waagerechten Platten der darüber befindlichen Kupferverkleidung ab.

droite Les lignes verticales sur la façade en verre du premier étage contrastent avec les panneaux horizontaux du revêtement en cuivre de la tour.

left above Cross section with stage area in the center, seating to the right.

links oben Querschnitt mit dem Bühnenbereich in der Mitte und den Sitzplätzen rechts.

ci-dessus à gauche Coupe avec la scène au centre, les sièges à droite.

left below Site plan showing how the wooden promenade envelops the square building and allows it to seemingly float on the water.

links unten Lageplan mit Ansicht der hölzernen Promenade, die das quadratische Gebäude umgibt und ihm den Anschein gibt, auf dem Wasser zu schwimmen.

ci-dessous à gauche Plan du site. L'allée en bois enveloppe le bâtiment carré, flottant sur l'eau en toute transparence.

level for work spaces and administration. The promenade and foyer are separated by slender mullions and large windows. The entire structure is crowned by a metallic scene tower.

The key materials are brick, glass, and copper. Brick was chosen to reflect the old warehouses in the surrounding dock area. This particular thin black brick, first developed by the architect Peter Zumthor, is a type made of English clay which can tolerate being fired to a very high temperature. It is water resistant; therefore, robust enough to be used beneath the water line. Glass was used to encase the first and second floors. Copper cladding, similar to that seen on the Copenhagen skyline of domes and spires, covers the scene tower at the top of the building.

Large glass walls allow for spectacular views to the surrounding harbor, while the dark interiors draw visitors in to the main 650-seat auditorium, a grotto-like space with staggered masonry walls and specially designed red velour chairs. The horizontal lines of the bricks on the first floor and copper cladding at the top contrast

Säulen verleihen dem Deck eine optische Leichtigkeit. Unter dem Foyer wurden zur Stützung des darüber liegenden dreistöckigen Bauwerks dickere Säulen errichtet. Neben der Promenade verfügt der Bau über zwei weitere Gestaltungselemente: das Theatergebäude im ersten Stockwerk, das das Foyer und die Zuschauerräume beherbergt, und das weitläufige, freitragende Obergeschoss mit Arbeitsräumen und der Verwaltung. Die Promenade und das Foyer werden von schlanken Pfosten und großen Fenstern optisch getrennt. Das gesamte Bauwerk wird von einem Kulissenturm aus Metall gekrönt.

Die Hauptmaterialien, die bei der Errichtung des Bauwerks verwendet wurden, sind Ziegel, Glas und Kupfer. Die Ziegel wurden in Anlehnung an die alten Lagerhäuser in der benachbarten Hafengegend gewählt. Diese besondere Art dünner, schwarzer Ziegel wurde erstmals von dem Architekten Peter Zumthor entwickelt. Sie wird von Hand aus einem englischen Ton gefertigt, der bei sehr hohen Temperaturen gebrannt werden kann. Die Ziegel

espaces de travail et l'administration. La promenade et le foyer sont séparés par de minces meneaux et de grandes fenêtres. La structure est couronnée d'une tour métallique.

La brique, le verre et le cuivre sont les matériaux principaux. La brique a été choisie pour rappeler les anciens entrepôts des quais voisins. La briquette noire, premièrement développée par l'architecte Peter Zumthor, est un type d'argile anglaise fait à la main et pouvant tolérer des températures très élevées. Elle est résistante à l'eau et donc suffisamment solide pour être immergée. Le rez-de-chaussée et le premier étage sont habillés de verre. Le revêtement en cuivre, similaire à celui que l'on perçoit à l'horizon de Copenhague, sur les dômes et les cimes, recouvre la tour au sommet de la construction.

Les hauts murs de verre offrent une vue spectaculaire sur le port tandis que les intérieurs plus sombres plongent les visiteurs dans le théâtre principal de 650 sièges, une sorte de grotte aux murs maçonnés et aux fauteuils de

left Thin, black bricks were employed on the building, specially designed to be water resistant.

links Für das Gebäude wurden dünne, schwarze Ziegel verwendet, die eigens so angefertigt wurden, dass sie wasserbeständig sind.

gauche Les briquettes noires, particulièrement résistantes à l'eau, ont été utilisées pour la construction.

left top Blond wood floors are used both outside and inside.

links oben Außen wie innen wurden Fußböden aus hellem Holz verlegt.

ci-dessus à gauche Parquet en bois clair, utilisé à l'intérieur comme à l'extérieur.

left middle The airy 26-feet high foyer with wide stairs leading to the balcony and upper levels.

links Mitte Das luftige, acht Meter hohe Foyer mit breiten Treppen, die zu den Balkon- und oberen Rängen führen.

au milieu à gauche Foyer de 8 mètres de haut dont les larges escaliers conduisent au balcon et aux niveaux supérieurs.

left bottom Recessed seating area on the second floor with stunning views.

links unten In den Boden eingelassener Sitzbereich im zweiten Stockwerk mit atemberaubender Aussicht.

ci-dessous à gauche Fauteuils intégrés au premier étage, avec vue stupéfiante.

right Balcony at second floor level looking down on the foyer and out to the river.

rechts Balkon im zweiten Stockwerk mit Blick auf das Foyer und auf den Fluss.

droite Balcon au premier étage avec vue sur le foyer et sur l'eau.

with the vertical lines of the middle green glass façade emphasizing the different levels.

The architects are keen to stress the importance of texture and detail in their work. "A building should work, be full of life and activity, be appreciated by users and those just passing by, age gracefully, be full of contrasts, appeal to the sensory, tell stories, surprise and delight."

sind wasserbeständig und daher robust genug, um auch unter der Wasseroberfläche verwendet zu werden. Zur Ummantelung des ersten und zweiten Stockwerks wurde Glas verwendet. Der Kulissenturm auf dem Gebäude wird von einer kupfernen Verkleidung ähnlich derjenigen, die das Kopenhagener Stadtbild mit seinen Kuppeln und Türmen prägt, bedeckt.

Riesige Glaswände geben spektakuläre Ausblicke auf den umgebenden Hafen frei, während die dunklen Innenräume Besucher in den mit 650 Sitzplätzen versehenen Hauptzuschauerraum locken, einem grottenartigen Raum mit versetzt gemauerten Wänden und eigens entworfenen Sitzen aus rotem Velours. Die waagerechten Linien der Ziegel im ersten Stockwerk und die kupferne Verkleidung auf dem Dach bilden einen Kontrast zu den senkrechten Linien der grünen Glasfassade in der Mitte und setzen so die verschiedenen Stockwerke voneinander ab.

Den Architekten ist es wichtig, die Bedeutung von Oberflächenstruktur und Detail in ihrem Werk hervorzuheben. „Ein Gebäude sollte funktionieren, voller Leben und Aktivität sein, von seinen Benutzern und Passanten geschätzt werden, mit Würde altern, voller Kontraste sein, die Sinne ansprechen, Geschichten erzählen, überraschen und erfreuen."

velours rouge. Les lignes horizontales de la brique au rez-de-chaussée et le revêtement de cuivre de la tour contrastent avec les lignes verticales de la façade de verre aux reflets verts du premier étage, ce qui accentue les différents niveaux.

Les architectes souhaitent souligner l'importance de la texture et des détails dans leur travail. « Un bâtiment doit travailler, être vivant, actif et apprécié des visiteurs et des passants. Il doit vieillir avec grâce, contraster, appeler aux sens, raconter des histoires, surprendre et enchanter. »

Liangzhu Culture Museum

Hangzhou, China
David Chipperfield Architects
2008

David Chipperfield is best known for the museums and galleries he has designed in the United States and Europe. His buildings are characterized by being simple and sophisticated, usually reduced down to a few key elements and materials. This new museum near the town of Hangzhou in China is no exception. It took five years to design and construct.

The Liangzhu Culture Museum forms the northern point of Liangzhu Cultural Village, a newly created park town, and houses a collection of archaeological artifacts from the Liangzhu culture, also known as the Jade culture (c.3000 BC). The building is surrounded by water on three sides and connected to a landscaped park via a footbridge. A second footbridge links the museum to a smaller island designed for outdoor exhibitions.

The museum is made up of four long rectangular volumes, each equal in width (59 feet) but differing in height and length. Within the volumes are five interior courtyards, which were inspired by the Chinese tradition of courtyard houses with stone walls. The intention was to create very quiet, contemplative spaces for the exhibitions, while the regular shapes allow for maximum flexibility for exhibition design and easy orientation for visitors.

David Chipperfield ist am bekanntesten für die von ihm entworfenen Museen und Galerien in den Vereinigten Staaten und in Europa. Seine Bauwerke zeichnen sich durch Schlichtheit und Raffinesse sowie durch die Beschränkung auf einige wenige Schlüsselelemente und Materialien aus. Dieses neue Museum in der Nähe der chinesischen Stadt Hangzhou bildet keine Ausnahme. Die Zeit für Entwurf und Fertigstellung des Gebäudes betrug fünf Jahre.

Das Liangzhu Kulturmuseum bildet den nördlichen Punkt des Liangzhu Kulturdorfes, einer neu geschaffenen Parkstadt, und beherbergt eine Sammlung archäologischer Artefakte der Liangzhu-Kultur, die auch als Jade-Kultur (ca. 3.000 v.Chr.) bekannt ist. Das Gebäude ist auf drei Seiten von Wasser umgeben und über eine Fußgängerbrücke mit einem Landschaftspark verbunden. Eine zweite Fußgängerbrücke verbindet das Museum mit einer kleineren Insel, die für Ausstellungen im Freien genutzt wird.

Das Museum besteht aus vier langen, rechteckigen Bauelementen, die alle gleich breit sind (18 Meter), sich aber in Höhe und Länge unterscheiden. Innerhalb dieser Bauelemente befinden sich fünf Innenhöfe, die ihre Inspiration von den traditionellen chinesischen Hofhäusern mit Steinmauern beziehen. Absicht des

David Chipperfield est reconnu pour ses musées et galeries conçus aux États-Unis et en Europe. Ses travaux se caractérisent par leur simplicité et leur sophistication et sont généralement réduits à quelques éléments et matériaux. Ce nouveau musée à proximité de Hangzhou en Chine ne fait pas exception. Sa conception et sa construction ont nécessité cinq ans.

Le musée de la culture de Liangzhu se trouve au nord de Liangzhu, village culturel récemment créé qui héberge une collection d'objets archéologiques de la culture de Liangzhu, également connue comme la culture de Jade (3000 av.J.-C.). Le bâtiment est entouré d'eau sur trois côtés et relié au parc par une passerelle. Une deuxième passerelle relie le musée à une île plus petite destinée aux expositions extérieures.

Le musée est composé de quatre longs rectangles d'une largeur identique de 18 mètres, mais de hauteur et de longueur différentes. Au sein de ces volumes se trouvent cinq cours intérieures, dont l'inspiration provient de la tradition chinoise des maisons avec cour et murs en pierre. L'objectif était de créer des espaces de calme et de contemplation pour les expositions. Les formes régulières laissent une grande souplesse à l'installation des expositions et permettent aux visiteurs de s'orienter facilement.

previous page David Chipperfield's work is noted for its combination of simplicity and sophistication—stone, wood, glass, and water.

vorherige Seite David Chipperfields Bauwerke sind für ihre Verbindung von Schlichtheit und Raffinesse bekannt – Stein, Holz, Glas und Wasser.

page précédente Le travail de David Chipperfield est reconnu pour ses alliances de simplicité et de sophistication (pierre, bois, verre et eau).

right The island museum is reached via a footbridge, and a further footbridge links the museum to a smaller island.

rechts Die Museumsinsel ist über eine Fußgängerbrücke erreichbar und über eine zweite Brücke mit einer kleineren Insel verbunden.

droite On accède au musée flottant par une passerelle. Une seconde relie le musée à une île plus petite.

left By isolating the museum on its own island with water all around, the building's dramatic monolithic façade is emphasized.

links Indem das Museum isoliert auf seiner eigenen, vollständig von Wasser umgebenen Insel errichtet wurde, hob der Architekt die dramatisch wirkende, monolithische Fassade des Gebäudes hervor.

gauche En isolant le musée sur une île et en l'entourant d'eau, l'aspect dramatique de la façade monolithique est accentué.

right Architect's sketch showing a series of interlocked rectangular volumes, each the same width, but varying in length.

rechts Architektenskizze mit einer Serie miteinander verzahnter, rechteckiger Körper, die alle gleich breit sind, sich jedoch in ihrer Länge unterscheiden.

droite Croquis de l'architecte présentant plusieurs rectangles emboîtés, de même largeur mais de longueurs différentes.

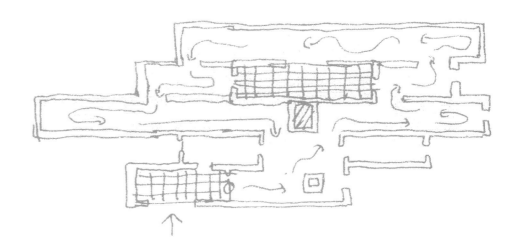

The concept was to use solid materials that age well. Iranian travertine stone was chosen for its texture and color in order to give the building depth and warmth. Travertine is known for its natural variation so the blocks were mixed to make the walls look homogeneous from a distance. Interiors feature Ipe, a dark wood noted for its durability, on the balustrades, doors, and benches. Contrasts between dark and light are clear to see, between the cream-colored stone and the water, and the open, bright courtyards and the huge multi-functional interior galleries.

Inspiration seems to have come as much from Japan as China. There is a strong element of Zen influence not only in the pared down simplicity of the stone walls, but also the interior courtyards with their minimal simplicity and small trees that bring to mind contemporary Japanese houses. Furthermore, the building itself, situated as it is in the middle of an artificial lake, has parallels with Zen rock gardens. The architect describes it so, "We were trying to strengthen the relationship between the lake and the building—a rock on an island in a lake."

Architekten war es, ruhige, kontemplative Räume für die Ausstellungen zu schaffen und mit den regelmäßigen Formen gleichzeitig ein Höchstmaß an Flexibilität für die Ausstellungsgestaltung und die einfache Orientierung der Besucher zu erzielen.

Das Konzept sah außerdem die Verwendung solider Materialien vor, die gut altern. Wegen seiner Oberflächenbeschaffenheit und Farbe wurde iranischer Travertin gewählt, um dem Gebäude ein Gefühl von Tiefe und Wärme zu verleihen. Travertin ist für seine natürlichen Variationen bekannt; die Blöcke wurden daher gemischt, um die Wände aus der Entfernung gleichförmig aussehen zu lassen. Für die Balustraden, Türen und Bänke in den Innenräumen wurde Ipé verwendet, ein dunkles Holz, das für seine Beständigkeit bekannt ist. Kontraste zwischen Hell und Dunkel werden deutlich in dem cremefarbenen Stein und dem Wasser sowie den offenen, hellen Innenhöfen und den riesigen vielseitig verwendbaren Galerien im Inneren.

Die Inspiration für das Gebäude scheint ebenso sehr aus Japan wie aus China gekommen zu sein. Ein starker Einfluss des Zen wird nicht nur in der auf das Allernotwendigste beschränkten Schlichtheit der Steinwände ersichtlich, sondern auch in den Innenhöfen mit ihrer minimalen Einfachheit und den kleinen Bäumen, die an zeitgenössische japanische Häuser denken lassen. Mit seiner Lage inmitten eines künstlichen Sees verfügt das Gebäude selbst ebenfalls über Parallelen mit den Steingärten des Zen. Der Architekt beschreibt es wie folgt: „Wir haben versucht, die Beziehung zwischen dem See und dem Gebäude zu verstärken – ein Felsen auf einer Insel in einem See."

Pour la construction, il fallait utiliser des matières solides et durables. Le travertin d'Iran a été choisi pour sa texture et sa couleur afin de conférer une certaine profondeur et chaleur à l'ouvrage. Le travertin est connu pour varier naturellement d'aspect. Les blocs ont donc été mélangés pour rendre les murs plus homogènes à distance. À l'intérieur, les balustrades, les portes et les bancs sont en Ipé, un bois sombre reconnu pour sa durabilité. Les contrastes entre le sombre et le clair sont évidents, entre la pierre crème et l'eau, et entre les cours ouvertes baignées de lumière et les immenses galeries intérieures multifonctionnelles.

L'inspiration semble provenir à la fois du Japon et de la Chine. On retrouve un élément important d'influence Zen dans la simplicité des murs en pierre et dans les cours intérieures minimalistes. Les petits arbres font également penser aux maisons japonaises contemporaines. Le bâtiment semble lui-même se trouver au milieu d'un lac artificiel, rappelant les jardins de pierre Zen. L'architecte le décrit ainsi : « Nous essayions de renforcer la relation entre le lac et le bâtiment – une roche perchée sur une île, au milieu d'un lac. »

left An interior courtyard. Benches and balustrades are of Ipe, a dark wood that contrasts with the light color of the stone.

links Ein Innenhof. Bänke und Balustraden wurden aus Ipé angefertigt, einem dunklen Holz, das sich von der hellen Farbe des Steins abhebt.

gauche Cour intérieure. Les bancs et les balustrades sont en Ipé, un bois sombre qui contraste avec la couleur claire de la pierre.

above A low-walled footbridge leads from the main museum to a smaller island intended for outdoor exhibitions.

oben Eine von einer niedrigen Mauer eingefasste Fuß-gängerbrücke führt vom Hauptgebäude des Museums zu einer kleineren Insel, die für Ausstellungen im Freien gedacht ist.

ci-dessus Une passerelle bordée de murets s'étend du musée à une plus petite île prévue pour les expositions extérieures.

below The inspiration for the design came from the Chinese tradition of building stone-walled courtyard houses.

unten Die Inspiration für den Entwurf stammt von den traditionellen chinesischen, um einen Hof herum angelegten Steinhäusern.

ci-dessous La conception s'inspire des maisons traditionnelles chinoises avec cour intérieure et murs en pierre.

above Walls are of Iranian travertine, a stone noted for its natural variation. By mixing bricks with different tones the architect achieved a warm and textured appearance.

oben Die Mauern bestehen aus iranischem Travertin, einem Stein, der für seine natürlichen Variationen bekannt ist. Durch die Mischung von Ziegeln mit unterschiedlichen Farbtönen erzielte der Architekt ein warmes, strukturiertes Erscheinungsbild.

ci-dessus Murs en travertin d'Iran, une pierre reconnue pour son aspect naturellement variable. En mélangeant des tons différents, l'architecte a réussi à obtenir une apparence chaude et texturée.

Oslo Opera House

Oslo, Norway
Snøhetta
2008

In 1999, the Norwegian National Assembly voted to build a new opera house in Bjørvika at the head of the Oslo fjord in the center of the city. A competition followed and the winners were the Norwegian studio Snøhetta. Nearly ten years later, their extraordinary "island" building was opened to the public. In 2008, it was the winner of the Culture category of the inaugural World Architecture Festival, and was described as a work that "in its scale, ambition and quality has raised the bar for Norwegian architecture."

The Opera House is a cool monument to Norway—a giant iceberg; a snow-covered mountain; a futuristic white liner. It is vast, covering the equivalent area of four soccer fields and containing 1,100 rooms. Access to the plaza and main entrance is via a marble-clad footbridge over a moat. The public areas, or "front of house," consisting of the foyer, large auditorium of 1,350 seats and a smaller one of 400 seats, are in the western section of building. "Back of house" areas, to the north and south, include workshops, changing rooms, offices, storage areas, rehearsal rooms, and every facility needed to stage an opera or ballet.

Snøhetta describe the building as having three main elements: the "wave wall," the "factory," and the "carpet." The wave wall is a huge wooden wall inside the building that represents the "line

1999 stimmte die Norwegische Nationalversammlung für den Bau eines neuen Opernhauses in Bjørvika in der Stadtmitte am oberen Ende des Oslofjords. Aus dem anschließenden Architekturwettbewerb ging das norwegische Studio Snøhetta als Sieger hervor. Fast zehn Jahre später wurde dieses außergewöhnliche „Inselgebäude" der Öffentlichkeit zugänglich gemacht. 2008 gewann es beim ersten World Architecture Festival den Preis in der Kategorie Kultur und wurde als ein Werk beschrieben, das „in seinem Umfang, seinem Anspruch und seiner Qualität die Messlatte für norwegische Architektur höher angesetzt hat."

Das neue Opernhaus ist ein cooles Monument für Norwegen – ein gigantischer Eisberg, ein schneebedeckter Berg, ein futuristischer, weißer Dampfer. Es ist gewaltig, mit einer Fläche, die derjenigen von vier internationalen Fußballfeldern entspricht und 1.100 Räume umfasst. Auf drei Seiten ist es von Wasser umgeben. Der Zugang zum Platz und zum Haupteingang erfolgt über eine mit Marmor verkleidete Fußgängerbrücke über einen Wassergraben. Die öffentlich zugänglichen Bereiche vor den Kulissen, die ein Foyer, einen großen Zuschauersaal mit 1.350 Sitzplätzen und einen kleineren Saal mit 400 Sitzplätzen umfassen, befinden sich im westlichen Teil des

En 1999, l'Assemblée nationale norvégienne a voté la construction d'un nouvel opéra à Bjørvika, à l'extrémité du fjord d'Oslo, en plein cœur de la ville. Le cabinet d'architectes norvégien Snøhetta a remporté la construction du bâtiment. Presque dix ans plus tard, cet extraordinaire ouvrage flottant ouvre ses portes au public. En 2008, il a terminé premier de la catégorie Culture du Festival mondial de l'architecture et a été décrit comme un travail qui par son échelle, ambition et qualité, élève le niveau de l'architecture norvégienne.

Le nouvel opéra est un monument froid pour la Norvège, un iceberg géant, une montagne enneigée, un paquebot blanc futuriste. D'une surface importante, il recouvre l'équivalent de quatre terrains de football et compte 1100 pièces. Il est entouré d'eau sur trois flancs. L'accès à la place et à l'entrée principale se fait par une passerelle de marbre enjambant un fossé. Les espaces publics, ou les salles, dont le foyer, un grand théâtre de 1 350 places et un plus petit de 400 places, se trouvent dans la partie ouest. Les zones réservées, au nord et au sud, comportent ateliers, vestiaires, bureaux, espaces de stockage, salles de répétition et toutes les installations nécessaires à l'organisation d'un opéra ou d'un ballet.

Selon Snøhetta, le bâtiment est composé de

above The promenade and roof—an accessible stone carpet of 193,750 square feet—incorporates various surface textures to prevent people slipping. The main material is white marble, but where the structure meets the water granite is used.

oben Die Promenade und das Dach – ein für die Öffentlichkeit zugänglicher Steinteppich aus 18.000 quadratischen Platten. Er besteht hauptsächlich aus weißem Marmor, wo die Struktur auf Wasser trifft, wurde jedoch Wassergranit verwendet.

ci-dessus L'allée et le toit, un tapis de pierre de 18 000 mètres carrés, présentent diverses textures pour offrir une adhérence maximale. Le marbre blanc est le matériau principal. Le granit est utilisé aux points de contact entre l'eau et la structure.

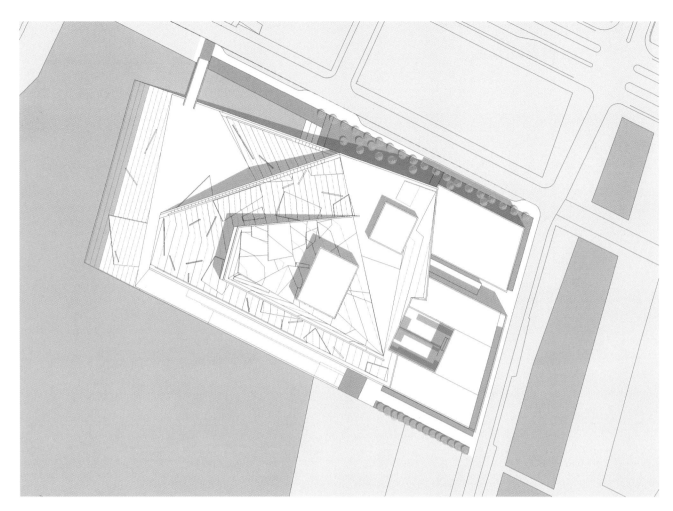

where the land and sea, Norway and the world, art and everyday life meet." The factory is the self-contained, rationally-planned production area. The carpet consists of a series of horizontal and sloping stone surfaces that flow down to the water's edge.

Enormous attention has been given to detail and materials. The predominant exterior material is La Facciata, a white Italian marble that retains its brilliance when wet. All stone cladding directly in contact with the water is a Norwegian granite called "Ice Green." The wave wall is made up of a complex series of oak joined cone shapes—chosen for acoustic reasons. An appropriate industrial material, aluminum cladding, was chosen for the factory area and tower—the polished panels have been patterned with circles and bumps in order to deflect light. Thick green glass was used for the windows in the 49-feet high façade.

The interiors are of an equally high architectural standard. Visitors are greeted in the foyer by the huge glass walls, the oak wave wall, and inclined massive white load-bearing columns needed to support the heavy roof. Craftsmanship is evident throughout, such as the grand staircase which is peeled out of the wooden wall leading up to three galleries or the perforated, illuminated cladding on the outside

Gebäudes. Die Bereiche hinter den Kulissen im Norden und Süden umfassen Werkstätten, Umkleideräume, Büros, Lagerräume, Proberäume und alle anderen zur Aufführung einer Oper oder eines Balletts erforderlichen Räume.

Snøhetta unterteilen das Gebäude in drei Hauptelemente: die „Wellenmauer", die „Fabrik" und den „Teppich". Die Wellenmauer ist eine riesige hölzerne Mauer innerhalb des Gebäudes, die „die Grenzlinie, an der Land und See, Norwegen und die Welt, die Kunst und das alltägliche Leben zusammentreffen, verkörpert." Die Fabrik ist ein in sich abgeschlossener, rational geplanter Produktionsbereich. Der Teppich besteht aus einer Reihe waagerechter und schräger Oberflächen aus Stein, die zum Rand des Wassers hinab fließen.

Details und Materialien wurden mit äußerster Sorgfalt und Aufmerksamkeit geplant. Außen ist das vorherrschende Material La Facciata, ein weißer italienischer Marmor, der seinen Glanz auch bei Nässe beibehält. Für alle Steinverkleidungen, die sich in unmittelbarem Kontakt mit dem Wasser befinden, wurde ein norwegischer Granit namens „Eisgrün" verwendet. Die Wellenmauer besteht aus einer komplexen Anordnung zusammengesetzter Kegelformen aus Eiche – die aus akustischen Gründen gewählt wurden. Der Fabrikbereich und der Turm sind mit

trois principaux éléments: « le mur de vagues », « l'usine » et « le tapis ». Le premier est un immense mur de bois à l'intérieur du bâtiment représentant « la ligne de rencontre entre la terre et la mer, la Norvège et le monde, l'art et la vie quotidienne ». L'usine est l'espace de production autonome et rigoureusement géré. Le tapis est une série de surfaces inclinées et horizontales en pierre, descendant jusqu'à l'eau.

Les détails et les matériaux ont fait l'objet d'une attention très particulière. Le matériau extérieur prédominant est La Facciata, un marbre blanc italien qui garde sa brillance même humide. L'intégralité du revêtement en pierre en contact direct avec l'eau est en « Ice Green », un granit norvégien coloré. Le mur de vagues est un assemblage complexe de formes coniques en chêne, choisi pour des raisons acoustiques. L'usine et la tour sont recouvertes d'aluminium, matériau industriel dont les panneaux polis ont été ornés de cercles et de bosses pour refléter la lumière. La façade est quant à elle composée d'épaisses baies vitrées de 15 mètres de haut.

L'intérieur est d'un niveau architectural tout aussi élevé. Les visiteurs sont accueillis dans le foyer par les imposantes parois vitrées, le mur de vagues en chêne et les énormes colonnes blanches inclinées qui supportent la charge du

above The green glass façade, up to 49 feet high, is made up of large panels and thin joints where the panels meet.

oben Die grüne Glasfassade, die bis zu 15 Meter hoch ist, besteht aus großen Platten und dünnen Verbindungsstücken, wo diese zusammentreffen.

ci-dessus La façade en verre vert, de 15 mètres de haut, est composée de grands panneaux et de joints filiformes.

left Main access to the Opera House island is by a footbridge, seen here on the left.

links Der Hauptzugang zum Opernhaus erfolgt über eine Fußgängerbrücke, die im Bild links sichtbar ist.

gauche L'accès principal à l'Opéra flottant se fait par une passerelle, que l'on aperçoit ici à gauche.

of the washrooms. Equally impressive is the main auditorium. The balcony fronts and oval ceiling are made of darkened strips of oak that give an intimate and warm feel in contrast to the more expansive lighter wood outside.

However, the most impressive element is the stone "carpet." This marble roofscape envelops the building like giant folded paper giving the public the freedom to walk everywhere. The New Opera House is a great and complex, but nonetheless welcoming, work of architecture.

Aluminium, einem geeigneten industriellen Material, verkleidet – die polierten Platten wurden mit einem Muster aus Kreisen und Erhebungen versehen, um das Licht abzuleiten.

Die Ausstattung der Innenräume erfolgte nach ebenso hohen architektonischen Standards. Besucher werden im Foyer von riesigen grünen Glasfenstern, der Wellenmauer aus Eichenholz und massiven schrägen, weißen tragenden Säulen willkommen geheißen, die zur Stützung der schweren Dachkonstruktion erforderlich sind. Handwerkliche Kunstfertigkeit wird überall deutlich, wie beispielsweise an dem prächtigen Treppenaufgang, der sich aus der hölzernen Wand schält und zu drei Galerien hinaufführt, oder an den perforierten, illuminierten Verkleidungen außerhalb der Waschräume. Der Hauptzuschauerraum ist ebenso beeindruckend. Die Balkonfronten und die ovale Decke sind aus nachgedunkelten Eichenholzstreifen gefertigt, die eine intime und warme Stimmung vermitteln und einen Kontrast zu dem großzügiger verwendeten, helleren Holz im Freien bilden.

Das beeindruckendste Element ist jedoch der steinerne „Teppich". Die Dachlandschaft aus Marmor umhüllt das Gebäude wie ein riesiges gefaltetes Papier und bietet Besuchern die Freiheit, sich überall hin zu bewegen. Das Neue Opernhaus ist ein großes und komplexes, aber dennoch einladendes architektonisches Kunstwerk.

toit. Le travail artistique est évident, comme le grand escalier longeant la paroi de bois conduisant aux trois théâtres ou le revêtement perforé et illuminé à l'extérieur des toilettes. Le théâtre principal est tout aussi impressionnant. Les balcons et le plafond ovale sont constitués de lattes de chêne plus foncées, ce qui donne une sensation de chaleur et d'intimité en contraste avec le bois plus clair de l'extérieur.

L'élément le plus impressionnant reste cependant « le tapis » de pierre. Ce toit en marbre enveloppe le bâtiment tel une feuille de papier géante, laissant le public libre de s'y promener en tout point. Le Nouvel Opéra est une architecture exceptionnelle et complexe, mais néanmoins accueillante.

left A grand staircase in oak leads up to three galleries that surround the auditorium.

links Ein prächtiger Treppenaufgang aus Eichenholz führt zu drei Galerien, die den Zuschauerraum umgeben.

gauche Un immense escalier en chêne mène aux trois galeries qui entourent le théâtre.

left The "wave wall" in the foyer is composed of a complex pattern of joined cone shapes.

links Die „Wellenmauer" im Foyer besteht aus einem komplexen Muster zusammengesetzter Kegelformen.

gauche Le « mur de vagues » dans le foyer est composé de motifs complexes de formes coniques.

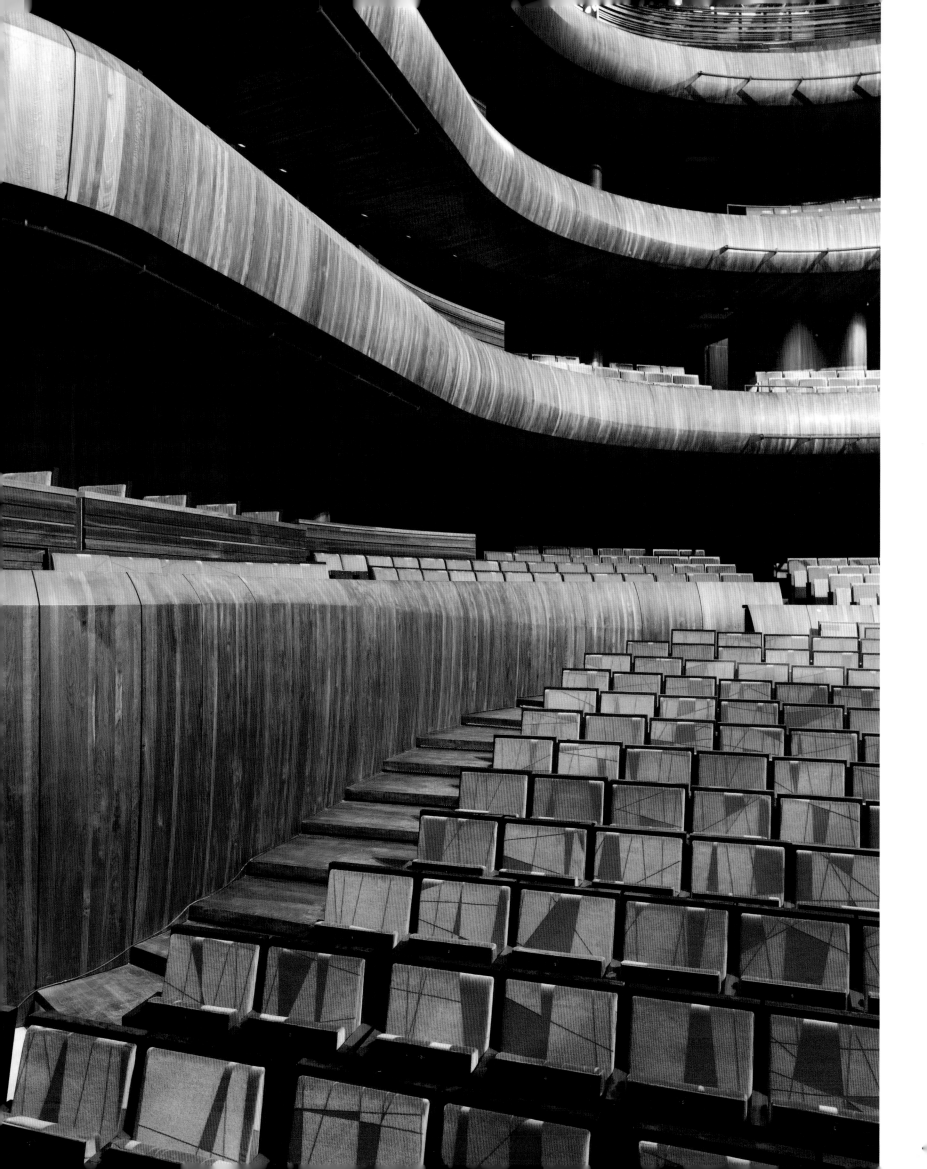

opposite The auditorium seats are designed to absorb as little sound as possible. Materials are dark timber and a specially designed orange fabric.

gegenüber Die Sitzplätze im Zuschauerraum sollen so wenig wie möglich Schall absorbieren. Als Materialien wurden ein dunkles Holz und ein eigens entworfener orangefarbener Stoff verwendet.

ci-contre Les sièges du théâtre absorbent le moins de son possible. Un bois sombre et un tissu orange spécialement conçu dans cette optique ont été utilisés.

below left The interior of the wooden staircase is in stark contrast to the white foyer. The architects describe it like "being inside a carved out piece of timber."

unten links Das Innere des hölzernen Treppenaufgangs bildet einen starken Gegensatz zu dem weißen Foyer. Die Architekten beschreiben es wie folgt: „als ob man sich in einem geschnitzten Stück Holz befände."

ci-dessous à gauche L'intérieur des escaliers en bois contraste vivement avec le foyer immaculé. Pour les architectes, on s'y déplace comme « à l'intérieur d'un tronc creusé. »

left Curved balcony fronts are made of pre-fabricated oak elements of solid stave glued together, treated with ammonia, before being oiled and polished.

links Die kurvenförmigen Balkonfronten wurden aus vorgefertigten Eichenholzelementen aus geleimten soliden Dauben hergestellt und mit Ammoniak behandelt, bevor sie schließlich geölt und poliert wurden.

gauche Les balcons incurvés sont composés d'éléments en chêne préfabriqués, collés, traités à l'ammoniac, puis huilés et polis.

above Looking out toward the fjord from one of the balconies with the tops of the inclined load-bearing columns.

oben Aussicht auf den Fjord von einem der Balkone aus, mit den oberen Enden der schrägen tragenden Säulen.

ci-dessus Vue sur le fjord depuis l'un des balcons. Le haut des colonnes inclinées soutient la charge.

Elbphilharmonie

Hamburg, Germany

Herzog & de Meuron Architekten

2011

HafenCity in the port of Hamburg is a new 360-acre neighborhood with apartments and office buildings that is due to complete in 2025. The centerpiece of this ambitious project is the Philharmonic Hall by the Swiss architects Herzog & de Meuron, best known for Tate Modern in London.

The cultural center is located at the tip of the Sandtor Harbor on top of the Kaispeicher, a warehouse built in 1966 and vacated in the 1990s. Perched on the edge of a promontory, it juts out into the River Elbe, a massive cultural tent, or as the architects have described it, a "pirate ship." It is designed to look like a "gigantic, iridescent crystal, whose appearance keeps changing as it catches the reflections of the sky, of the water, and of the city."

Because the warehouse originally had to bear the weight of thousands of heavy bags of cocoa beans, it is solid enough to support the new structure above. The contrast between the two halves is very striking. Below the massive brick structure is quiet and plain, while above the glass building is unusual and fluid. An undulating roof rises to 355 feet at the tip of the peninsula and slopes down to the eastern end where it is 65 feet lower. The glass façade is made up of curved panels some of which are cut open. A grid of white dots printed on the façade

Die HafenCity im Hafen von Hamburg ist ein neues, 145 Hektar großes Viertel mit Apartments und Bürogebäuden, dessen Fertigstellung für 2025 vorgesehen ist. Das Herzstück dieses ehrgeizigen Projekts ist die von Herzog & de Meuron entworfene Elbphilharmonie – die Architekten haben sich mit dem Entwurf der Tate Modern in London einen Namen gemacht, für die sie wohl am bekanntesten sind.

Das Kulturzentrum befindet sich an der Spitze des Sandtorhafens über dem Kaispeicher, einem 1966 erbauten und seit den Neunziger Jahren leerstehenden Lagerhaus. Das am Rande eines Vorsprungs befindliche Bauwerk ragt wie ein massives Kulturzelt oder – wie es die Architekten beschreiben – ein „Piratenschiff" auf die Elbe hinaus. Der Entwurf soll wirken wie ein „gigantischer, schillernder Kristall, dessen Aussehen sich durch das Einfangen der Spiegelungen des Himmels, des Wassers und der Stadt in ständigem Wandel befindet."

Das Lagerhaus musste ursprünglich das Gewicht Tausender schwerer Säcke voller Kakaobohnen aushalten und ist daher ausreichend solide, um den neuen auf ihm entstehenden Bau zu tragen. Der Kontrast zwischen den beiden Hälften fällt sofort ins Auge. Die massive Ziegelstruktur im unteren Teil sieht ruhig und schlicht aus, während das darüber

HafenCity, dans le port de Hambourg, est un nouveau quartier de 145 hectares, comprenant des appartements et des bureaux, prévu pour 2025. La pièce maîtresse de ce projet ambitieux est la construction de la Elbphilharmonie par les architectes suisses Herzog & de Meuron, reconnus pour la galerie Tate Modern de Londres.

Le centre culturel se trouve à l'extrémité du port de Sandtor, au sommet du Kaispeicher, un entrepôt conçu en 1966 et libéré dans les années 1990. Perché au bord d'un promontoire, il dépasse sur l'Elbe tel un imposant chapiteau culturel, ou comme le décrivent les architectes, un « bateau pirate ». Il devrait ressembler à un « gigantesque cristal irisé, à l'apparence perpétuellement changeante suivant les reflets du ciel, de l'eau et de la ville ».

L'entrepôt devait à l'origine supporter le poids de milliers de sacs de fèves de cacao. Il est donc suffisamment solide pour supporter la nouvelle structure. Le contraste entre les deux moitiés est frappant : la partie inférieure, une structure massive en briques, est discrète et épurée tandis que la partie supérieure, en verre, est élancée et inhabituelle. Un toit ondulé s'élève à 108 mètres au sommet de la péninsule et redescend vers l'extrémité est, 20 mètres plus bas. La façade en verre est composée de panneaux incurvés, ouverts pour certains. Une

previous page A glass tent-like structure sits on top of an old brick warehouse that was originally built to store cocoa beans.

vorherige Seite Eine zeltähnliche, gläserne Struktur sitzt auf einem alten Lagerhaus aus Ziegeln, das ursprünglich zur Lagerung von Kakaobohnen erbaut wurde.

page précédente Une structure de verre en forme de chapiteau repose sur un vieil entrepôt en briques, où étaient à l'origine stockés des sacs de fèves de cacao.

below The main entrance to the east. The glass façade has a series of portholes that act as balconies for residents.

unten Der Haupteingang im Osten. In die gläserne Fassade sind eine Reihe Luken eingelassen, die als Balkone für die Bewohner dienen.

ci-dessous L'entrée principale se trouve à l'est. La façade en verre se caractérise par plusieurs hublots et les balcons des résidents.

opposite Foyer of the auditorium perched on top of the Kaispeicher.

gegenüber Foyer des Auditoriums über dem Kaispeicher.

ci-contre Foyer de la salle de concert perché au sommet du Kaispeicher.

is designed to give protection from the sun.

The main entrance lies to the east. Immediately on entering, an elongated escalator curves slightly as it leads up to a plaza, so that each end is obscured from the other. At this level, there are restaurants, bars, the ticket office and hotel entrance, as well as access to the lobby for the new concert hall. Below, the old warehouse has been converted into a car park. The core of the complex is the Elbphilharmonie itself, a major concert hall with 2,100 seats and a chamber music hall for 500. This is encased in a 220-room hotel and 45 luxury apartments. Residents have access to balconies via horse-shaped recesses in the glass, giving spectacular views and wind protection.

liegende Gebäude aus Glas ungewöhnlich und flüssig erscheint. Ein wellenförmiges Dach erhebt sich an der Spitze der Halbinsel bis zu einer Höhe von 108 Metern und fällt zum östlichen Ende hin ab, wo es 20 Meter niedriger ist. Die Glasfassade besteht aus gewölbten Scheiben, von denen einige aufgeschnitten sind. Ein auf die Fassade gedrucktes Gitter aus weißen Punkten soll als Schutz vor Sonneneinstrahlung dienen.

Der Haupteingang liegt im Osten. Unmittelbar nach dem Betreten des Gebäudes führt eine verlängerte Rolltreppe in einer leichten Kurve hinauf zu einem Platz, so dass beide Enden der Rolltreppe voreinander verborgen sind. Auf diesem Stockwerk finden sich Restaurants, Bars, der Kartenverkauf und ein Hoteleingang sowie der Zugang zur Lobby des neuen Konzertsaals. Das darunter liegende alte Lagerhaus wurde in ein Parkhaus umgewandelt. Im Kern des Komplexes befinden sich die Elbphilharmonie selbst, ein großer Konzertsaal mit 2.100 Sitz-plätzen sowie ein Saal für Kammermusikkonzerte mit 500 Sitzplätzen. Diese Säle sind von einem Hotel mit 220 Zimmern und 45 Luxusapartments umgeben. Die Bewohner erhalten über hufeisenförmige Einlassungen in dem Glas Zugang zu den windgeschützten Balkonen, die ihnen spektakuläre Aussichten bieten.

grille de points blancs recouvre la façade pour offrir une protection contre le soleil.

L'entrée principale se trouve à l'est. En entrant, un grand escalator légèrement incurvé conduit vers une esplanade, de manière à ce que chaque extrémité reste invisible à l'autre. Ce niveau accueille les restaurants, les bars, le guichet et l'entrée de l'hôtel, ainsi que l'accès au hall pour la nouvelle salle de concert. En dessous, le vieil entrepôt a été transformé en parking. Le cœur du complexe est l'Elbphilharmonie, une grande salle de concert de 2 100 places et une salle de musique de chambre de 500 sièges. Un hôtel de 220 chambres et de 45 appartements de luxe embrasse le tout. Les résidents ont accès aux balcons par des niches en forme de fer à cheval, offrant une vue spectaculaire et une protection contre le vent.

Louvre Abu Dhabi

Saadiyat Island, Abu Dhabi, UAE

Ateliers Jean Nouvel

2012

Along with Tadao Ando, Zaha Hadid, and Frank O. Gehry, the French architect Jean Nouvel was invited to create a new museum on Saadiyat Island near Abu Dhabi. Saadiyat Island, which means "Island of Happiness" in Arabic, covers 10.7 square miles and has 18.6 miles of water frontage. When finished in 2018 it will accommodate 150,000 residents and include a 667-acre cultural district where the architects' museums will be built. Each of the museums will be perched on the edge of Saadiyat surrounded by the sea—individual islands of culture.

Jean Nouvel describes his building like this: "We have covered it with a large dome, a form common to all civilizations. Made of a web of different patterns and interlaced into a translucent ceiling, the dome lets a diffuse magical light enter the space in the tradition of great Arabian architecture." Nouvel already has an architectural link with the Arab world through his Arab World Institute in Paris that was completed in 1987. Transparency, a key element in much of his work, plays an important role here. Inspired by the way light passes through date palm fronds in an oasis, the giant roof is a series of abstract weaves that allow light to pass through at different angles. Such a construction is obviously ideal for a very hot

Neben Tadao Ando, Zaha Hadid, Norman Foster und Frank O. Gehry wurde auch der französische Architekt Jean Nouvel gebeten, ein neues Museum auf der Saadiyat-Insel bei Abu Dhabi zu schaffen. Die Saadiyat-Insel – im Arabischen „Insel des Glücks" – bedeckt eine Fläche von 27 Quadratkilometern und verfügt über eine Küste von insgesamt 30 Kilometern Länge. Nach ihrer Fertigstellung im Jahr 2018 wird sie 150.000 Bewohner und einen 270 Hektar großen Kulturbezirk beherbergen, in dem die Museen der zuvor genannten Architekten erbaut werden. Jedes der Museen wird sich am Rand der Saadiyat-Insel befinden und vom Meer umgeben sein – einzelne Inseln der Kultur.

Jean Nouvel beschreibt sein Gebäude wie folgt: „Wir haben es mit einer großen Kuppel bedeckt, einer Form, die allen Kulturen gemein ist. Die aus einem Netz verschiedener Muster gefertigte und in eine lichtdurchlässige Decke verflochtene Kuppel lässt ein diffuses, magisches Licht in den Raum dringen, ganz in der Tradition der großen arabischen Architektur." Mit dem Institut du Monde Arabe in Paris, das 1987 fertig gestellt wurde, verfügte Nouvel bereits über eine architektonische Verbindung mit der arabischen Welt. Transparenz ist ein Schlüsselelement in den meisten seiner Bauwerke, das auch hier wieder auftritt.

Avec Tadao Ando, Zaha Hadid, Norman Foster et Frank O. Gehry, l'architecte français Jean Nouvel a été invité à créer un nouveau musée sur l'île de Saadiyat, à proximité d'Abu Dhabi. L'île de Saadiyat, signifiant « île du bonheur » en arabe, couvre 27 kilomètres carrés et possède 30 kilomètres de rive. Achevée en 2018, l'île accueillera 150 000 résidents et un centre culturel de 270 hectares où les musées des architectes seront construits. Chaque musée sera situé sur les rives de l'île de Saadiyat, entouré par la mer, tel un îlot de culture.

Jean Nouvel décrit sa construction ainsi: « Nous l'avons recouvert d'un dôme imposant, une forme commune à toutes les civilisations. Cette immense toile aux motifs variables est intégrée dans un plafond translucide: le dôme laisse ainsi une lumière diffuse et magique envahir l'espace, dans la tradition architecturale arabe. » Jean Nouvel possède déjà un lien architectural avec le monde arabe grâce à son Institut du monde arabe situé à Paris et achevé en 1987. La transparence, que l'on constate ici est un élément clé dans la plupart de ses travaux. S'inspirant de la manière dont la lumière traverse les frondes des palmiers dans une oasis, le toit gigantesque est une série de nattes abstraites laissant entrer la lumière sous des angles différents. Une telle construction

climate. At the same time, it gives the place a sense of mystery.

Under the 258,000 square foot floating dome there is a micro-city with its own micro-climate. Water plays an important role here, in cooling the environment as well as reflecting the buildings. Steps leading down to large pools and canals bring to mind island cities such as Venice. This "Arab Louvre" responds to the local natural environment of the sea and desert. As Nouvel says, "The island offers a harsh landscape, tempered by its meeting with the channel, a striking image of the aridity of the earth versus the fluidity of the waters."

A small cluster of low buildings will house classical art exhibits lent by the Louvre in Paris. The main museum will include sections on Asian Art, Classical Antiquities, European Painting and Sculpture, Islamic Art, and European Decorative Arts and Furniture. Other buildings will include a special exhibition area, offices, and an education center. There will be two ways of entering the island, with the main museum entrance to the south. A massive underground car park will be situated under an artificial lake situated between the shore and the museum island.

The inspiration for the buildings came from the idea of a lost city, undiscovered under deep

Inspiriert von der Art, in der Licht durch die Palmwedel von Dattelpalmen in einer Oase fällt, besteht das gigantische Dach aus einer Reihe abstrakter Verflechtungen, die das Licht aus unterschiedlichen Winkeln einfallen lassen. Eine solche Bauweise ist ideal für ein sehr heißes Klima und verleiht dem Ort zugleich eine geheimnisvolle Atmosphäre.

Unter der 24.000 Quadratmeter großen, schwebenden Kuppel befindet sich eine Mikro-Stadt mit ihrem eigenen Mikro-Klima. Wasser spielt hier eine wichtige Rolle bei der Abkühlung der Umgebung und der Spiegelung der Gebäude. Stufen führen hinab zu weitläufigen Becken und Kanälen und lassen an Inselstädte wie Venedig denken. Dieser „arabische Louvre" ist eine Erwiderung auf die natürliche Umgebung vor Ort, der Verbindung von Wüste und Meer. Wie Nouvel sagt: „Die Landschaft der Insel ist karg, diese Wirkung wird jedoch durch den Kanal abgemildert – ein eindrucksvolles Bild der Trockenheit der Erde gegenüber der Flüssigkeit des Wassers."

Eine kleine Gruppe niedriger Gebäude wird die vom Louvre und anderen französischen Museen geliehenen Kunstgegenstände beherbergen. Das Hauptgebäude des Museums wird Abteilungen für Asiatische Kunst, Klassische Altertümer, Europäische Malerei und Skulptur,

convient à l'évidence à un climat extrêmement chaud et confère en même temps un certain mystère au lieu.

Sous le dôme flottant de 24 000 mètres carrés se trouve une minuscule ville ayant son microclimat. L'eau joue un rôle important ici puisqu'elle rafraîchit l'environnement et reflète les bâtiments. Les marches conduisent à de grands bassins et d'importants canaux, rappelant les villes flottantes telles que Venise. Ce « Louvre arabe » répond à l'environnement naturel de la mer et du désert. Selon Jean Nouvel, « l'île offre un paysage dur, tempéré par sa rencontre avec le canal, une image frappante de l'aridité de la terre face à la fluidité de l'eau. »

Un petit groupe de bâtiments peu élevés accueillera les expositions d'art classique du Louvre et d'autres musées français. Le musée principal sera divisé en sections sur l'art asiatique, les antiquités classiques, la peinture et la sculpture européennes, l'art islamique, les arts décoratifs et le mobilier européen. D'autres bâtiments comprendront des bureaux, un espace réservé aux expositions et un centre d'éducation. L'accès à l'île se fera par deux entrées possibles, dont l'entrée principale du musée située au sud. Un immense parking souterrain occupera l'espace situé sous le lac artificiel, entre la rive et l'île musée.

previous page A microclimate is created through the use of shade and water.

vorherige Seite Durch die Verwendung von Schatten und Wasser wird ein Mikroklima geschaffen.

page précédente L'ombre et l'eau créent un microclimat.

left Clusters of small buildings are given a grandeur through the device of the dome.

links Durch die Kuppel wird den Gruppen kleiner Gebäude Größe verliehen.

gauche Les groupes de petits bâtiments semblent grandioses à travers le dôme.

top Detail of the model of the dome.

oben Detail des Modells für die Kuppel.

haut Détail de la maquette du dôme.

above Cross section showing the mainland to the right and underground parking beneath the lake.

oben Querschnitt mit Ansicht des Festlands auf der rechten Seite und dem unterirdischen Parkhaus unter dem See.

ci-dessus Coupe présentant la terre à droite et le parking souterrain sous le lac.

below The museum, the first overseas outpost of the Louvre, will exhibit Eastern and Western antiquities.

unten Das Museum, die erste Außenstelle des Louvre in Übersee, wird Altertümer aus Ost und West ausstellen.

ci-dessous Le musée, première bouture du Louvre à l'étranger, accueillera des antiquités orientales et occidentales.

below opposite With direct access to the water's edge, the masterplan is reminiscent of Venice.

unten gegenüber Mit seinem direkten Zugang zum Rand des Wassers erinnert der Masterplan an Venedig.

ci-dessous ci-contre Avec un accès direct au bord de l'eau, le plan principal rappelle Venise.

sands or at the bottom of the sea. "These dreamy thoughts have merged into a simple plan of an archaeological field revived as a small city, a cluster of nearly one-row buildings along a leisurely promenade."

Islamische Kunst und Europäisches Kunsthandwerk und Möbel umfassen. Die anderen Gebäude werden einen Bereich für Sonderausstellungen, Büros und ein Bildungszentrum enthalten. Es wird zwei Zugänge zur Insel geben, wobei der Haupteingang zum Museum über eine Fußgängerbrücke im Süden erreichbar sein wird.

Nouvels Anspruch ist es, das Traumähnliche in Wirklichkeit zu verwandeln. Er bezog seine Inspiration von der Idee einer verlorenen Stadt, die unter tiefen Schichten von Sand oder auf dem Grund des Meeres unentdeckt verborgen liegt. „Diese Gedanken an Träume sind zu einem einfachen Entwurf eines archäologischen Feldes verschmolzen, das als kleine Stadt wieder ersteht, als Cluster von Gebäuden, die nahezu in einer Reihe entlang einer gemächlichen Promenade liegen."

Jean Nouvel souhaite transformer le rêve en réalité. S'inspirant de l'idée d'une ville perdue, cachée sous des sables profonds ou engloutie. « Ces pensées ont fusionné pour résulter en un plan simple d'un champ archéologique revenu à la vie tel une petite ville, un groupe de bâtiments assez bas, alignés le long d'une promenade tranquille. »

Performing Arts Center

Saadiyat Island, Abu Dhabi, UAE

Zaha Hadid Architects

2012

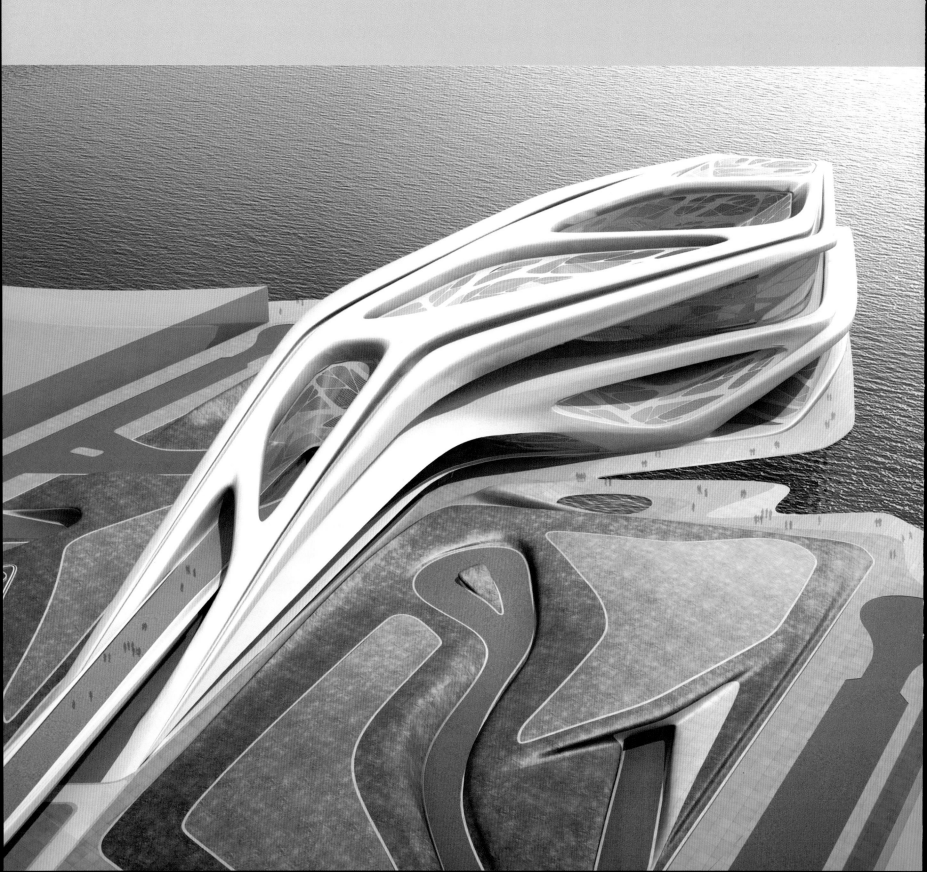

Saadiyat's Cultural District, just offshore from the city of Abu Dhabi, is to be the setting of five new major cultural buildings. The ensemble of institutions will start with the Maritime Museum at the southern tip and finish with the Contemporary Art Museum at the northern tip. A new performing arts center by Zaha Hadid will sit in the middle of this group along the seafront.

Facing west, the 202-feet high building will tower over the ocean below. Surrounded by water on three sides, its sculptural form will house five auditoria—an opera house, drama theater, concert hall, flexible theater, and music hall—with a total seating capacity of 6,200. The main concert hall will be located above the four other theaters. A huge window over the stage will allow natural light to flood in and offer spectacular views of the surrounding seascape. Lobbies for each theater will be orientated toward the sea and a shaded rooftop restaurant on the north side of the building will allow for alfresco eating.

From above, the center resembles a sea creature sliding across the surface of the water. However, the architect's true inspiration came

Der Kulturbezirk auf der Saadiyat-Insel vor der Küste der Stadt Abu Dhabi wird in naher Zukunft den Hintergrund für fünf neue bedeutende kulturelle Bauwerke bilden. Das Ensemble der Institutionen beginnt mit dem Schifffahrtsmuseum an der Südspitze und endet mit dem Museum für Zeitgenössische Kunst an der Nordspitze der Insel. In der Mitte dieser Gebäudegruppe entlang des Meeresufers wird ein neues, von Zaha Hadid entworfenes Zentrum für Darstellende Künste errichtet.

Das 62 Meter hohe Gebäude ist nach Westen hin ausgerichtet und wird über den Ozean hinausragen. Seine auf drei Seiten von Wasser umgebene bildhauerische Form wird fünf Zuschauerräume mit einer Gesamtkapazität von 6.200 Sitzplätzen beherbergen – ein Opernhaus, ein Schauspielhaus, einen Konzertsaal, ein flexibles Theater und einen Musiksaal. Der Hauptkonzertsaal befindet sich über den anderen vier Räumlichkeiten. Ein riesiges Fenster über der Bühne lässt natürliches Licht hereinfluten und bietet spektakuläre Aussichten über die umliegende Meereslandschaft. Die Eingangshallen zu jedem der Säle sind auf das Meer hin ausgerichtet, und Besucher können

Le District culturel de Saadiyat, au large de la ville d'Abu Dhabi, devrait accueillir cinq nouveaux grands bâtiments culturels. L'ensemble des institutions commencera par le Musée de la marine à la pointe sud et s'achèvera avec le Musée d'art contemporain à la pointe nord. Une nouvelle salle de spectacles conçue par Zaha Hadid règnera au cœur de ce groupe le long du front de mer.

Dirigée vers l'ouest, la construction de 62 mètres de haut surplombera l'océan. Entourée d'eau sur trois côtés, sa forme sculpturale accueillera cinq salles de spectacle: un opéra, un théâtre, une salle de concert, un théâtre aménageable et un cabaret. La capacité totale d'accueil sera de 6 200 personnes. La salle principale sera située au-dessus des quatre autres théâtres. Une immense fenêtre sur la scène laissera entrer la lumière naturelle et offrira une vue spectaculaire sur le paysage environnant. Les entrées de chaque théâtre seront orientées vers la mer et un restaurant ombragé situé au nord du bâtiment offrira une restauration en plein air.

Vu de haut, le centre ressemble à une créature marine glissant à la surface de l'eau. Cependant,

left Footpaths intersect at the back of the Performing Arts Center forming a series of entrances.

links Fußgängerwege überkreuzen sich auf der Rückseite des Performing Arts Center und führen zu einer Reihe von Eingängen.

gauche Des sentiers se croisent à l'arrière du Centre des arts scéniques formant plusieurs entrées.

right Web-like glass ceiling above the main concert hall takes its inspiration from organizational systems in the natural world.

rechts Die netzartige Glasdecke über dem Hauptkonzertsaal wurde durch in der Natur vorliegende Organisations-systeme inspiriert.

droite Le plafond en verre tel une toile au-dessus de la salle de concert principale rappelle les systèmes organisationnels du monde naturel.

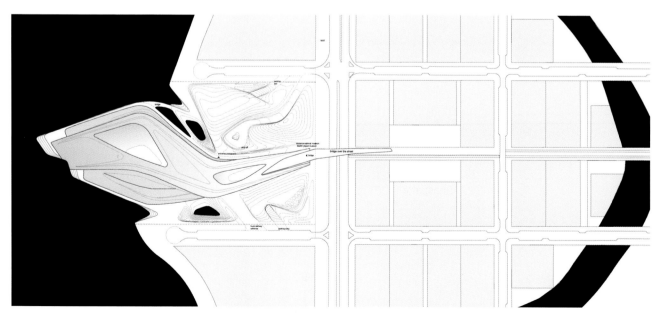

from structures found in nature, such as leaves, stems, branches, and fruit. Vast windows in the concert hall dominate the design, their transparency emphasized by their leaf-like forms. A series of pedestrian paths intersect each other cutting through the surrounding grass landscape, with a main footbridge entrance leading directly into the tail of the building where a retail section will be located. Hadid describes it as: "gradually developing into a growing organism that sprouts a network of successive branches. As it winds through the site, the architecture increases in complexity, building up in height and depth and achieving multiple summits in the bodies housing the performance spaces, which spring from the structure like fruits on a vine and a face westward, toward the water."

darüber hinaus in einem schattigen Dachrestaurant auf der Nordseite des Gebäudes im Freien speisen.

Von oben gleicht das Zentrum einem Meereswesen, das über die Wasseroberfläche gleitet. Die eigentliche Inspirationsquelle der Architektin waren jedoch Strukturen, wie sie in der Natur auftreten: Blätter, Halme, Zweige und Früchte. Das Bauwerk wird von den gigantischen Fenstern des Konzertsaals dominiert, deren Transparenz von ihren blattähnlichen Formen betont wird. Eine Reihe von Fußgängerwegen überkreuzen einander und durchschneiden die das Gebäude umgebende Graslandschaft. Eine Fußgängerbrücke am Haupteingang führt unmittelbar in das schwanzförmig auslaufende Ende des Gebäudes, in dem einige Einzelhandelsgeschäfte eingerichtet werden

l'architecte s'est inspiré des structures naturelles telles que les feuilles, les tiges, les branches et les fruits. De larges fenêtres en forme de feuille, accentuant leur transparence, prédominent dans la salle de concert. Plusieurs allées piétonnes se croisent, coupant les zones herbeuses environnantes. Une entrée principale conduit directement à l'arrière du bâtiment où seront installées quelques boutiques. Selon Zaha Hadid, « son ouvrage se transforme progressivement en un organisme vivant qui grandit tel un réseau de branchages. À mesure qu'elle pénètre le site, l'architecture se fait plus complexe, plus haute et plus profonde; formant les membres multiples, qui accueillent les espaces de spectacle, ils naissent de la structure, tels les fruits d'une vigne et un visage tourné vers l'ouest, en direction de la mer. »

Its branching geometry and abstract shapes are combined to create a building of enormous energy, as if it, literally, were snaking forward. Spectacular views will be offered across the bay and at night the entire edifice will light up—a cultural lighthouse on its own island.

sollen. Hadid beschreibt es wie folgt: „Das Bauwerk entwickelt sich allmählich zu einem wachsenden Organismus, dem ein Netzwerk aufeinanderfolgender Zweige entsprießt. Je länger es sich durch das Gelände schlängelt, desto komplexer wird die Architektur, die an Höhe und Tiefe zunimmt und in den Körpern, die die Veranstaltungsräume beherbergen, mehrfach Gipfelpunkte erreicht. Diese wachsen aus dem Gebäude wie Früchte an einem Weinstock und richten sich nach Westen aus, zum Wasser hin."

Die verzweigte Geometrie und die abstrakten Formen vereinen sich zu einem Gebäude von enormer Energie, gleichsam als ob es vorwärts schlängeln würde. Nach der Fertigstellung werden sich Besuchern spektakuläre Aussichten über die Bucht eröffnen, und bei Nacht wird das gesamte Bauwerk erleuchtet sein – ein kultureller Leuchtturm auf seiner eigenen Insel.

Sa géométrie branchue et ses formes abstraites se marient pour former un bâtiment d'une énergie exceptionnelle, comme avançant pour se jeter à l'eau. Une vue spectaculaire s'offre aux visiteurs par-dessus la baie. La nuit, l'édifice s'éclaire tel un phare culturel sur sa propre île.

left A restaurant is located at the top of the center in the tip, the opera house is directly below.

links Oben in der Spitze des Gebäudes befindet sich ein Restaurant, das Opernhaus liegt unmittelbar darunter.

gauche Un restaurant se trouve au sommet du bâtiment, à la pointe. L'opéra se trouve directement en dessous.

below Two sections. The top drawings shows reception and service areas. The bottom the theaters, restaurant, and cafés.

unten Zwei Querschnitte. Die obere Zeichnung zeigt die Empfangs- und Dienstleistungsbereiche, die untere die Theater, das Restaurant und die Cafés.

ci-dessous Deux parties. Le dessin du haut présente la réception et les espaces de services. Le dessin du bas montre les théâtres, le restaurant et les cafés.

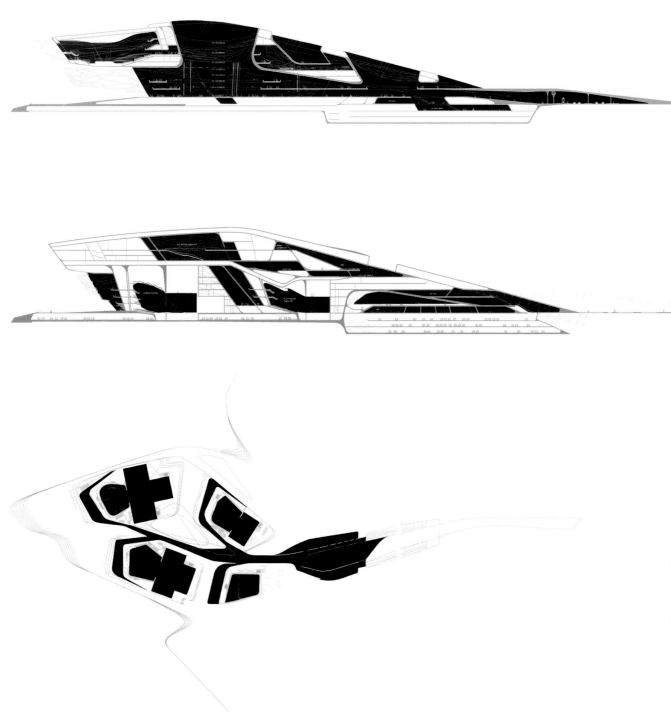

left Plan showing the balcony level of the center. There are four theaters—Opera House, Musical Hall, Experimental Theater, and Playhouse Theater.

links Grundriss der Balkonetage des Gebäudes. Es verfügt über vier Theater – ein Opernhaus, einen Musiksaal, ein experimentelles Theater und ein Schauspielhaus.

gauche Plan montrant le niveau désaxé du balcon. Le bâtiment compte quatre théâtres: l'Opéra, le Cabaret, le théâtre expérimental et la salle de théâtre.

Maritime Museum

Saadiyat Island, Abu Dhabi, UAE
Tadao Ando Architect & Associates
2012

As part of the Saadiyat "Culture Island" project, the Japanese architect, Tadao Ando, was commissioned to build a new maritime museum for Abu Dhabi. Ando is an obvious and clever choice as water is a constant theme in his work. He has used it both internally and externally on many of his buildings—in courtyards, on roofs, as infinity pools, and for artificial ponds and lakes.

The central element is a water courtyard, 354 feet long, 118 feet wide, and 88.5 feet high. When completed it will cover 355,000 square feet. Above the courtyard a massive arch rises, as if a solid mass had been carved by the sea winds. As the architect explains it, "Our response was a proposal for a building in which an upside-down shell-shaped void, tracing the swelling of a boat's sail inflated by sea breezes, is excavated from a rectangular volume." The main material will be exposed concrete, something that Ando is an acknowledged master of.

Inside the arch a series of ramps, decks, and viewing platforms guide the general public up and down the building through the exhibition spaces. Within the huge interior space, floors float at different levels with slopes running between them, rather like the decks inside a ship. Below ground level, a second space

Als Teil des „Kulturinsel-Projekts" auf der Saadiyat-Insel erhielt der japanische Architekt Tadao Ando den Auftrag, ein neues Schifffahrtsmuseum für Abu Dhabi zu bauen. Ando ist eine naheliegende und kluge Wahl, da Wasser in seinem Werk ein konstantes Thema bildet. Er hat es bei vielen seiner Bauwerke innen wie außen verwendet – in Höfen, auf Dächern, als Überlaufbecken und für künstliche Teiche und Seen.

Das zentrale Element des Museums ist ein Wasserhof von 108 Metern Länge, 36 Metern Breite und 27 Metern Höhe. Nach seiner Fertigstellung wird er 33.000 Quadratmeter bedecken. Über dem Hof erhebt sich ein massiver, wie das Segel einer Dau geformter Bogen. Der Architekt erläutert: „Unsere Antwort war der Vorschlag für ein Gebäude, in dem ein auf dem Kopf stehender muschelförmiger Hohlraum, der das von Meeresbrisen geschwellte Segel eines Bootes nachvollzieht, aus einem rechteckigen Körper herausgeschält wird." Das Baumaterial ist hauptsächlich Sichtbeton, dessen Verwendung Ando bekanntlich meisterhaft beherrscht.

Innerhalb des Bogens führen eine Reihe von Rampen, Decks und Sichtplattformen Besucher durch die Ausstellungsflächen hinauf und hinunter, die die Geschichte der Schifffahrt des Landes erzählen. Die verschiedenen Etagen

Participant au projet de « l' île culturelle » de Saadiyat, l'architecte japonais Tadao Ando a été chargé de créer un nouveau musée de la marine pour Abu Dhabi. Faire appel à ces architecte est un choix intelligent et pertinent puisque l'eau est un thème omniprésent dans ses travaux. On la retrouve à la fois à l'intérieur et à l'extérieur d'un bon nombre de ses ouvrages, notamment dans les cours, sur les toits, en piscines ou en bassins et lacs artificiels.

L'élément central du musée est une cour pleine d'eau, de 108 mètres de long, 36 mètres de large et 27 mètres de haut. Une fois achevée, elle couvrira 33 000 mètres carrés. Au-dessus de la cour s'élève une arche imposante aux formes arrondies, comme érodée par le vent. Comme l'explique l'architecte, Nous avons proposé un bâtiment rectangulaire dans lequel est taillée une ouverture en coquillage, imitant une voile gonflée par la brise marine. La construction sera principalement en béton apparent, une matière que Tadao Ando maîtrise parfaitement.

À l'intérieur de l'arche, plusieurs rampes, ponts et plates-formes guident les visiteurs dans les espaces d'exposition supérieurs et inférieurs qui racontent l'histoire maritime du pays. À l'intérieur, l'espace immense est constitué d'étages à différents niveaux reliés par des rampes, comme les ponts d'un navire. Le sous-

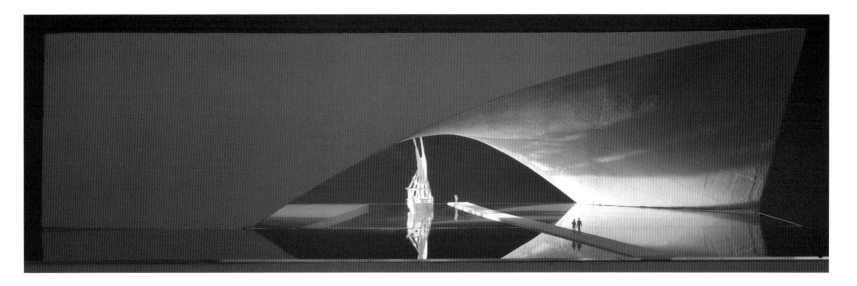

left A *dhow*, a traditional arabic sailing boat, sails under the arch of the new Abu Dhabi Maritime Museum.

links Eine *Dau*, ein traditionelles arabisches Segelboot, segelt unter dem Bogen des neuen Schifffahrtsmuseums von Abu Dhabi.

gauche Un boutre, voilier arabe traditionnel, navigue sous l'arche du nouveau Musée de la marine d'Abu Dhabi.

above The huge arch floats on a water court as if carved out by sea winds.

oben Der riesige Bogen schwebt über einem Wasserhof, als ob er von den Meereswinden herausgemeißelt worden wäre.

ci-dessus L'arche imposante flotte sur une cour d'eau comme si elle avait été sculptée par les vents marins.

above The arch is designed to be both a geometric sculpture and a frame for the seascape.

oben Der Bogen ist als geometrische Skulptur wie auch als Rahmen für die Meereslandschaft gedacht.

ci-dessus L'arche est conçue comme une sculpture géométrique et sert de cadre au paysage.

below The site plan clearly shows the arch sitting in an artificial water court, which itself is surrounded by the sea.

unten Der Plan zeigt deutlich die Lage des Bogens in einem künstlichen Wasserhof, der selbst vom Meer umgeben ist.

ci-dessous Le plan du site montre clairement l'arche au milieu d'une cour artificielle remplie d'eau, elle-même entourée par la mer.

right A wooden model of the Maritime Museum. The building itself will be principally made of exposed concrete.

rechts Ein hölzernes Modell des Schifffahrtsmuseums. Das Gebäude selbst wird vorwiegend aus Sichtbeton hergestellt.

droite Maquette en bois du Musée de la marine. La construction sera essentiellement composée de béton apparent.

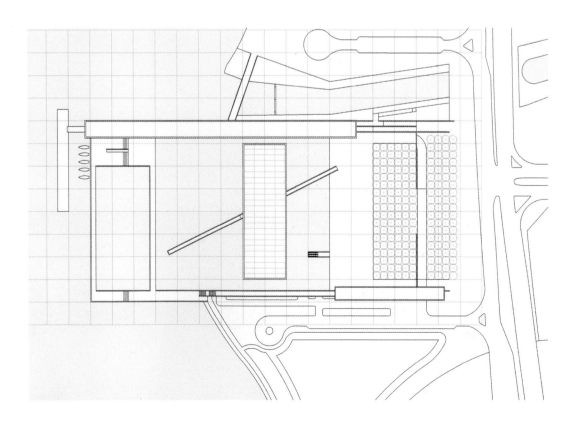

contains a giant aquarium and reception hall. The water court itself is the inverted shape of the arch above and visitors can look into this huge water tank from the lobby below.

The museum's concept is inspired by Abu Dhabi's natural landscape and maritime traditions. Here the land meets the water. Ando likes to think of it as an independent sculpture, an object of simple geometry. The void space between the aquarium and the arch frames the sea of the Saadiyat Island coast, and its gentle curves draw the viewer closer to the magnificent seascape. As Ando puts it, "The solitary form stands like a gate over a vast water court, defining a space of encounter between two important landscape elements of the city's culture: the land and the sea. With its reflective surface, the water court visually merges site and sea, reinforcing the maritime theme of the museum."

schweben im riesigen Innenraum des Gebäudes wie die Decks eines Schiffes auf unterschiedlicher Höhe und sind über schräge Rampen miteinander verbunden. Im Untergeschoss befindet sich ein zweiter Raum mit einem gigantischen Aquarium und einer Empfangshalle. Der Wasserhof selbst bildet die spiegelverkehrte Form des darüber liegenden Bogens ab, und Besucher können aus der darunter liegenden Lobby in den riesigen Wassertank schauen.

Das Konzept des Museums wurde von der einheimischen Landschaft und den Schifffahrtstraditionen Abu Dhabis inspiriert. Hier treffen Land und Wasser zusammen. Ando sieht das Bauwerk gern als unabhängige Skulptur, ein Objekt von einfacher Geometrie. Der Hohlraum zwischen dem Aquarium und dem Bogen umrahmt das Meer um die Küste der Saadiyat-Insel, und seine sanfte Kurvenform zieht den Betrachter enger zur der wunderbaren Meereslandschaft hin. Ando drückt es so aus: „Die einsame Form steht wie ein Tor über einem riesigen Wasserhof und definiert den Raum, in dem zwei wesentliche Landschaftselemente der Kultur dieser Stadt zusammentreffen: Land und Meer. Mit seiner spiegelnden Oberfläche verschmilzt der Wasserhof den Ort optisch mit dem Meer und betont so das Schifffahrtsthema des Museums."

sol abrite un aquarium géant et le hall d'accueil. La cour d'eau est la forme inversée de l'arche qui la surplombe. Les visiteurs peuvent observer l'intérieur de cet immense bassin depuis le hall situé dessous.

Le paysage naturel et les traditions marines d'Abu Dhabi se reflètent dans ce musée. Ici, la terre rencontre la mer. Tadao Ando aime le définir comme une sculpture indépendante, un objet géométrique simple. L'espace vide entre l'aquarium et l'arche forme un cadre à la mer qui entoure l'île de Saadiyat, et ses douces courbes rapprochent le visiteur du splendide paysage marin. Comme l'affirme Tadao Ando, « La forme solitaire s'élève telle une porte sur une immense cour d'eau, définissant un espace de rencontre entre deux éléments importants de la culture de la ville: la terre et la mer. Avec sa surface réfléchissante, la cour fait entrer en fusion le site et la mer, accentuant le thème marin du musée. »

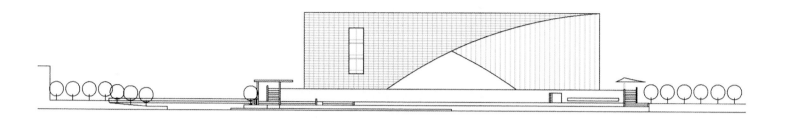

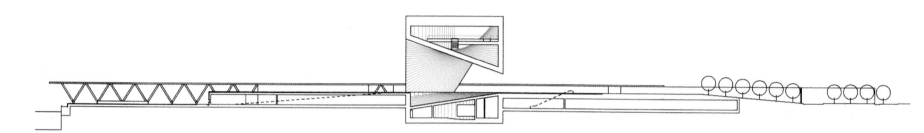

above Elevations of the Maritime Museum. A modern interpretation of the classical arch.

oben Zeichnungen des Schifffahrtsmuseums. Eine moderne Interpretation des klassischen Bogens.

ci-dessus Élévations du Musée de la marine. Une interprétation moderne de l'arche classique.

right Drawing showing the giant aquarium and reception hall below ground. A series of decks, ramps, and viewing platforms lead visitors up and down the museum.

rechts Zeichnung mit Ansicht des gigantischen Aquariums und der Empfangshalle im Untergeschoss. Eine Reihe von Decks, Rampen und Sichtplattformen führt Besucher durch die Räume des Museums hinauf und hinunter.

droite Dessin présentant l'aquarium géant et le hall d'accueil au sous-sol. Plusieurs ponts, rampes et plates-formes conduisent les visiteurs aux niveaux supérieurs et inférieurs du musée.

right Cross section. The excavated water court is the inverted shape of the arch above, shaped like the underside of a boat.

rechts Querschnitt. Der ausgegrabene Wasserhof bildet die seitenverkehrte Form des darüber liegenden Bogens ab und ist wie die Unterseite eines Boots geformt.

droite Coupe. La cour d'eau, en forme de coque de bateau, est l'inverse de l'arche qui la surplombe.

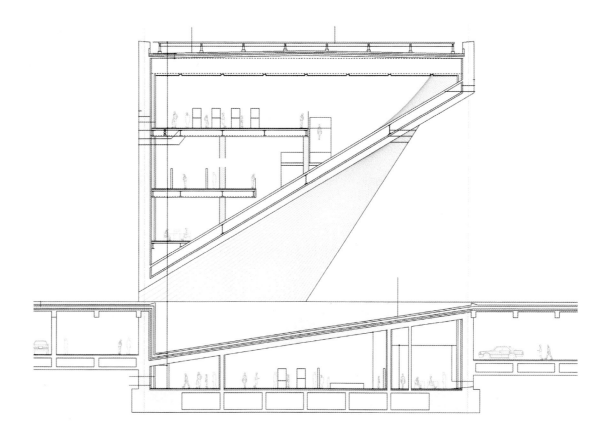

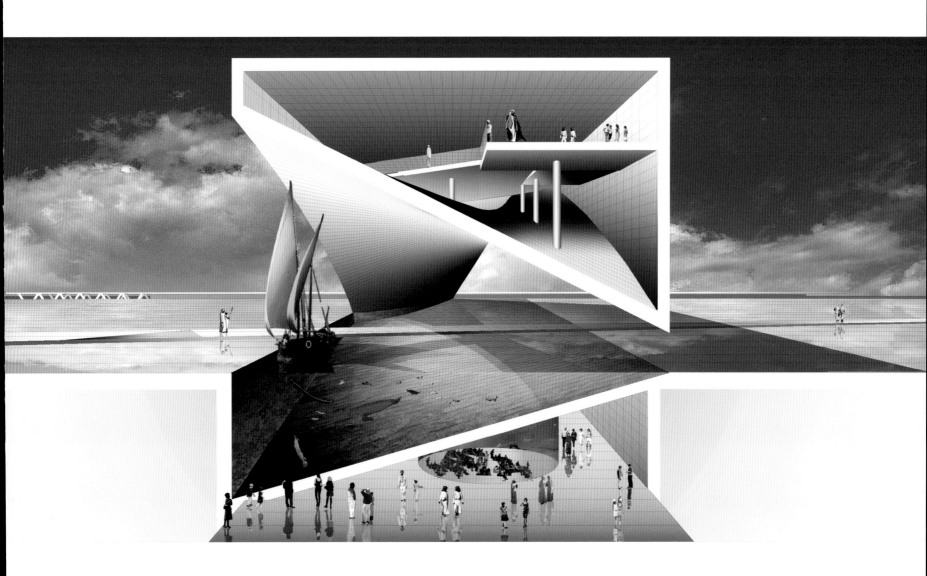

Guggenheim
Abu Dhabi Museum

Saadiyat Island, Abu Dhabi, UAE
Gehry Partners
2012

above A series of galleries radiate out from the center with water on all sides.

oben Eine Reihe von Galerien strahlt von der Mitte aus und ist auf allen Seiten von Wasser umgeben.

ci-dessus Plusieurs galeries partent du centre, entourées d'eau.

Frank O. Gehry's best-known building is the titanium-clad Guggenheim Museum in Bilbao, Spain. His trademark style is experimental shapes that are asymmetrical and quirky; buildings that look like sculptural objects. As part of the development on Saadiyat Island in Abu Dhabi, he has now been commissioned to build a new Guggenheim museum. At 323,000 square feet, including 130,000 square feet of exhibition space, it will be the largest Guggenheim ever built and will contain permanent exhibitions, galleries of special exhibitions, a center for art and technology, archives, library, and conservation laboratory.

The site, virtually on the water or with water on all sides, is almost an island. The surrounding landscape of desert and sea, combined with the light quality, were all important considerations for the architect. Its design plays off the blue of the water and the sky against the color of sand. "Approaching the design of the museum for Abu Dhabi made it possible to consider options for design of a building that would not be possible in the United States or Europe. It was clear from the beginning that this had to be a new invention."

Four stories of central core galleries are stacked on top of each other and designed around a courtyard. Each gallery will be a

Frank O. Gehrys bekanntestes Bauwerk ist das mit Titan verkleidete Guggenheim Museum im spanischen Bilbao. Sein Markenzeichen sind experimentelle, asymmetrische und ungewöhnliche Formen, Gebäude, die wie bildhauerisch gestaltete Objekte aussehen. Als Teil des Bauvorhabens auf der Saadiyat-Insel in Abu Dhabi hat er nun den Auftrag für den Bau eines neuen Guggenheim Museums erhalten. Mit 30.000 Quadratmetern – 12.000 Quadratmeter davon Ausstellungsfläche – wird es das größte jemals erbaute Guggenheim Museum werden und Dauerausstellungen, Galerien mit Sonderausstellungen, ein Zentrum für Kunst und Technologie, Archive, eine Bibliothek und eine Restaurierungswerkstatt umfassen.

Der Standort, gleichsam auf dem Wasser gelegen oder auf allen Seiten von Wasser umgeben, ist beinahe eine Insel. Die umliegende Landschaft aus Wüste und Meer in Verbindung mit der Qualität des Lichts waren für den Architekten allesamt wichtige Faktoren. Der Entwurf spielt mit dem Blau des Wassers und des Himmels im Gegensatz zur Farbe des Sandes. „Die Annäherung an den Entwurf für das Museum in Abu Dhabi ermöglichte die Erwägung verschiedener Optionen für die Gestaltung eines Gebäudes, das in den Vereinigten Staaten oder in Europa so nicht

La construction la plus connue de Frank O. Gehry est le musée Guggenheim de Bilbao, en Espagne, revêtu de titane. On reconnaît son style par ses formes expérimentales asymétriques et biscornues. Ses constructions ressemblent davantage à des sculptures. Dans le projet de l'île de Saadiyat, à Abu Dhabi, Frank O. Gehry est chargé de concevoir un nouveau musée Guggenheim. Sur 30 000 mètres carrés, dont 12 000 d'espace d'exposition, ce musée Guggenheim sera le plus grand au monde. Il accueillera en permanence des expositions, des galeries d'exposition spéciales, un centre artistique et technologique, des archives, une bibliothèque et un laboratoire de conservation.

Le site, quasiment sur l'eau, ou entouré d'eau de toutes parts, s'apparente à une île. Le désert, la mer et la qualité de la lumière ont été des facteurs importants pour l'architecte. Sa conception fait contraster le bleu de la mer et du ciel à la couleur du sable. « Pour aborder le design du musée d'Abu Dhabi, nous avons considéré les options nous permettant de concevoir un bâtiment impossible à réaliser aux États-Unis ou en Europe. Nous avons donc dès le début pensé que cet ouvrage devait être une invention. »

Quatre étages de galeries sont empilés les uns sur les autres autour d'une cour intérieure.

above This cultural center, at 323,000 square feet, will be the largest Guggenheim Museum ever built.

oben Dieses Kulturzentrum wird mit 30.000 Quadratmetern das größte jemals erbaute Guggenheim Museum sein.

ci-dessus Ce centre culturel, de 30 000 mètres carrés, sera le plus grand musée Guggenheim jamais construit à ce jour.

different height and size. The central spaces will be used for classical contemporary galleries and will incorporate skylights, air-conditioning, and sophisticated lighting. From the core, a series of rings of galleries radiate out. The next ring will house larger galleries in a variety of shapes, while the third ring will accommodate even larger galleries—raw, unfinished industrial spaces with exposed lighting. These galleries will allow contemporary artists to make enormous site-specific works on a scale not possible in most existing museums.

This cultural island, with its conical stone-clad shapes and water walls, is a thrilling example of Gehry's imagination. It is a jungle of spaces with light and air.

möglich wäre. Es war von vornherein klar, dass es sich bei diesem Auftrag um eine völlig neue Erfindung handeln musste."

Vier Stockwerke mit Galerien im Kern des Gebäudes sind aufeinander gestapelt und um einen Hof herum angelegt. Jede dieser Galerien unterscheidet sich von den anderen in Höhe und Größe. Die zentralen Räumlichkeiten werden als Galerien für klassische, zeitgenössische Kunst dienen und mit Oberlichtern, Klimaanlage und raffinierter Beleuchtung ausgestattet sein. Vom Kern aus wird eine Reihe ringförmig angelegter Galerien ausstrahlen. Der nächste Ring wird größere Galerien in einer Vielfalt von Formen beherbergen, während der dritte Ring sogar noch größere Galerien enthalten wird – rohe, unfertige industrielle Räume mit freiliegender Beleuchtung. Diese Galerien werden es zeitgenössischen Künstlern ermöglichen, ortsspezifische Arbeiten in gewaltigem Umfang auszuführen, die so in den meisten vorhandenen Museen nicht möglich wären.

Diese Kulturinsel mit ihren kegelförmigen, steinverkleideten Formen und Wasserwänden ist ein aufregendes Beispiel für Gehrys Vorstellungskraft. Sie ist ein Dschungel von Räumen mit Licht und Luft.

Chaque galerie sera de taille et de hauteur différentes. Les espaces du centre accueilleront les galeries contemporaines classiques et seront équipés de lucarnes, de la climatisation et d'un éclairage sophistiqué. Du cœur de la construction rayonnent plusieurs anneaux de galeries ; le second anneau accueillera des galeries plus grandes sous diverses formes et le troisième des galeries encore plus vastes, des espaces bruts, inachevés, avec un éclairage apparent. Ces galeries permettront aux artistes contemporains de réaliser des travaux spécifiques au site, à une échelle inenvisageable dans la plupart des autres musées existants.

Cette île culturelle, constituée de cônes de pierre et de murs d'eau, est un exemple exaltant de l'imagination de Frank O. Gehry. C'est une jungle d'espaces d'air et de lumière.

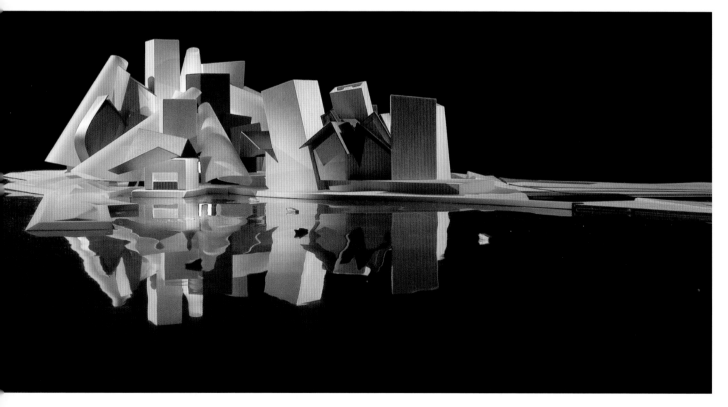

above A combination of abstract conical and rectangular shapes—a typical example of a Gehry vision.

oben Eine Kombination abstrakter, kegelförmiger und rechteckiger Formen – ein typisches Beispiel für eine von Gehrys Visionen.

ci-dessus Mariage de formes rectangulaires et coniques abstraites, un exemple typique de la vision de Frank O. Gehry.

Villas, Houses, and Apartments

Villen, Häuser und Wohnungen

Villas, maisons et appartements

Water/Glass Guest House I Watervilla

Sphinxes Lake Side Housing I Watervilla I Floating House

Lakeside Studio I Hong Luo Club I Periscope Houses I Maison Flottante

The examples here show what is possible for island living. They respond to their environment in different ways, offering solutions to building on water through a combination of form, shape, and material. Sometimes the reason for building on water is necessity, such as in the Netherlands where over a quarter of the land is below sea level. On other occasions, the need is to create a home that is totally isolated, a form of retreat. The desire to play in water, be it swimming or sailing, is another factor. Or the main drive can be aesthetic, water offering the added drama of reflected light and uninterrupted views. The projects include a villa on the Great Lakes, a guesthouse in Japan, a clubhouse in China, an art studio in California, and several floating homes. All the designs have one thing in common—a relationship to water that is inspiring and dynamic.

previous page Lakeside studio in California, USA.

vorherige Seite Seeuferstudio in Kalifornien, USA.

page précédente Studio de Lakeside en Californie, États-Unis.

left Looking out over the lake at the Clubhouse in Hong Luo, China.

links Blick über den See aus dem Klubhaus in Hong Luo, China.

gauche Vue sur le lac, au Club de Hong Luo, en Chine.

Les exemples présentés ici montrent les différentes possibilités d'habitat îlien et répondent de différentes manières à leur environnement, en offrant des solutions de construction sur l'eau mariant diverses formes et matériaux. Les constructions sur l'eau sont parfois nécessaires, comme aux Pays-Bas où plus d'un quart du territoire se trouve sous le niveau de la mer. Il peut s'agir d'un simple besoin d'isolement, de retrait, ou bien encore du désir de jouer dans l'eau, de nager ou de naviguer. La raison peut également être esthétique, l'eau apportant une certaine théâtralité grâce à la réflexion de la lumière et aux vues ininterrompues. Les projets présentés ci-après sont, entre autres, une villa sur les Grands lacs, une maison au Japon, un pavillon en Chine, un studio artistique en Californie, et plusieurs autres maisons flottantes. Toutes les constructions ont en commun une relation inspirante et dynamique avec l'eau.

Die folgenden Beispiele zeigen verschiedene Möglichkeiten des Insellebens. Sie reagieren in unterschiedlicher Weise auf ihre Umgebung und bieten durch ihre Verbindung aus Form, Gestalt und Material Lösungen für die Errichtung von Bauwerken auf dem Wasser. Bisweilen besteht eine schlichte Notwendigkeit, auf Wasser zu bauen, wie etwa in den Niederlanden, wo sich mehr als ein Viertel der Landmasse unter dem Meeresspiegel befindet. In anderen Fällen ist das Ziel, ein Heim zu schaffen, das vollkommen isoliert ist, eine Art Zuflucht. Der Wunsch, in oder mit Wasser zu spielen – sei es zu schwimmen oder zu segeln – ist ein weiterer Faktor. Oder die Ästhetik bildet den Hauptantrieb, denn Wasser schafft zusätzlich mit Lichtspiegelungen und freien Aussichten Raum für dramatische Effekte. Zu den hier vorgestellten Projekten gehören eine Villa an den Großen Seen, ein Gästehaus in Japan, ein Klubhaus in China, ein Kunststudio in Kalifornien und mehrere schwimmende Häuser. Alle Entwürfe haben eine Gemeinsamkeit: eine inspirierende und dynamische Verbindung mit dem Wasser.

Water/Glass Guest House

Shizuoka, Japan
Kengo Kuma & Associates
1996

The Japanese architect Kengo Kuma is well-known for his "water" buildings, including Stone Museum and Lotus House. But arguably his most dramatic statement is his Water/Glass Guest House from 1996. Perched high up on a headland in the seaside resort of Atami, this three-story villa takes much of its inspiration from the German architect Bruno Taut who designed the Glass Pavilion for the Werkbund Exhibition in Cologne in 1914 and who worked on the Hyuga Villa in Japan in 1935. Taut was particularly interested in the idea of how traditional Japanese architecture frames nature with nature: the wooden eaves and bamboo verandas creating frames for the viewer inside the building. In the Water/Glass Guest House, the layer of water which surrounds the building is the equivalent of a bamboo veranda, while the stainless steel louvers on the roof are like traditional Japanese eaves.

By far the most dramatic element of the building is on the third floor, where a glass pavilion and guest rooms are located. All the rooms have glass walls and look out over a spectacular 270 degree panorama. The main element is the pavilion, an oval shaped glass box with transparent walls and floor and a glass walkway leading to it. Here the room is a floating island—shallow water completely

Der japanische Architekt Kengo Kuma ist weltberühmt für seine „Wassergebäude", darunter das Steinmuseum und das Lotushaus. Sein wohl dramatischster Entwurf ist jedoch dieses Glas-/Wassergästehaus aus dem Jahr 1996. Die hoch auf einer Landzunge im Seebad von Atami errichtete dreistöckige Villa ist in hohem Maße von dem deutschen Architekten Bruno Taut inspiriert, der den Glaspavillon für die Werkbundausstellung von 1914 in Köln entwarf und 1935 an der Hyuga-Villa in Japan arbeitete. Taut interessierte sich insbesondere für die Idee, nach dem Vorbild der traditionellen japanischen Architektur Natur mit Natur zu umrahmen: Die hölzernen Dachvorsprünge und Bambusveranden schaffen Rahmen für den Blick des Betrachters im Gebäude. Im gläsernen Gästehaus bildet die Lage Wasser, die das Haus umgibt, eine Entsprechung zu einer Bambusveranda, während die Edelstahlgitter auf dem Dach traditionellen japanischen Dachvorsprüngen ähneln.

Die bei weitem eindrucksvollsten Elemente des Gebäudes, ein Glaspavillon und Gästezimmer, befinden sich im zweiten Stockwerk. Alle Räume haben gläserne Wände und bieten ein spektakuläres Panorama, das sich über 270 Grad erstreckt. Der Pavillon ist das Hauptelement: ein ovaler Glaskasten mit durchsichtigen Wänden und Böden, der über einen gläsernen Gang erreicht

L'architecte japonais Kengo Kuma est connu pour ses constructions flottantes, dont le Musée de pierre et la Maison Lotus. Son plus grand ouvrage reste sans aucun doute sa Maison d'eau et de verre conçue en 1996. Perchée sur un promontoire dans la station balnéaire d'Atami, cette villa à trois étages est grandement inspirée par l'architecte allemand Bruno Taut, qui a conçu le Pavillon de verre pour l'exposition de Werkbund à Cologne en 1914 et a travaillé sur la Villa Hyuga au Japon en 1935. Bruno Taut s'intéressait particulièrement à la manière dont l'architecture japonaise traditionnelle encadrait la nature avec la nature: les débordements de toitures en bois et les vérandas en bambous créent des cadres pour le spectateur qui se trouve à l'intérieur du bâtiment. Dans la Maison de verre, l'eau qui entoure le bâtiment joue le rôle de la véranda en bambou, alors que les persiennes en acier inoxydable sur le toit font penser aux avant-toits traditionnels japonais.

L'élément le plus spectaculaire de la construction se trouve au troisième étage, qui accueille un pavillon de verre et les chambres. Toutes les chambres possèdent des murs de verre et offrent une vue spectaculaire à 270°. Le pavillon est l'élément principal: on accède par une passerelle en verre à cette boîte de verre

far left An oval glass pavilion sits in the middle of a shallow pond, an island in itself.

ganz links Ein ovaler Glaspavillon sitzt in der Mitte eines seichten Teiches, eine Insel in sich selbst.

au loin à gauche Un pavillon en verre ovale repose au milieu d'un bassin peu profond, une île en lui-même.

left The site plan shows the house perched on top of a cliff looking out over the Pacific Ocean.

links Der Lageplan zeigt die Anlage des Hauses auf einem Felsvorsprung mit Aussicht über den Pazifischen Ozean.

gauche Le plan du site présente la maison perchée au sommet d'une falaise, avec vue sur l'océan Pacifique.

surrounds it, forming part of an infinity pool that gently flows over the edge to blend with the Pacific Ocean below. Boundaries vanish and everything dissolves in the ocean. As the architect puts it, "The ocean has brought about a radical change in my architecture…, it has drawn my eyes to water, it has reminded me of the value of the horizontal plane…"At night the dining room and walkway light up like a glass beacon with lights located at floor level.

In an interview in 2005, Kuma stated, "Transparency is a characteristic of Japanese architecture. I try to use light and natural materials to get a new kind of transparency." Although today he is more interested in using natural materials to create this lightness, clearly he achieved his aim here using water and glass.

werden kann. Der Raum bildet hier eine schwimmende Insel – als Teil eines Überlaufbeckens, aus dem das Wasser sanft über den Rand fließt und mit dem darunter liegenden Pazifischen Ozean verschmilzt, ist er vollkommen von Wasser umgeben. Die Grenzen verschwimmen, und alles löst sich im Ozean auf. Der Architekt beschreibt es wie folgt: „Der Ozean hat ein radikales Umdenken in meiner Architektur bewirkt…, er hat meine Augen zum Wasser hin gelenkt und mich an den Wert der waagerechten Fläche erinnert…" Bei Nacht leuchten das Esszimmer und der Gang auf wie ein gläserner Leuchtturm mit Lichtern im Fußboden.

Im Jahr 2005 sagte Kuma in einem Interview: „Transparenz ist ein Kennzeichen der japanischen Architektur. Ich versuche Licht und natürliche Materialien zu verwenden, um eine neue Art der Transparenz zu erreichen." Obgleich er heute mehr daran interessiert ist, natürliche Materialien zu verwenden, um diese Leichtigkeit zu erzeugen, hat er im vorliegenden Fall sein Ziel mit Wasser und Glas eindeutig erreicht.

ovale dont les murs et le sol sont transparents. La pièce ici est une île flottante; elle est entourée d'eaux peu profondes, appartenant à un plus grand bassin à débordement, se mêlant finalement à l'océan Pacifique au-dessous. Les frontières disparaissent et tout se dissout dans l'océan. Comme l'explique l'architecte. « L'océan a apporté un changement radical à mon architecture, il a attiré mon regard sur l'eau, m'a rappelé la valeur du plan horizontal. » La nuit, la salle à manger et la passerelle s'illuminent comme un phare de verre grâce à un éclairage situé au sol.

En 2005, lors d'un entretien, Kengo Kuma a déclaré que « La transparence est une caractéristique de l'architecture japonaise. J'essaie d'utiliser la lumière et les matières naturelles pour en créer un nouveau type. » Bien qu'il soit aujourd'hui plus intéressé par l'usage de matières naturelles pour créer cette légèreté, il parvient clairement à ses fins ici grâce à l'eau et au verre.

left A stainless steel louver brings to mind traditional Japanese eaves. The layer of water is the equivalent of a bamboo veranda.

links Ein Edelstahlgitter erinnert an traditionelle japanische Dachvorsprünge. Die Lage Wasser entspricht einer Bambusveranda.

gauche Une persienne en acier inoxydable rappelle les avant-toits japonais. L'eau fait penser aux vérandas de bambous.

right An infinity pool is designed so the edge of the building blends with the ocean below.

rechts Ein Überlaufbecken wurde so entworfen, dass der Rand des Gebäudes mit dem darunter liegenden Ozean verschmilzt.

droite La piscine est conçue pour que le bord du bâtiment se mêle à l'océan en contrebas.

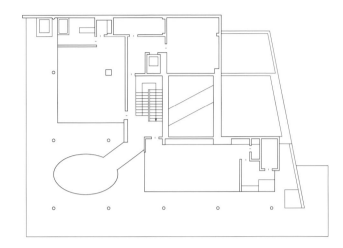

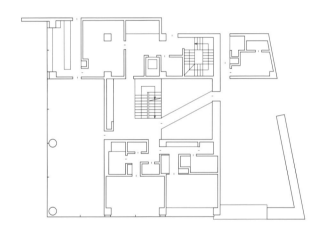

left above Plan of top floor with oval glass pavilion.

links oben Grundriss des obersten Stockwerks mit dem ovalen Glaspavillon.

ci-dessus à gauche Plan du dernier étage et pavillon ovale en verre.

left middle Plan of middle floor with guest rooms off a central staircase.

links Mitte Grundriss des mittleren Stockwerks mit Gästezimmern, die von einem zentralen Treppenaufgang abgehen.

au milieu à gauche Plan du deuxième étage, chambres et escalier central.

left bottom Plan of first floor with water pool and glass rocks.

links unten Grundriss des Erdgeschosses mit Wasser- becken und gläsernen Felsen.

en bas à gauche Plan du premier étage avec la piscine et les rochers en verre.

left This pool with sculpted rocks, two floors below the pavilion, continues the theme of glass and water. It surrounds a *tatami* room.

links Zwei Stockwerke unter dem Pavillon setzt dieses Becken mit bildhauerisch geformten, gläsernen Felsen die Themen Glas und Wasser fort. Es umgibt einen Tatami-Raum.

gauche Ce bassin orné de rochers en verre, deux étages en dessous du pavillon, reste dans le thème de l'eau et du verre. Il entoure la pièce aux tatamis.

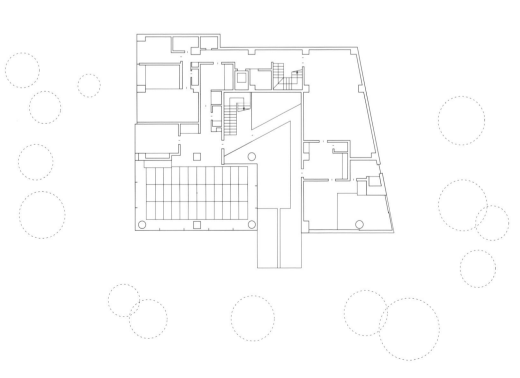

Watervilla

Middelburg, the Netherlands
Architectuurstudio HH
2002

This compact and cylindrical steel-and-glass villa is a pioneering example of a modernist floating house. It was first designed in 1986 by the Dutch architect Herman Hertzberger before a prototype was built at Middelburg in the Netherlands in 2002.

It has a very flexible design whose layout can be changed if wished—the living room, for example, can be on the ground floor or the floor above. The maximum number of floors that the house can have is three. The house is permanently attached to the shore, but can revolve approximately 90 degrees on the water via a manual winch. Therefore, it has the advantage of being able to turn around to change the view and to revolve with the sun, or away from it. Full-height windows and terraces allow the occupants to take full advantage of this. This also has obvious energy-saving implications.

It borrows its technology from offshore oil rigs. The flotation system consists of a hexagon of six interconnected 0.7 in. thick steel pipes, 6.5 feet in diameter. These pipes are built to last, so little maintenance is needed. In addition, even if one of the flotation tubes is removed, it will still remain afloat. A 26-feet long wooden gangway with steel railings links the house to the shore and acts as a form of anchor to stop the house from drifting in

Diese kompakte, zylindrische Villa aus Stahl und Glas ist ein bahnbrechendes Beispiel für ein modernistisches schwimmendes Haus. Es wurde bereits 1986 von dem niederländischen Architekten Herman Hertzberger entworfen, bevor 2002 schließlich im niederländischen Middelburg ein Prototyp erbaut wurde.

Das Gebäude verfügt über ein äußerst flexibles Design, dessen Layout, falls gewünscht, verändert werden kann – beispielsweise kann das Wohnzimmer entweder im Erdgeschoss oder im darüber liegenden Stock eingerichtet werden. Das Haus kann jedoch höchstens drei Stockwerke haben. Obgleich es dauerhaft am Ufer befestigt ist, kann es mit Hilfe einer manuellen Winde um etwa 90 Grad gedreht werden. Aufgrund dieser Beweglichkeit hat es den Vorteil, dass die Aussicht verändert werden kann oder das Gebäude in die Sonne oder von ihr fort gedreht werden kann. Mit vom Boden bis zur Decke reichenden Fenstern und Terrassen können die Bewohner diesen Vorteil so weit wie möglich ausnutzen, der sich darüber hinaus positiv auf den Energieverbrauch auswirkt.

Seine Technologie entlehnt das Gebäude Ölplattformen auf hoher See. Das Flotations-system besteht aus einem Sechseck aus miteinander verbundenen, 18 mm dicken Stahlrohren von jeweils 2 Metern Durchmesser.

Cette villa compacte et cylindrique, de verre et d'acier, est un exemple avant-gardiste d'une maison flottante moderniste. Elle a été conçue en 1986 par l'architecte néerlandais Herman Hertzberger avant la construction d'un prototype en 2002, à Middelburg, aux Pays-Bas.

Le design est très flexible puisque les pièces peuvent être déplacées. Le salon peut être situé au rez-de-chaussée ou au premier étage et le nombre de pièces est limité à trois. La maison est en permanence reliée à la côte mais peut tourner de 90° sur l'eau grâce à un levier manuel. Elle a donc l'avantage de pouvoir pivoter pour changer la vue ou suivre la direction du soleil. Les portes-fenêtres et les terrasses permettent aux occupants de profiter pleinement de cette fonctionalité. Elles permettent également de réaliser des économies d'énergies significatives.

Cette technologie est empruntée aux appareils de forages pétroliers. Le système de flottaison est un hexagone de six conduits en acier de 18 mm d'épaisseur et de 2 mètres de diamètre. Ces conduits ont une durée de vie assez longue et demandent très peu de maintenance. Si l'un des tubes de flottaison est retiré, la maison reste tout de même à la surface de l'eau. Une passerelle en bois de 8 mètres de long, avec une balustrade en acier, relie la

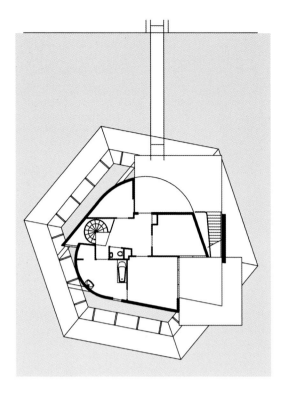

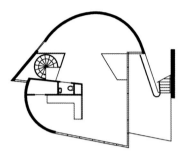

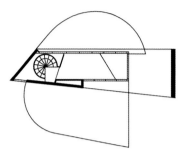

above First floor plan; second floor plan; third floor plan.

oben Grundriss des Erdgeschosses, des ersten und des zweiten Stockwerks.

ci-dessus Plan du rez-de-chaussée; plan du premier étage; plan du deuxième étage.

strong winds. Winch cables also help to hold the house in position. In Middelburg, the water level is shallow and fairly stable so light flotation units were suitable. In other places where the water is deeper, a flotation system using a concrete box turned upside down and filled with polystyrene can be used.

Construction is simple, a steel skeleton with low-maintenance exterior and interior metallic façades which can be further finished according to the owner's needs. The floor is of steel plate concrete and the window frames are in wood. Much of the building is prefabricated, including the load-bearing structure and façade, so construction is relatively quick, taking around four months. Floating gardens next to the homes can also be included with the house, and the roofs can be made to take vegetation.

Diese Rohre haben eine lange Lebensdauer und nur wenige Instandhaltungsarbeiten sind erforderlich. Außerdem bleibt die Plattform selbst dann über Wasser, wenn eines der Flotationsrohre entfernt wird. Das Haus ist über einen 8 Meter langen Steg mit Stahlgeländer mit dem Ufer verbunden, der eine Art Anker bildet, um das Haus bei starken Winden an seinem Platz zu halten. Auch die Windenkabel halten das Gebäude in Position. Der Wasserspiegel in Middelburg ist niedrig und verhältnismäßig stabil, daher waren leichte Flotationseinheiten ausreichend. An anderen Orten, wo das Wasser tiefer ist, kann ein Flotationssystem mit einem umgedrehten Betonkasten und einer Styroporfüllung verwendet werden.

Die Bauweise ist einfach: ein Stahlskelett mit einem wartungsarmen Äußeren und metallischen Fassaden im Inneren, die nach den Bedürfnissen und Wünschen des Besitzers weiter umgestaltet werden können. Die Böden bestehen aus Stahlbeton und die Fensterrahmen aus Holz. Der größte Teil des Gebäudes ist vorgefertigt, einschließlich der tragenden Struktur und der Fassade, daher kann die Erbauung mit ungefähr vier Monaten verhältnismäßig schnell erfolgen. Schwimmende Gärten neben den Häusern können zusätzlich erworben werden, und auf den Dächern kann Vegetation angepflanzt werden.

maison à la rive et joue le rôle d'ancre pour éviter que la maison ne dérive en cas de vent violent. Les câbles du levier permettent également de stabiliser la maison. À Middelburg, l'eau est peu profonde et assez stable, ce qui permet d'avoir un matériel de flottaison relativement léger. Lorsque l'eau est plus profonde, on peut utiliser un système de flottaison avec une boîte en béton retournée et remplie de polystyrène.

La construction est simple: un squelette en acier, avec des façades intérieures et extérieures métalliques, nécessitant peu de maintenance, et auquel d'autres éléments peuvent être ajoutés en fonction des besoins de l'occupant. Le sol est en acier et en béton et les châssis des fenêtres sont en bois. La plupart du bâtiment est préfabriqué, dont la structure porteuse et la façade, ayant nécessité environ quatre mois de travail. Des jardins flottants juxtaposés aux maisons peuvent être ajoutés et le toit peut accueillir de la végétation.

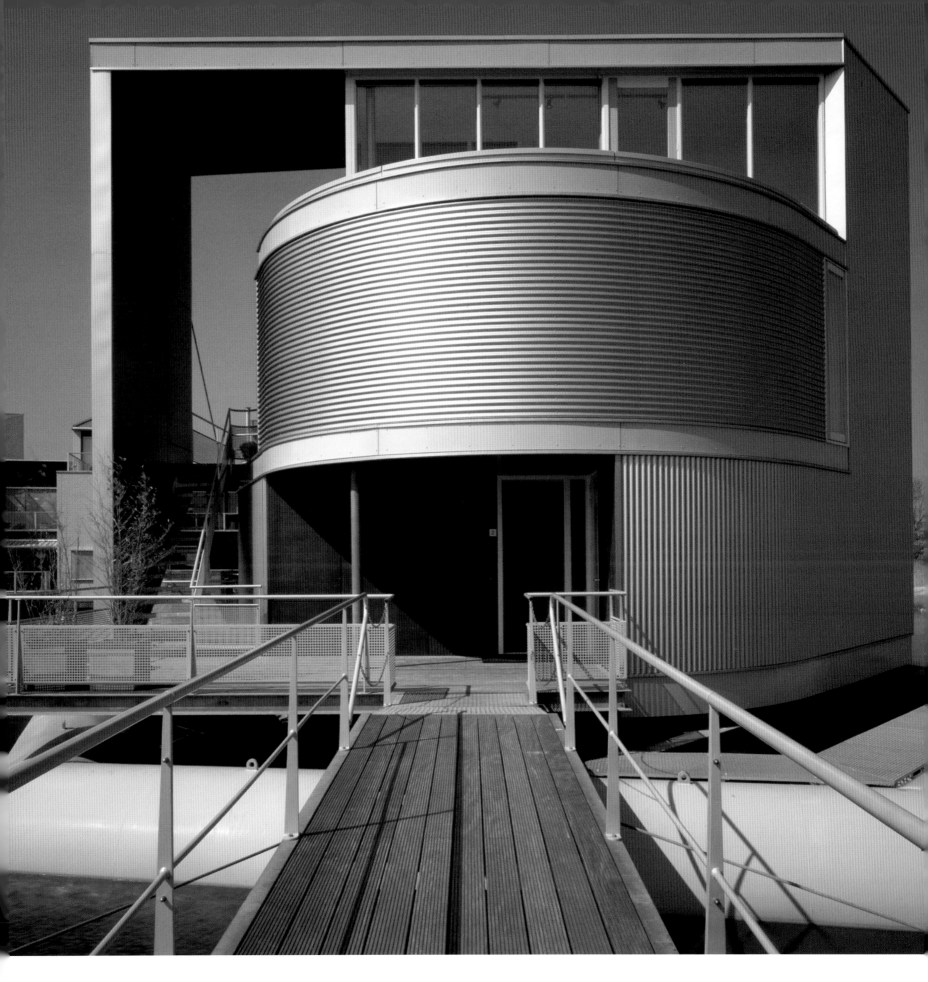

above A 26-feet long wooden gangway with metal railings links the steel-and-glass villa to the shore.

oben Ein 8 Meter langer hölzerner Steg mit Metall-geländer verbindet die Villa aus Glas und Stahl mit dem Ufer.

ci-dessus Une passerelle en bois de 8 mètres de long aux rambardes métalliques relie la villa de verre et d'acier à la rive.

Sphinxes
Lake Side Housing

Huizen, the Netherlands

Neutelings Riedijk Architects

2003

opposite A concrete bridge, that can be used by cars and pedestrians, is the only link to the land.

gegenüber Eine Brücke aus Beton, die von Fahrzeugen und Fußgängern überquert werden kann, ist die einzige Verbindung zum Ufer.

ci-contre Un pont en béton, pouvant être emprunté par les voitures et les piétons, est le seul lien à la terre.

right Floor plans starting with first floor at the top; cross section.

rechts Grundrisse, beginnend mit dem Erdgeschoss oben; Querschnitt.

droite Plans des étages, en commençant par le premier étage en haut; coupe.

below Dutch architects are the masters of design when it comes to building on water.

unten Niederländische Architekten sind Meister des Entwurfs, wenn Gebäude auf dem Wasser erbaut werden sollen.

ci-dessous Les architectes néerlandais sont les maîtres du design lorsqu'il s'agit de construire sur l'eau.

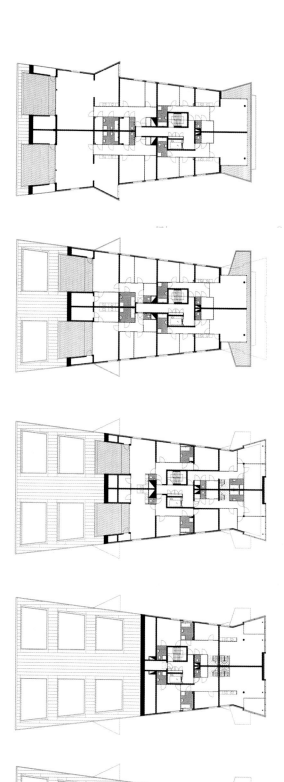

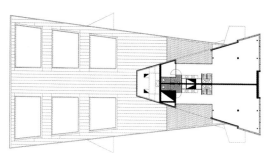

Five large "sphinxes" rise up out of the water in Huizen on the shores of Lake Gooimeer in northern Holland. Designed to give maximum light and provide the occupants with spectacular unobstructed views, each housing tower tapers down from top to bottom. Each "sphinx" contains 13 apartments, six on each side and a penthouse at the top. As one moves up the building, each floor contains one fewer room. Kitchens and bathrooms are located along the center of the building with living spaces around the outer wall. North-facing roof terraces are situated away from the lake in the slanting back of the creature, positioned so as to catch as much sun as possible.

The design of each of the penthouses is slightly different—the height and angle of the roof changes—so that each "sphinx" has an individual head. The buildings are totally isolated, each connected to the shore by their own concrete bridge for cars and pedestrians. Surrounding the buildings is a fringe of reeds that acts as both a hydrophytic filter for water treatment and serves as a gentle transition from the water to the massive apartment blocks. Garages are situated in the first floor and double as foundation tanks. Above the first floor are five more stories, culminating in the penthouse.

Each building is clad in rough unpolished

Fünf große „Sphinxen" erheben sich im nordholländischen Huizen am Ufer des Gooimeers aus dem Wasser. Jeder dieser Wohntürme wurde so entworfen, dass er maximalen Lichteinfall ermöglicht, seinen Bewohnern spektakuläre, ungehinderte Ausblicke bietet und sich von oben nach unten verjüngt. Alle „Sphinxen" beherbergen 13 Apartments, sechs auf jeder Seite, und 1 Penthouse in den obersten Stockwerken. Von unten nach oben ansteigend enthält jeder Stock einen Raum weniger. Küchen und Badezimmer befinden sich in der Mitte der Gebäude und die Wohnräume an den Außenwänden. Nach Norden hin ausgerichtete Dachterrassen wurden auf der vom See abgewandten Seite im abgeschrägten Rücken der Kreaturen angelegt, um so viel Sonne wie nur möglich einzufangen.

Die Entwürfe der einzelnen Penthouses unterscheiden sich leicht voneinander – Höhe und Winkel der Dächer ändern sich – so dass jede „Sphinx" ihren eigenen Kopf hat. Sie stehen vollkommen isoliert und jede ist über ihre eigene Betonbrücke für Fahrzeuge und Fußgänger vom Ufer aus erreichbar. Die Gebäude sind rundherum von Schilf gesäumt, das zugleich als Filter zur Wasseraufbereitung und sanfter Übergang zwischen dem Wasser und den massiven Apartmenthäusern dient. Die

Cinq grands « Sphinx » s'élèvent hors de l'eau à Huizen, sur les rives du lac Gooimer au nord des Pays-Bas. Conçu pour offrir un maximum de lumière et une vue dégagée spectaculaire à leurs occupants, chaque bâtiment est plus large à sa base. Chaque « Sphinx » compte 13 appartements, dont six de chaque côté et 1 appartement de luxe au dernier étage. À mesure que l'on monte, les étages comptent une pièce de moins. Les cuisines et salles de bain sont placées au centre et les espaces de vie autour. Les terrasses, dirigées vers le nord et situées sur la pente de la construction, tournent donc le dos au lac et sont positionnées de manière à capturer le plus de soleil possible.

Les appartements de luxe diffèrent légèrement: la hauteur et l'angle du toit changent, de manière à ce que chaque « Sphinx » ait une tête individuelle. Les maisons sont totalement isolées. Chacune est reliée à la rive par un pont que peuvent emprunter les voitures et les piétons. Une frange de roseaux entoure les bâtiments, joue le rôle de filtre hydrophyte pour le traitement des eaux et permet une transition entre l'eau et les blocs imposants des bâtiments. Les garages sont situés au premier étage et appartiennent également aux fondations. Au-dessus du premier étage se trouvent cinq étages supplémentaires, dominés par les appartements de luxe.

aluminum sheets that dramatically reflect the surrounding water. Indeed the studio is renowned for its innovative façades, such as the red clay jacket of the Minnaert Building (1997) and the transparent front with letters of Veenman Printers (1997). As the architects themselves have said, buildings are "born naked" and their job is to clothe them.

This development of 65 apartments also has a public space behind it that has been designed to be an integral part of the development. At five points along the esplanade, there are different public spaces—a look-out bastion, a surf beach, a village square, a wind balcony, and a fishing jetty.

Garagen befinden sich im Erdgeschoss und dienen gleichzeitig als Fundamenttanks. Darüber liegen fünf weitere Stockwerke, die in den Penthouses gipfeln.

Jedes der Gebäude ist mit rauen, unpolierten Aluminiumblechen verkleidet, die das umgebende Wasser widerspiegeln. Das Architekturstudio ist berühmt für seine innovativen Fassaden, wie etwa die rote Tonumhüllung des Minnaert-Gebäudes (1997) und die transparente, mit Buchstaben versehene Glasfront der Druckerei Veenman (1997). Wie die Architekten selbst sagen: Gebäude werden „nackt geboren" und ihre Arbeit als Architekten besteht darin, sie zu bekleiden.

Dieses Bauprojekt mit 65 Apartments verfügt außerdem über öffentliche Bereiche, die hinter den Gebäuden liegen und als wesentlicher Bestandteil der Anlage entworfen wurden. An fünf Punkten entlang der Promenade liegen eine Aussichtsbastion, ein Strand zum Surfen, ein Dorfplatz, ein Windbalkon und ein Steg zum Fischen.

Chaque bâtiment est revêtu de feuilles d'aluminium non poli qui reflètent l'eau de manière spectaculaire. Le cabinet d'architectes est en effet reconnu pour ses façades innovantes, comme le revêtement en argile rouge du Bâtiment Minnaert (1997) et la façade transparente recouverte de lettres de Veenman Printers (1997). Comme l'ont affirmé les architectes eux-mêmes, les bâtiments « naissent nus » et leur travail consiste à les habiller.

Ce projet de 65 appartements comprend également un espace public, faisant partie intégrante du développement. L'esplanade accueille des espaces publics en cinq points: un bastion en porte-à-faux, une plage pour le surf, une place centrale, une terrasse et une jetée pour la pêche.

left The tapered shape allows the large terraces at the back to catch the sun, while at the front panoramic windows give unobstructed views of the lake.

links Durch die abgeschrägte Form können die großen Terrassen auf der Rückseite die Sonne einfangen, während die Panoramafenster auf der Vorderseite ungehinderte Blicke auf den See zulassen.

gauche La forme fuselée permet l'ensoleillement aux grandes terrasses situées à l'arrière, tandis que les fenêtres panoramiques à l'avant permettent une vue sur le lac.

below The first floor is used as a garage. Above that, there are five floors of apartments, with a penthouse at the very top.

unten Das Erdgeschoss wird als Garage verwendet. Darüber befinden sich fünf Stockwerke mit Apartments und einem Penthouse an der Spitze.

ci-dessous Le premier niveau abrite le garage. Au-dessus, cinq niveaux accueillent des appartements, dont un de luxe au dernier étage.

Watervilla

Aalsmeer, the Netherlands
Waterstudio.NL
2004

Waterstudio is an architectural studio with a difference. The firm works exclusively in water-based designs and floating structures. Koen Olthuis, the founder of the studio, is acutely aware of the problems of rising water levels, especially in his country, the Netherlands, where 50 percent of the land is only 3 feet above sea level and 27 percent actually below sea level. As a consequence, much of the country is built on polders—parcels of land reclaimed from the sea, protected by a complex system of dykes, canals, and pumps. However, it is forecasted that by 2100 the sea will rise by a further 20 feet. So as Olthuis says, "We can't keep extending our cities with tower blocks above. And the rising water level is swallowing up more and more land. If we were to stop pumping round-the-clock, we would be underwater within 42 hours."

One of the first buildings Waterstudio made was a villa in Aalsmeer, a region that was particularly badly hit during North Sea flood of 1953. Because the council stipulated that the building could be no more than 13 feet above water level, the architects built a floor under water. The two-story villa was prefabricated in a factory and floated to its final destination next to a 9,687 square feet garden on the shores of Lake Westeinderplassen. It floats on a hollow box-like concrete core—a system patented by the

Waterstudio ist ein Architekturstudio mit einem kleinen Unterschied. Das Unternehmen arbeitet ausschließlich an Entwürfen im Wasser und schwimmenden Bauwerken. Der Gründer des Studios, Koen Olthuis, ist sich des Problems der steigenden Wasserspiegel sehr bewusst, insbesondere in seinem eigenen Land: In den Niederlanden befinden sich 50 Prozent des Landes nur 1 Meter über dem Meeresspiegel und 27 Prozent gar darunter. Infolgedessen ist ein Großteil des Landes auf Poldern erbaut – Landflächen, die aus dem Meer zurück gewonnen wurden – und wird von komplexen Systemen aus Deichen, Kanälen und Pumpen geschützt. Gemäß den meisten Voraussagen soll der Meeresspiegel bis 2100 jedoch um weitere sechs Meter ansteigen. Deshalb sagt Olthuis: „Wir können unsere Städte nicht mit immer höheren Hochhäusern erweitern. Und der steigende Wasserspiegel schluckt immer mehr Land. Wenn wir aufhören würden, rund um die Uhr zu pumpen, wären wir 42 Stunden später ganz unter Wasser."

Eines der ersten von Waterstudio entworfenen Gebäude war eine Villa in Aalsmeer, einer von der Nordseeflut im Jahr 1953 besonders hart betroffenen Region. Da die Kommunalbehörden vorschrieben, dass der Bau nicht mehr als 4 Meter über dem Wasserspiegel liegen durfte,

Waterstudio est un cabinet d'architectes différent des autres, travaillant exclusivement sur des conceptions ayant trait à l'eau et aux structures flottantes. Koen Olthuis, le fondateur du cabinet, est très conscient des problèmes concernant la montée du niveau de l'eau, notamment dans son pays, les Pays-Bas, où 50% du territoire ne se trouve qu'à 1 mètre au-dessus du niveau de la mer et 27% en dessous. Par conséquent, la plupart du pays est bâti sur des polders, ces parcelles de terre sur la mer protégées par des systèmes complexes de digues, de canaux et de pompes. Il est prévu d'ici 2100 que la mer monte de six mètres supplémentaires. Donc, comme l'affirme Koen Olthuis, « Nous ne pouvons pas continuer d'étendre nos villes avec des tours. La montée du niveau de la mer nous prend de plus en plus de terre. Si nous devions arrêter de pomper en continu, nous nous retrouverions sous l'eau en moins de 42 heures. »

L'une des premières constructions de Waterstudio est une villa dans la région d'Aalsmeer, particulièrement frappée par les inondations de la mer du Nord en 1953. L'administration ayant indiqué que le bâtiment ne pouvait dépasser les 4 mètres au dessus du niveau de la mer, les architectes ont construit un étage sous l'eau. La villa à deux niveaux a été

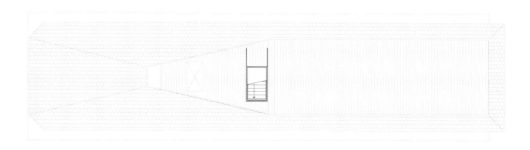

previous page The two-story house was constructed in a factory before being towed to its present mooring.

vorherige Seite Das zweigeschossige Haus wurde in einer Fabrik vorgefertigt, bevor es auf dem Wasserweg zu seinem gegenwärtigen Standort geschleppt wurde.

page précédente La maison à deux niveaux a été montée en usine avant d'être amenée à son mouillage actuel.

right Plans of the roof, first floor, and basement area.

rechts Grundrisse des Dachs, des Erdgeschosses und des Untergeschosses.

droite Plans du toit, du niveau au-dessus de l'eau et du niveau en dessous de l'eau.

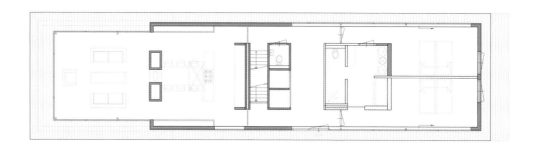

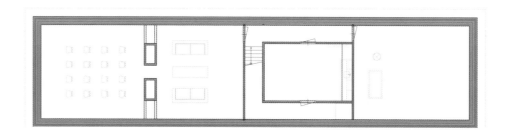

studio—and like a ship is moored to the bottom of the lake and the land. In order to give the house stability, it was designed to be symmetrical. As Olthuis puts it, "We build to make you feel as if you're on terra firma no matter how strong the wind."

Built for a flower farmer, wife, and son, this rectangular 2-bedroom villa has 3,229 square feet of living space and a roof terrace. The client did not like the idea of sleeping under water so the bedrooms and bathroom are located above water on the main floor. On the same level, there are a living room and kitchen, separated by a modern fireplace. A green, glass staircase—part of the water theme—leads to the lower floor where there is a lounge, 20-seater cinema, and storage space. Both inside and outside, the design is intended to be streamlined and "timeless." The black aluminum exterior helps it blend in with the water landscape, while the reflective materials used in the interior—chrome metal kitchen surfaces and polished granite floors—continue the water theme. Glass doors, which open directly onto the lake, are mirrored

legten die Architekten ein Stockwerk unter Wasser an. Die zweigeschossige Villa wurde in einer Fabrik vorgefertigt und anschließend auf dem Wasserweg zu ihrem endgültigen Standort neben einem 900 Quadratmeter großen Garten an den Ufern der Westeinderplassen transportiert. Sie schwimmt auf einem hohlen, kastenförmigen Betonkern – einem von Waterstudio patentierten System – und ist wie ein Schiff auf dem Grund des Sees und am Land festgezurrt. Der Entwurf des Hauses ist symmetrisch, um ihm mehr Stabilität zu verleihen. Olthuis sagt: „Wir haben so gebaut, dass Sie sich wie auf dem Festland fühlen, ganz gleich wie stark der Wind bläst."

Die für einen Blumenzüchter, seine Frau und beider Sohn erbaute rechteckige Zweizimmer-villa verfügt über 300 Quadratmeter Wohnraum und eine Dachterrasse. Da der Kunde nicht gerne unter Wasser schlafen wollte, befinden sich die Schlafräume und das Badezimmer über Wasser im Erdgeschoss. Auf diesem Stockwerk liegen außerdem ein Wohnzimmer und eine Küche, die von einem modernen Kamin getrennt

préfabriquée en usine puis mise à l'eau pour sa destination finale, à côté d'un jardin de 900 mètres carrés sur les rives du lac Westeinderplassen. Elle flotte sur une boîte creuse en béton, un système breveté par le cabinet, et est amarrée au fond du lac et à la terre comme un bateau. Pour être stable, la construction devait être symétrique. Comme l'explique Koen Olthuis, « Nous construisons pour que vous vous sentiez comme sur la terre ferme, quelle que soit la force du vent. »

Construite pour un cultivateur de fleurs, sa femme et son fils, cette villa rectangulaire de 2 chambres compte 300 mètres carrés d'espace de vie et une terrasse sur toit. Le client n'aimait pas l'idée de dormir sous l'eau donc les chambres et la salle de bain sont au niveau principal, au-dessus de l'eau. Au même niveau se trouve un salon et une cuisine, séparés par une cheminée moderne. Un escalier en verre vert – rappelant le thème de l'eau – conduit au niveau inférieur où se trouvent un home cinéma avec canapés pour 20 personnes et un espace de rangement. À l'intérieur comme à l'extérieur,

left Black aluminum panels line the side of the house, designed to make it blend in with the water.

links Schwarze Aluminiumplatten verkleiden die Seite des Hauses, um es mit dem Wasser verschmelzen zu lassen.

gauche Des panneaux en aluminium noir sont alignés sur le côté de la maison pour la fondre dans le paysage.

above Living room designed like an elongated piece of rock. The house has a massive, yet streamlined, appearance.

oben Wohnzimmer, das wie ein verlängertes Stück Felsen gestaltet wurde. Das Haus hat eine massive und doch windschnittige Form.

ci-dessus Le salon est conçu comme un rocher allongé. La maison a un aspect imposant mais épuré.

right Polished metal surfaces were chosen for the kitchen to mirror the reflective effect of the water.

rechts Für die Küche wurden polierte Metalloberflächen gewählt, um die Spiegelungen des Wassers wiederzugeben.

droite Des surfaces en métal poli ont été choisies pour la cuisine afin de rappeler l'effet réfléchissant de l'eau.

above Living room on the first floor has views onto the lake and glass walls that can be fully opened.

oben Das Wohnzimmer im Erdgeschoss bietet Aussichten auf den See und Glaswände, die sich zur Gänze öffnen lassen.

ci-dessus Salon au premier étage avec vue sur le lac et parois en verre s'ouvrant entièrement.

right Like a waterfall glass stairs cascade down to the basement area where there is a cinema.

rechts Glastreppen fallen wie ein Wasserfall hinunter zum Untergeschoss, in dem sich ein Kino befindet.

droite Comme une chute d'eau, les escaliers en verre descendent au sous-sol où se trouve le home cinéma.

to give privacy and increase reflectivity. The overall effect is "like a piece of rock that is carefully shaped by a sculptor."

werden. Eine grüne Treppe aus Glas – eine Fortsetzung des Wasserthemas – führt ins Untergeschoss, wo sich ein Wohn- und Aufenthaltsraum, ein Kino mit 20 Sitzen und Stauraum befinden. Das Design soll innen wie außen windschnittig und „zeitlos" wirken. Die Außenwand aus schwarzem Aluminium lässt das Gebäude mit der Wasserlandschaft verschmelzen, während die spiegelnden Materialien im Inneren – die Metalloberflächen aus Chrom in der Küche und die Böden aus poliertem Granit – das Thema der Spiegelung fortsetzen. Die Glastüren, die unmittelbar auf den See hinausführen, sind zur Wahrung der Privatsphäre und für weitere Reflektionen verspiegelt. Die Gesamtwirkung lässt sich beschreiben als „ein Stück Fels, das von einem Bildhauer sorgfältig bearbeitet wurde."

le design se veut moderne et intemporel. L'extérieur en aluminium noir se fond aisément dans l'eau tandis que les matières réfléchissantes utilisées à l'intérieur telles que les surfaces en métal chromé de la cuisine et le sol en granit poli, restent dans ce thème de réflexion. Les portes en verre miroir, qui s'ouvrent directement sur le lac, offrent une plus grande intimité et augmentent la réflexion. La construction, dans sa globalité, fait penser à « un rocher délicatement sculpté ».

Floating House

Lake Huron, Ontario, Canada
MOS
2004

below Living areas—sitting room, kitchen, office, and bedroom—are all located on the second floor.

unten Wohnbereiche – Wohnzimmer, Küche, Büro und Schlafzimmer – befinden sich alle im ersten Stockwerk.

ci-dessous Les espaces de vie – salon, cuisine, bureau et chambre – sont tous au premier étage.

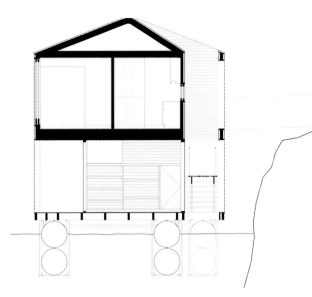

left The house floats on a steel platform with pontoons below the water level.

links Das Haus schwimmt auf einer Stahlplattform mit Pontons unter dem Wasserspiegel.

gauche La maison flotte sur une plate-forme en acier avec des pontons au-dessous du niveau de l'eau.

below Located on a remote island on one of the Great Lakes, the design experiments with the idea of the wooden vernacular house.

unten Der Entwurf dieses auf einer abgelegenen Insel in einem der Großen Seen befindlichen Wohnhauses experimentiert mit der Idee eines landestypischen Holzhauses.

ci-dessous Située sur une île isolée de l'un des Grands lacs, la construction revisite le concept de la maison classique en bois.

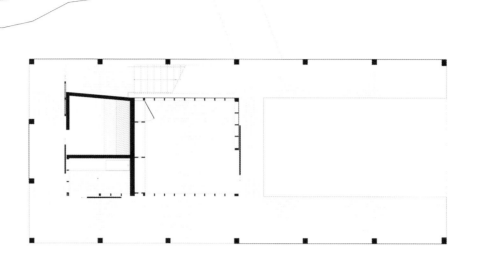

left Floor plan of first floor with surrounding decking at water level.

links Grundriss des Erdgeschosses mit Holzbodenterrasse auf Höhe des Wasserspiegels.

gauche Plan du rez-de-chaussée entouré d'une plate-forme au niveau de l'eau.

right Floor plan of the second floor with footbridge.

rechts Grundriss des ersten Stockwerks mit der Fußgängerbrücke.

droite Plan du premier étage avec la passerelle.

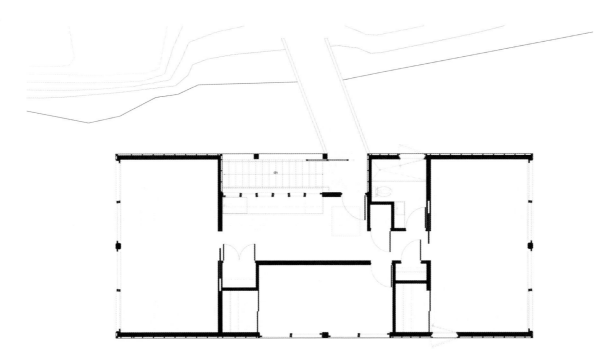

One of the most beautiful floating houses to be built in recent years is Michael Meredith's house on the Great Lakes in Canada. Although very straightforward in design—a two-story wooden rectangular box with gable roof—its clear lines and light-brown cedar cladding allow it to stand out against the surrounding natural landscape of pine trees, rock, and flowing water. At night the building is further transformed with its lights making it glow like a lantern against the dark.

As it would have been prohibitively expensive to build the house using traditional construction processes on site in this inaccessible area, the architects had the house prefabricated on another part of the lake. Construction materials were delivered to a fabrication shop on the lake shore where the house was built on frozen water during winter. Once it was completed, the entire house was towed along the water to its present location, a remote island on Lake Huron. Because the lake's water levels change drastically from season to season, it was also decided that the house had to float—a steel platform structure with incorporated pontoons allows it to rise and fall with the water level.

The layout of the house is very simple. On the first floor, there are a series of rooms for

Eines der schönsten schwimmenden Häuser, das in den letzten Jahren gebaut wurde, ist Michael Merediths Haus auf den Großen Seen in Kanada. Obgleich sehr schlicht in seinem Design – ein zweistöckiger, rechteckiger Kasten aus Holz mit einem Satteldach – hebt es sich durch seine klaren Linien und seine hellbraune Verkleidung aus Zedernholz von der umgebenden Landschaft aus Kiefern, Felsen und fließendem Wasser deutlich ab. Nachts verwandelt sich das Gebäude mit seinen Lichtern, die es wie eine Laterne im Dunklen aufleuchten lassen, noch mehr.

Da es unerschwinglich teuer gewesen wäre, das Haus in dieser unzugänglichen Gegend mit traditionellen Bauweisen vor Ort zu errichten, ließen die Architekten das Haus auf einem anderen Teil des Sees vorfertigen. Die Baumaterialien wurden zu einer Werkstätte am Seeufer geliefert, wo das Haus während des Winters auf gefrorenem Wasser erbaut wurde. Nach seiner Fertigstellung wurde das gesamte Haus über das Wasser an seinen gegenwärtigen Standort, einer abgelegenen Insel im Huronsee, geschleppt. Da der Wasserspiegel des Sees sich mit den Jahreszeiten drastisch ändert, wurde außerdem beschlossen, dass das Haus schwimmen musste – eine Stahlplattform mit eingebauten Pontons lässt es mit dem Wasser des Sees steigen und fallen.

L'une des plus belles maisons flottantes de ces dernières années est celle de Michael Meredith sur les Grands Lacs au Canada. Bien que son design soit très simple (une maison en bois à deux niveaux, rectangulaire, avec un toit à pignon), ses lignes lumineuses et son revêtement en cèdre marron clair la font ressortir sur le paysage naturel composé de pins, de rochers et d'eau. La nuit, la construction se transforme en une lanterne dans l'obscurité, grâce à un éclairage particulier.

Comme il aurait été excessivement coûteux de construire cette maison sur le site, inaccessible, les architectes l'ont préfabriquée sur une autre partie du lac. Les matériaux ont été livrés au bord du lac où la maison a été construite, sur l'eau gelée en hiver. Une fois achevée, la maison a été tractée le long de la rive jusqu'à son emplacement actuel, une île isolée sur le Lac Huron. Le niveau de l'eau changeant constamment d'une saison à une autre, la maison devait également flotter. Une plate-forme en acier avec des pontons intégrés lui permettent de suivre les fluctuations de l'eau.

La disposition de la maison est très simple: le rez-de-chaussée comporte plusieurs pièces de détente, dont un sauna et une véranda conduisant directement sur le lac. Le premier étage est l'espace de vie: on y trouve salon, cuisine, bureau et chambre. De grandes portes

left Wooden slats work as a screen, allowing in natural light, keeping out rain, and giving privacy.

links Holzleisten dienen als Schutzschild, der natürliches Licht einfallen lässt, Regen abhält und die Privatsphäre schützt.

gauche Les lattes en bois protègent la maison de la pluie, laissent entrer la lumière naturelle et offrent une certaine intimité.

right The house is linked to the shore on one side by a footbridge, and to the rocks on the other by planks.

rechts Das Haus ist auf einer Seite über eine Fußgängerbrücke mit dem Ufer und auf der anderen Seite über Planken mit den Felsen verbunden.

droite La maison est reliée à la terre d'un côté par une passerelle, et aux rochers d'un autre côté par des planches.

right At night, the floating house glows spectacularly against the natural setting of the lake and woods.

rechts Nachts ist das schwimmende Haus in seiner natürlichen Umgebung mit See und Wäldern spektakulär beleuchtet.

droite La nuit, la maison flottante brille de manière spectaculaire face au lac et au bois.

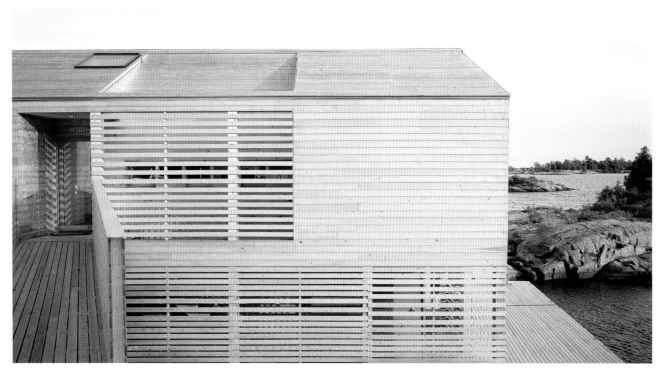

below A wooden footbridge at second floor level acts as an entrance. Access to the rocks is via a platform at the water level.

unten Eine hölzerne Fußgängerbrücke im ersten Stockwerk dient als Eingang. Der Zugang zu den Felsen erfolgt über eine Plattform auf Höhe des Wasserspiegels.

ci-dessous Une passerelle en bois au premier étage permet d'accéder à la maison. Un accès par les rochers se fait au rez-de-chaussée.

relaxing on the water, including a sauna, and a veranda leading directly onto the lake. The second floor is the living space, with living room, kitchen, office, and bedroom. Large glass sliding doors in the living room allow for spectacular views. The house is linked to the shore via a gangway at second story level, while on the first floor there is a simple footbridge leading to the rocks. An outer layer of wooden slats with small openings has been designed as a rainscreen and to allow light to radiate softly out of the windows. The screen also helps reduce heat gain and wind load and encloses exterior spaces on the veranda.

Das Layout des Hauses ist sehr einfach: Im Erdgeschoss befinden sich eine Reihe von Räumen zur Entspannung auf dem Wasser, einschließlich einer Sauna, und eine Veranda, die unmittelbar auf den See hinausführt. Im ersten Stockwerk sind die Wohnräume mit Wohnzimmer, Küche, Büro und Schlafzimmer. Im Wohnzimmer bieten große Schiebetüren aus Glas spektakuläre Aussichten. Auf der Höhe des ersten Stockwerks ist das Gebäude über einen Steg mit dem Ufer verbunden, während aus dem Erdgeschoss eine einfache Fußgängerbrücke auf die Felsen führt. Eine äußere Schicht aus Holzleisten mit kleinen Öffnungen wurde als Schutz vor Regen entworfen und lässt Licht sanft aus den Fenstern strahlen. Der Schutzschild hilft außerdem, Überhitzung und Windeinfall zu vermeiden und umschließt Außenbereiche auf der Veranda.

coulissantes dans le salon offrent une vue spectaculaire. La maison est reliée à la rive par une passerelle au premier étage, tandis qu'une simple planche de bois posée sur les rochers permet d'accéder au rez-de-chaussée. Des lattes en bois espacées protègent la maison de la pluie et laissent la lumière rayonner en douceur par les fenêtres. Cette protection permet également de réduire la chaleur et la charge du vent, tout en abritant la véranda.

Lakeside Studio

California, USA
Mark Dziewulski Architect
2005

Mark Dziewulski is a British architect with offices in San Francisco and London whose work is gaining an increasing international reputation. In 2005, he completed a highly successful studio for a private client that won the American Institute of Architects Design Award and the Pacific Coast Builders Award.

The shape of the building was influenced by the site itself. A man-made lake was created in the surrounding garden and an open-plan space to be used for entertaining, as a studio, and for exhibiting art was added to an existing house. Views of the nearby river were required so the new studio was raised to allow for this. Dziewulski concluded that the new building would only work well if it was south-facing with a cantilevered floor over the water and large roof overhangs. The design is reminiscent of work by Oscar Niemeyer, but the architect is quick to point out that this has more to do with site and climate issues. The building is located in northern California near San Francisco and the climate dictated much of the design. As there are huge areas of triple-glazed glass, a roof overhang over the south side was necessary to give shade; the west wall in contrast to the glass walls is solid in order to offer protection from the climate.

Materials and colors are subtly balanced. Steel was used for the main structure, with dark

Mark Dziewulski ist ein junger britischer Architekt mit Büros in San Francisco und London, dessen Werk zunehmende internationale Bekanntheit erlangt. Im Jahr 2005 stellte er ein äußerst erfolgreiches Studio für einen Privatkunden fertig, das den Design Award des American Institute of Architects und den Pacific Coast Builders Award gewann.

Die Form des Gebäudes wurde vom Standort selbst beeinflusst. In dem umliegenden Garten wurde ein künstlicher See angelegt und ein offen angelegter Raum, der als Empfangsraum für Gäste, als Studio und für Kunstausstellungen genutzt werden sollte, wurde zu dem bereits vorhandenen Haus hinzugefügt. Da Aussichten auf den nahe gelegenen Fluss möglich sein sollten, wurde das Studio angehoben. Dziewulski glaubte, dass das neue Gebäude nur dann funktionieren würde, wenn es nach Süden hin ausgerichtet mit einem Vorsprung über dem Wasser und einem ausladenden Dach errichtet würde. Der Entwurf erinnert an Arbeiten von Niemeyer, der Architekt weist jedoch schnell darauf hin, dass er mehr vom Standort und von Klimafragen beeinflusst wurde. Das Gebäude befindet sich in Nordkalifornien nahe bei San Francisco und der Entwurf ist in hohem Maße von dem dortigen Klima beeinflusst. Da das Gebäude über riesige Bereiche mit

Mark Dziewulski est un jeune architecte dont les cabinets se trouvent à San Francisco et Londres et dont le travail est en train de gagner une réputation internationale. Il a terminé en 2005 un studio pour un particulier, qui a rencontré un énorme succès et a remporté le prix American Institute of Architects Design et le prix Pacific Coast Builders Award.

Le site lui-même a influencé la forme de sa construction. Un lac artificiel a été créé dans le jardin, et un espace ouvert, pour les loisirs (comme un studio) et pour les expositions artistiques, a été ajouté dans une maison préexistante. Le nouveau studio a été surélevé pour offrir une vue sur la rivière. Selon Mark Dziewulsky, le nouveau bâtiment ne serait réussi que dirigé vers le sud avec un sol en porte-à-faux sur l'eau et d'importants débords de toiture. La conception rappelle le travail de Niemeyer, mais l'architecte s'empresse de souligner qu'elle se rapproche davantage des questions géographiques et climatiques. La construction se trouve au nord de la Californie, près de San Francisco et le climat en a en grande partie dicté le design. Une partie importante des parois étant conçue en triple vitrage, un débord de toiture était nécessaire du côté sud pour apporter de l'ombre; la façade ouest, en contraste avec les parois en verre, est

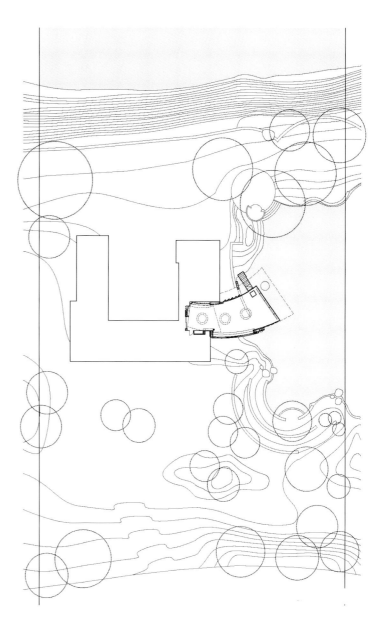

previous page The building is a combination of flexible living space, art studio, and gallery.

vorherige Seite Das Gebäude ist eine Mischung aus flexiblem Wohnraum, Kunststudio und Galerie.

page précédente Le bâtiment est une combinaison d'espaces de vie flexibles, d'un studio artistique et d'une galerie.

above Site plan showing the river to the east (top) and the man-made lake to the south (right).

oben Lageplan mit dem Fluss im Osten (oben) und dem künstlich angelegten See im Süden (rechts).

ci-dessus Plan du site montrant la rivière à l'est (en haut) et le lac artificiel au sud (à droite).

left Rectangular shapes are cut out of the west wall to frame windows. An oculus is cut into the overhanging roof.

links Aus der westlichen Wand wurden rechteckige Formen herausgeschnitten, um Fenster zu umrahmen. In das überhängende Dach wurde ein Rundfenster geschnitten.

gauche Des formes rectangulaires sont taillées dans le mur du côté ouest pour encadrer les fenêtres. Un oculus est creusé dans le débord de toiture.

green limestone encasing two large concrete vertical piers, pale limestone on the floor, and white painted plaster on the solid walls. Various shapes—rectangles and circles—have been cut out of the floor, walls, and ceiling to create a balanced composition that is intentionally asymmetrical. The architect was aiming for the same kind of simplicity and order found in the work of Rietveld or Mondrian. Water was also very important. In a way, the building is a garden pavilion, peacefully perched like a sculpture above a pond within a landscaped garden. The tranquil environment is enhanced by sunlight reflecting off the water that dapples the ceiling with dancing patterns.

Lighting comes from natural and recessed lighting. There are skylights throughout. Four circles in the roof allow light in, the fourth being a simple hole, or oculus, in the outside roof—the idea here being to link the inside to the outside.

dreifachverglasten Fenstern verfügt, war eine Dachüberkragung erforderlich, um den nötigen Schatten zu spenden; im Gegensatz zu den Glaswänden ist die Westwand solide, um Schutz vor dem Klima zu bieten.

Die Materialien und Farben sind auf subtile Weise ausgewogen. Für die Hauptstruktur wurde Stahl verwendet, dunkelgrüner Kalkstein umgibt zwei große senkrechte Betonpiers, die Böden bestehen aus hellem Kalkstein und die harten Wände aus weißem, bemaltem Putz. Aus dem Boden, den Wänden und der Decke wurden verschiedene Formen – Rechtecke und Kreise – herausgeschnitten, um eine ausgewogene Komposition zu schaffen, die mit Absicht asymmetrisch ist. Der Architekt strebte dieselbe Schlichtheit und Ordnung an, die sich auch in Werken von Rietveld oder Mondrian finden. Wasser war ebenfalls sehr wichtig. Das Gebäude ist gewissermaßen ein Gartenpavillon, der wie eine Skulptur friedlich über einem Teich mit einem landschaftlich gestalteten Garten steht. Die ruhige Umgebung wird durch Sonnenlicht verschönert, das sich im Wasser widerspiegelt und die Decke mit tanzenden Mustern verziert.

Die Beleuchtung kommt aus natürlichen und eingelassenen Lichtquellen. Überall wurden Oberlichter eingebaut. Im Dach lassen vier Kreise das Licht einfallen, wobei es sich bei dem vierten um ein einfaches Loch oder Rundfenster im äußeren Dach handelt – die Idee war hier, das Innere mit dem Äußeren zu verbinden.

compacte, pour offrir une protection contre le climat.

Les matières et les couleurs s'équilibrent très subtilement. La structure principale est en acier et en faux calcaire vert foncé dans lequel sont emboîtées deux grandes plates-formes verticales. Du calcaire clair est utilisé au sol et du plâtre blanc sur les murs. Les sols, murs et plafonds ont été taillés de diverses formes (cercles et rectangles) pour créer une composition équilibrée volontairement asymétrique. L'architecte recherchait le même genre de simplicité et d'ordre que celui du travail de Rietveld ou Mondrian. L'eau était également très importante: d'une certaine manière, le bâtiment est un pavillon de jardin, paisiblement perché tel une sculpture sur un bassin de jardin paysager. La tranquillité de l'environnement est accentuée par la réflexion du soleil sur l'eau qui tachète le plafond de motifs en mouvement.

La lumière provient de l'éclairage naturel et de sources encastrées. Des ouvertures sont faites au plafond; quatre cercles laissent entrer la lumière, le quatrième étant un simple orifice, ou oculus, dans le débord de toiture. L'idée ici était de relier l'intérieur et l'extérieur.

left Along the east wall, the glass is louvered to frame views and act as a place to put sculptures.

links Entlang der östlichen Wand fassen Glasrippen die Aussicht ein und bieten Platz zur Ausstellung von Skulpturen.

gauche Le long de la paroi du côté est, des panneaux de verre forment des persiennes pour cadrer la vue et servir d'espace d'exposition pour les sculptures.

below Plan showing the studio extension sweeping over the lake. Most of the studio is surrounded by the lake.

unten Lageplan mit Ansicht des Studioanbaus, der über den See hinausragt. Der größte Teil des Studios ist von einem See umgeben.

ci-dessous Plan montrant l'extension du studio sur le lac, qui en entoure une grande partie.

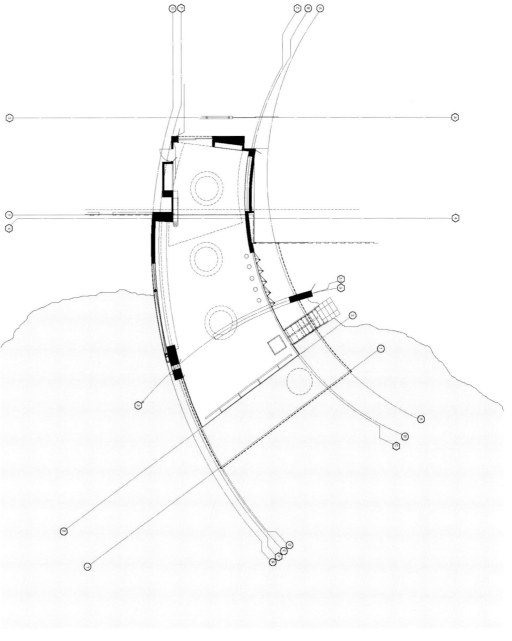

above Uninterrupted glass walls allow water reflections to bounce off the ceiling. The landscape design is by Edgar Haag.

oben Ununterbrochene Glaswände reflektieren die Spiegelungen des Wassers auf der Decke. Der Garten wurde von Edgar Haag entworfen.

ci-dessus Des parois continues en verre laissent le reflet de l'eau frapper le plafond. Le jardin est conçu par Edgar Haag.

right Three materials—white painted plaster, green limestone, and tripled-glazed glass.

rechts Drei Materialien – weißer, bemalter Putz, grüner Kalkstein und dreifachverglaste Scheiben.

droite Trois matières – plâtre blanc, calcaire vert et verre à triple vitrage.

Hong Luo Club

Hong Luo, China
MAD
2006

MAD in Beijing, China, is one of the country's most dynamic and exciting new architecture studios—the name is short for Ma Design, named after the founder Yansong Ma who started the company in 2002. They were named as Young Architects of 2006 by the Architectural League of New York and won the competition to build the Absolute Towers in Toronto, Canada, making them the first Chinese practice to undertake a large-scale urban project abroad.

One of their most startling projects, however, is a very small-scale building. The Hong Luo Club is a clubhouse and swimming pool for residents living in the Hong Luo Villa district, a gated community north of Beijing an hour's drive from the city center. The area is noted for its natural environment, in particular a lake and impressive mountain range. As the area has grown in popularity, it has attracted increasing amounts of investment.

The building is approached from two ways, one a wooden footbridge, the other a sunken path 4.26 feet below the level of the lake. The wooden bridge already existed, but the architects created the house in the middle of the lake and the sunken entrance path to the shore. The sunken approach of two concrete walls with water either side is designed to make visitors feel as if they are walking through the

MAD aus Peking ist eines der dynamischsten und aufregendsten neuen Architekturstudios in China – der Name ist eine Abkürzung für Ma Design, benannt nach Yansong Ma, der das Unternehmen 2002 gründete. Das Studio bekam von der Architectural League of New York den Titel Young Architects of 2006 verliehen und gewann den Wettbewerb um die Erbauung der Absolute Towers in Toronto, Kanada. Die Architekten sind damit das erste chinesische Unternehmen, das ein städtisches Projekt von solch großem Umfang in Übersee ausführt.

Eines ihrer aufregendsten Projekte ist jedoch ein sehr kleines Bauwerk. Der Hong Luo Club ist ein Klubhaus mit Schwimmbecken für die Anwohner des benachbarten Hong Luo-Villenviertels, einer bewachten Wohnsiedlung nördlich von Peking, eine Stunde Fahrt vom Stadtzentrum entfernt. Das Gebiet ist für seine natürliche Schönheit bekannt, insbesondere für einen See und eine beeindruckende Bergkette. Aufgrund ihrer wachsenden Beliebtheit hat die Gegend zunehmend neue Investitionen angezogen.

Das Gebäude kann über zwei Zugänge erreicht werden, über eine hölzerne Fußgängerbrücke und über einen versunkenen Pfad 1,3 Meter unter dem Wasserspiegel des Sees. Die hölzerne Brücke bestand bereits, die

MAD est l'un des nouveaux cabinets d'architectes les plus dynamiques et innovants. Le nom, raccourci de Ma Design, vient du fondateur Yansong Ma qui a créé le cabinet en 2002, à Pékin. Le cabinet a été élu Jeunes Architectes de 2006 par la Ligue architecturale de New York et a remporté le concours des Absolute Towers à Toronto, au Canada. MAD est donc devenu le premier cabinet chinois à entreprendre un projet urbain d'une telle échelle à l'étranger.

L'un de leurs projets les plus surprenants est cependant une construction à très petite échelle. Le Club de Hong Luo abrite un pavillon et une piscine pour les résidents du district de Hong Luo Villa, une zone résidentielle située au nord de Pékin, à une heure de route du centre ville. La zone est réputée pour son environnement naturel, en particulier le lac et l'impressionnante chaîne de montagnes. Gagnant en popularité, elle attire un nombre croissant d'investisseurs.

On accède au pavillon par deux chemins, une passerelle en bois et une allée en contrebas, à 1,3 mètre en dessous du niveau du lac. La passerelle existait déjà et les architectes ont créé le pavillon au milieu du lac et l'allée en contrebas le reliant à la rive. Cette allée immergée constituée de deux murs de béton

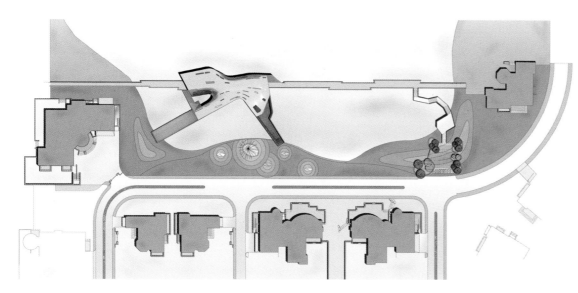

above The clubhouse has two distinct branches, the under-water platform, and the swimming pool (left of the building).

oben Das Klubhaus hat zwei von einander getrennte Ausleger, die Unterwasser-Plattform und das Schwimmbecken (rechts vom Gebäude).

ci-dessus Le pavillon est composé de deux parties distinctes, la plate-forme sous l'eau et la piscine (à gauche du bâtiment).

left Site plan with wooden footbridges running either side of the clubhouse.

links Lageplan mit den hölzernen Fußgängerbrücken auf beiden Seiten des Klubhauses.

gauche Plan du site avec passerelles en bois de chaque côté du pavillon.

right Plan with footbridges, rectangular swimming pool, and sunken entrance with steps.

rechts Plan mit Fußgängerbrücken, rechteckigem Schwimmbecken und versunkenem Eingang mit Stufen.

droite Plan avec les passerelles, la piscine rectangulaire, l'entrée immergée et les escaliers.

lake and is reminiscent of the entrance to Tadao Ando's Water Temple (1991) on Awaji Island, Japan. Where the path reaches the building, there are a series of steps that lead up to ground level. The other branch out from the building is a rectangular swimming pool set into the surrounding lake where the natural and artificial water are at the same level.

The most impressive architectural element is the thick silver fiberglass roof that flows down to the entrance and which also acts as the interior wall. Its shape expresses the transition from liquid (the lake) to solid (the house). Floor-to-ceiling glass walls allow for natural light to fill the internal space and act as a light counterbalance to the solid roof.

Locating the building on water was crucial to the architects as they wanted the residents to have a point of contact with the environment they live in, to get them in touch with nature. Although it does not use typical Chinese elements in its construction, it has been compared to a Chinese waterside pavilion. Visitors can feel the same peace and tranquility, the same connection with nature, as they would in an old-style pavilion.

Architekten schufen jedoch das Haus in der Mitte des Sees und den versunkenen Eingangspfad zum Ufer neu. Durch den versunkenen Zugang zwischen zwei Betonmauern mit Wasser auf beiden Seiten fühlen sich Besucher, als ob sie durch den See gingen; er erinnert eindeutig an den Eingang zu Tadao Andos Wassertempel (1991) auf der japanischen Insel Awajishima. Sobald der Pfad das Gebäude erreicht, führt eine Reihe Stufen den Besucher hinauf zum Erdgeschoss. Der andere Ausleger des Gebäudes ist ein rechteckiges, in den umgebenden See eingelassenes Schwimmbecken, wobei sich das natürliche und das künstliche Wasser auf derselben Höhe befinden.

Das beeindruckendste architektonische Element ist das dicke, silberne Glasfaserdach, das zum Eingang hinabfließt und außerdem als Innenwand fungiert. Seine Form drückt den Übergang vom Flüssigen (dem See) zum Festen (dem Haus) aus. Vom Boden bis zur Decke verglaste Wände lassen natürliches Licht in den Innenraum einfallen und bilden ein leichtes Gegengewicht zu dem soliden Dach.

Für die Architekten war die Erbauung des Gebäudes auf dem Wasser wesentlich, weil sie bestrebt waren, die Besucher mit der Umgebung, in der sie leben, und mit der Natur in Berührung kommen zu lassen. Obgleich für den Bau keine typischen chinesischen Elemente verwendet wurden, ist das Gebäude mit chinesischen Wasserpavillons verglichen worden. Besucher verspüren hier denselben Frieden und dieselbe Ruhe, dieselbe Verbindung mit der Natur, wie sie dies auch in einem Pavillon alten Stils empfinden würden.

donne l'impression de marcher dans le lac et rappelle clairement l'entrée du Temple de l'eau de Tadao Ando (1991) sur l'île d'Awaji au Japon. Au bout de l'allée, à l'entrée du bâtiment, plusieurs marches conduisent le visiteur au rez-de-chaussée. La seconde issue du bâtiment forme une piscine rectangulaire installée dans le lac où l'eau naturelle et l'eau artificielle sont au même niveau.

L'élément architectural le plus impressionnant est le toit épais et argenté en fibre de verre qui chute à la manière d'un cours d'eau vers l'entrée et qui sert également de paroi intérieure. Sa forme est l'expression de la transition du liquide (le lac) au solide (la maison). Les parois en verre du sol au plafond laissent la lumière naturelle envahir l'intérieur et contrebalancent le toit compact.

Le choix de l'emplacement, sur l'eau, était crucial pour les architectes puisqu'ils souhaitaient que les résidents aient un point de contact avec leur environnement et se rapprochent de la nature. Bien que la construction ne soit pas composée d'éléments chinois classiques, elle a été comparée à un pavillon chinois traditionnel situé au bord de l'eau. Le visiteur peut y ressentir la même quiétude et tranquillité ainsi que le même lien avec la nature.

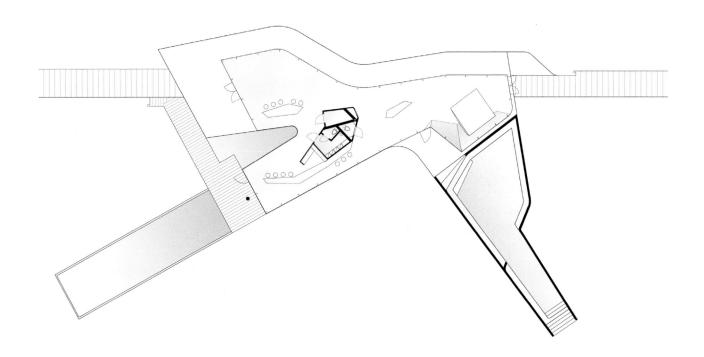

above Floor-to-ceiling glass walls give the open plan interior spaces a cool, modernist feel.

oben Vom Boden bis zur Decke verglaste Wände verleihen den offen angelegten Innenräumen ein kühles, modernistisches Ambiente.

ci-dessus Les parois en verre du sol au plafond confèrent aux espaces intérieurs ouverts une sensation froide et moderniste.

right Pillars are made of steel, while the roof structure is fiberglass.

rechts Die Pfeiler bestehen aus Stahl, während die Dachstruktur aus Glasfasern hergestellt wurde.

droite Les piliers sont en acier tandis que la toiture est en fibre de verre.

left below The clubhouse has been compared to a traditional Chinese waterside pavilion, a place offering peace and tranquility.

links unten Das Klubhaus ist mit traditionellen japanischen Wasserpavillons verglichen worden, Orten der Ruhe und des Friedens.

ci-dessous à gauche Le pavillon a été comparé à un pavillon traditionnel chinois au bord de l'eau, un espace de paix et de tranquillité.

above The flowing roof acts as a link between the building and the water.

oben Das fließende Dach dient als Verbindung zwischen dem Gebäude und dem Wasser.

ci-dessus La fluidité de la toiture relie le bâtiment à l'eau.

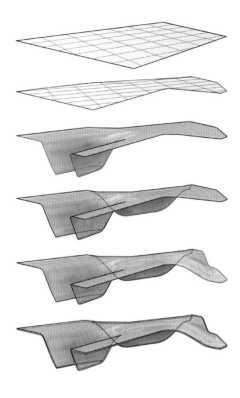

left Diagram of roof development indicating how the curving shape was designed from a single, flat plain.

links Diagramm der Dachentwicklung, die zeigt, wie die gebogene Form aus einer einfachen, flachen Ebene entwickelt wurde.

gauche Schémas présentant les étapes du développement de la toiture et la conception de sa courbe à partir d'une seule forme plane.

below At one end of the building the roof becomes the interior walls. The swimming pool is to the right.

unten An einem Ende des Gebäudes verwandelt sich das Dach in eine der Innenwände. Das Schwimmbecken befindet sich rechts.

ci-dessous À l'une des extrémités du pavillon, le toit sert également de paroi intérieure. À droite se trouve la piscine.

Periscope Houses

Nesselande, Rotterdam, the Netherlands

Joke Vos Architecten

2006

left Small boats can moor alongside the houses where wooden platforms offer direct access to the lake.

links Kleine Boote können an den Häusern anlegen, an denen hölzerne Plattformen unmittelbaren Zugang zum See bieten.

gauche De petits bateaux peuvent s'amarrer le long des maisons où des plates-formes en bois offrent un accès direct au lac.

above Like submarine periscopes, the houses seemingly peer out from the water.

oben Die Häuser scheinen wie U-Boot-Periskope über das Wasser zu schauen.

ci-dessus Les maisons émergent de l'eau à la manière des périscopes des sous-marins..

The Dutch architects Joke Vos won a competition in the early 2000s to design a series of 12 houses in a comfortable suburb of Rotterdam, popular with professional couples working in the nearby city. The houses had to be both expressive and visually appealing, and at the same time, be built to a very high standard. As the area was renowned for its unregulated housing—in terms of aesthetics—this project was designed to stand out.

The Periscope Houses are surrounded by water on three sides, with an entrance at the back of the house on the land side. The houses are clustered into four groups of three, each one its own little island. In addition, each house is slightly different—the position of the entrance, the width of the loggia, and the shape of the aluminum volumes. Like submarine periscopes, the houses look in different directions over the surrounding lake, thereby allowing each house privacy from the other. This also cleverly breaks up any monotony of design and gives the entire complex a vibrancy.

On the first floor next to the main entrance, there is a garage and behind the garage a room that can either be used as a water room or a kitchen. All fixed elements, the bathrooms and stairs, are located in narrow central sections running up the middle of the houses. The living

In den frühen 2000er Jahren gewann das niederländische Architektenbüro Joke Vos einen Wettbewerb zum Entwurf einer Serie von 12 Häusern in einem wohnlichen Vorort von Rotterdam, sehr beliebt bei berufstätigen Paaren, die in der nahegelegenen Stadt arbeiten. Die Häuser sollten sowohl ausdrucksstark als auch optisch ansprechend wirken und gemäß äußerst hohen Standards erbaut werden. Da die Gegend für ihr – vom ästhetischen Standpunkt aus – unkontrolliertes Bauwesen bekannt war, sollte dieses Projekt etwas Außergewöhnliches darstellen.

Die Periskophäuser sind auf drei Seiten von Wasser umgeben, ihr Eingang befindet sich auf der Landseite an der Rückseite der Häuser. Sie sind in vier Gruppen von jeweils drei Häusern angelegt, wobei jede Gruppe ihre eigene Insel bildet. Außerdem unterscheidet sich jedes Haus leicht von den anderen – in der Lage des Eingangs, der Breite der Loggia und der Form der Aluminiumkörper. Wie U-Boot-Periskope blicken die Häuser in verschiedene Richtungen auf den umgebenden See hinaus und wahren dadurch die Privatsphäre ihrer Bewohner. Dadurch wird außerdem auf intelligente Weise jegliche Monotonie im Design vermieden und der gesamte Komplex erhält eine gewisse Lebendigkeit.

Im Erdgeschoss befinden sich neben dem Haupteingang eine Garage und dahinter ein

Le cabinet d'architectes néerlandais Joke Vos a remporté un concours au début des années 2000 visant à concevoir douze maisons dans la banlieue riche de Rotterdam, où vivent des couples travaillant en ville. Les maisons devaient être expressives, attirantes, et d'un niveau très élevé. Le quartier étant reconnu pour ses maisons esthétiquement hors-normes, le projet devait se distinguer.

Les maisons périscopes sont entourées d'eau sur trois côtés. Leur entrée se trouve à l'arrière, du côté de la rive. Elles sont rassemblées en quatre groupes de trois petites îles distinctes légèrement différentes les unes des autres au niveau de l'emplacement de l'entrée, la largeur de la loggia et la forme des volumes en aluminium. Comme des périscopes de sous-marins, les maisons regardent toutes dans différentes directions sur le lac, ce qui leur confère une intimité les unes par rapport aux autres. Cet aspect rompt également avec intelligence la monotonie de la conception et donne vie au complexe.

Au premier niveau, à côté de l'entrée, se trouve le garage. Derrière celui-ci, une pièce peut être utilisée comme cuisine ou salle de bain. Tous les éléments fixes, les salles de bain et les escaliers, se trouvent dans des parties centrales étroites qui montent à l'intérieur des maisons. Les espaces de

areas are on the second and third floors. The second floor ideally is for kitchen and living room, whereas the bedrooms are located on the third floor.

Each house has its own south-facing wooden loggia on the second floor, and below, on the first floor level, there is a cantilevered terrace designed for direct access to the water and where small boats can moor. Large south-facing windows on the second floor allow light and heat to enter deep into the houses, while movable wooden shutters can be used to keep the sun out and cool the building.

The materials used have a very organic look, are durable and need little maintenance. Walls are encased in a dark brick that has been given a metallic finish, while light aluminum panels enclose the periscopes. Warm hardwoods are used throughout: floors and internal walls are of the same bilinga hardwood; window shutters are made of western red cedar; and the wooden sliding doors of meranti.

Raum, der entweder als Wasserraum oder als Küche genutzt werden kann. Alle festen Elemente, Badezimmer und Treppen befinden sich in engen, zentralen Abschnitten in der Mitte der Häuser. Die Wohnbereiche liegen im ersten und zweiten Stockwerk, wobei der erste Stock idealerweise für Küche und Wohnzimmer und der zweite für die Schlafzimmer gedacht ist.

Jedes Haus verfügt im ersten Stockwerk über seine eigene, nach Süden ausgerichtete Loggia, und darunter befindet sich auf Höhe des Erdgeschosses eine ausladende Terrasse mit direktem Zugang zum Wasser und einem Anlegeplatz für kleinere Boote. Große, nach Süden weisende Fenster im ersten Stock lassen Licht und Wärme in die Häuser fallen, während bewegliche Holzläden dazu dienen, die Sonne fernzuhalten und das Gebäude zu kühlen.

Die verwendeten Materialien haben ein sehr organisches Aussehen, sind beständig und benötigen nur wenig Pflege. Die Wände sind mit einem dunklen Ziegel verkleidet, der eine metallische Endbearbeitung erhalten hat, während die Periskope von hellen Aluminiumblechen ummantelt sind. Im ganzen Haus wurden warme Laubhölzer verwendet: Die Böden und Innenwände bestehen aus demselben Laubholz namens *Billinga*, die Fensterläden aus Riesen-Lebensbäumen und die hölzernen Schiebetüren aus *Meranti*.

vie se trouvent au deuxième et au troisième niveau. Le deuxième niveau est idéalement destiné à la cuisine et au salon. Les chambres se trouvent à l'étage supérieur.

Au deuxième niveau, les maisons ont leur propre loggia en bois orientées sud. Au niveau inférieur, une terrasse en porte-à-faux permet d'accéder directement à l'eau et aux petits bateaux amarrés. Au deuxième niveau, les baies vitrées, au sud, laissent entrer la chaleur tandis que les stores en bois permettent de se protéger du soleil et de rafraîchir la maison.

Les matériaux utilisés ont un aspect très naturel, sont durables et nécessitent peu d'entretien. Les murs sont recouverts de brique foncée à laquelle a été ajoutée une finition métallique, tandis que des panneaux en aluminium clair habillent les périscopes.

Le bois est utilisé dans toute la maison, ce qui lui confère une certaine chaleur: le sol et les murs intérieurs sont en bilinga, les stores en cèdre rouge occidental et les portes coulissantes en meranti.

left North-facing backs of the houses, where the entrances and garages are located.

links Die nach Norden ausgerichteten Rückseiten der Häuser, wo sich die Eingänge und Garagen befinden.

gauche À l'arrière des maisons, au nord, se trouvent les entrées et les garages.

right Each house is cleverly designed so it does not overlook its neighbor.

rechts Jedes Haus ist auf intelligente Weise so entworfen, dass das Nachbarhaus nicht eingesehen werden kann.

droite Chaque maison est intelligemment conçue et sans vis-à-vis.

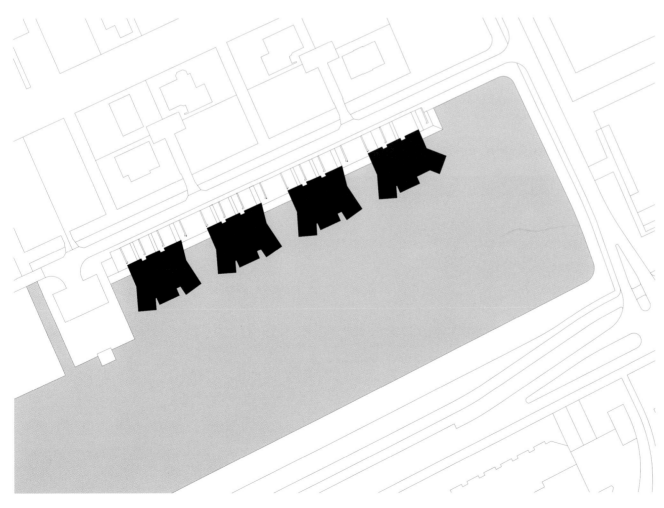

left Masterplan. Each block of houses is slightly different in shape.

links Masterplan. Alle Häusergruppen unterscheiden sich leicht in ihrer Form.

gauche Plan directeur. Chaque bloc de maisons diffère légèrement au niveau de la forme.

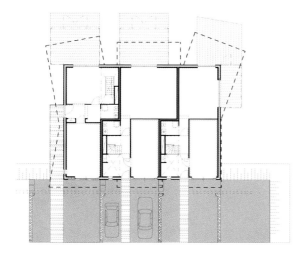 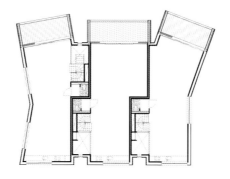 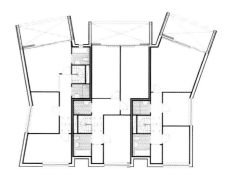

above Floor plans first floor with waterside platforms; second floor with balconies; third floor.

oben Grundrisse des Erdgeschosses mit den Plattformen am Wasserrand, des ersten Stockwerks mit Balkonen und des zweiten Stockwerks.

ci-dessus Plans d'étage. Premier niveau avec les terrasses au bord de l'eau. Deuxième niveau avec les balcons. Troisième niveau.

below Warm hardwoods are used throughout, such as western red cedar for the shutters on this second floor balcony.

unten Im gesamten Gebäude wurden warme Laubhölzer verwendet, wie etwa Riesen-Lebensbaum für die Fensterläden auf diesem Balkon im ersten Stockwerk.

ci-dessous Le bois est utilisé dans toute la maison comme le cèdre rouge occidental pour les stores et sur le balcon du second niveau.

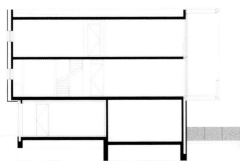

left Cross section showing the three stories.

links Querschnitt mit Ansicht der drei Stockwerke.

gauche Coupe présentant les trois niveaux.

above A living room on the second floor. The balcony is reached through sliding glass doors.

oben Ein Wohnraum im ersten Stockwerk. Der Balkon kann über gläserne Schiebetüren erreicht werden.

ci-dessus Salon du deuxième niveau. On accède au balcon par les baies vitrées coulissantes.

left Detail of the aluminum cladding and dark bricks with metallic finish.

links Detail der Aluminium-verkleidung und der dunklen Ziegel mit metallischer Endbearbeitung.

gauche Revêtement en aluminium et briques noires avec finition métallique.

left Main entrance and garage door to the right. All the bathrooms and stairs are in a narrow central section.

links Haupteingang und Garagentür rechts. Alle Badezimmer und Treppen befinden sich in einem engen, zentralen Abschnitt des Hauses.

gauche Entrée principale et porte du garage à droite. Toutes les salles de bains et les escaliers sont dans la partie centrale étroite.

above Low walls of black and white rocks encased in metal mesh act as dividers between each of the four blocks.

oben Niedrige, von einem Metallgitter umgebene Mauern aus schwarzen und weißen Steinen dienen als Trennwände zwischen jedem der vier Häuserblöcke.

ci-dessus Les murets en pierres noires et blanches enveloppés d'un grillage métallique servent de séparation entre chacun des quatre blocs.

Maison Flottante

Chatou, France

Ronan & Erwan Bouroullec, Jean-Marie Finot, Denis Daversin

2006

left A wooden trellis envelops the boat, the idea being that it will blend with its environment as plants cover its surface.

links Hölzernes Flechtwerk umgibt das Boot. Gemäß dem Entwurf soll es mit seiner Umgebung verschmelzen, je mehr seine Oberfläche von den Pflanzen bedeckt wird.

gauche Un treillis de bois enveloppe le bateau, l'idée étant de le marier à son environnement en recouvrant sa surface de plantes.

right The houseboat was prefabricated in Le Havre before being pushed to its final destination.

rechts Das Hausboot wurde in Le Havre vorgefertigt, bevor es zu seinem endgültigen Ziel geschleppt wurde.

droite La maison flottante a été préfabriquée au Havre avant d'être remorquée jusqu'à sa destination finale.

The Paris-based brothers, Ronan and Erwan Bouroullec, are established stars in the European design scene. They have made furniture for Vitra, Cappellini, and Ligne Roset, had their works exhibited in museums throughout the world, and designed interiors for Issey Miyake. Although not architects they apply their knowledge of furniture at a larger scale. Together with the architect Denis Daversin and the renowned naval architect Jean-Marie Finot they have come up with a modern interpretation of the classic house boat.

In 2002 the Centre National de l'Estampe et de l'Art Imprimé, or Cneai—a contemporary art center devoted to artist publications, prints, and multiples—commissioned a new habitation for its artists-in-residence. The center is based at Chatou on an island on the Seine made famous by the Impressionists who painted there (known as L'Ile des Impressionistes). Cneai specifically asked for a houseboat to be designed in reference to the laundry boats that used to be seen on the river in the late 19th century. The result is a very contemporary intepretation that is characterized by clean and uncluttered lines typical of the Bouroullecs' work.

Working to a very tight budget the brothers designed a 1,184 square feet space that is both a residence and studio for artists and authors.

Die in Paris ansässigen Brüder Ronan und Erwan Bouroullec sind etablierte Stars der europäischen Designszene. Sie haben Möbel für Vitra, Cappellini und Ligne Roset hergestellt, ihre Werke in Museen rund um die Welt ausgestellt und Inneneinrichtungen für Issey Miyake entworfen. Obgleich sie keine Architekten sind, wenden sie ihre Fachkenntnisse über Möbel auch in größerem Maßstab an. Gemeinsam mit dem Architekten Denis Daversin und dem renommierten Schiffbau-architekten Jean-Marie Finot haben sie eine moderne Interpretation des klassischen Hausboots geschaffen.

Im Jahr 2002 gab der Centre National de l'Estampe et de l'Art Imprimé (Cneai) – ein zeitgenössisches Kunstzentrum, das sich den Veröffentlichungen, Drucken und Auflagen von Künstlern widmet – eine neue Wohnstätte für seine im Zentrum ansässigen Gastkünstler in Auftrag. Das Zentrum befindet sich in Chatou auf einer Insel in der Seine, die durch die dort malen-den Impressionisten berühmt wurde (sie ist als Insel der Impressionisten bekannt). In Anlehnung an die Wäschereischiffe, die im späten 19. Jahr-hundert auf dem Fluss zu sehen waren, bat Cneai ausdrücklich um den Entwurf eines Hausboots. Das Ergebnis ist eine sehr zeitgenössische Interpretation, die sich durch die für das Werk der

Les frères Ronan et Erwan Bouroullec, situés à Paris, sont des stars reconnues sur la scène architecturale européenne. Ils ont créé du mobilier pour Vitra, Cappellini et Ligne Roset. Leurs travaux sont exposés dans des musées du monde entier ; ils ont également conçu des intérieurs pour Issey Miyake. Bien qu'ils ne soient pas architectes, ils mettent en application leurs connaissances du mobilier à plus grande échelle. Avec l'architecte Denis Daversin et l'architecte naval reconnu Jean-Marie Finot, ils sont parvenus à créer une interprétation moderne de la maison flottante classique.

En 2002, le Centre national de l'estampe et de l'art imprimé, ou CNEAI, un centre artistique contemporain consacré aux publications et impressions artistiques, a commandé une nouvelle habitation pour ses artistes-résidents. Le centre basé à Chatou, sur une île de la Seine, est devenu célèbre grâce aux Impressionnistes qui y ont peint (on l'appelle également l'île des Impressionnistes). Le CNEAI a spécifiquement demandé une maison flottante rappelant les bateaux-lavoirs que l'on trouvait sur le fleuve au XIXe siècle. Il en résulte une interprétation très contemporaine, caractérisée par des lignes épurées typiques du travail des frères Bouroullec.

Travaillant avec un budget très serré, les frères Bouroullec ont conçu un espace de 360

An aluminum shell, 75.5 feet long by 16.4 feet wide, is covered by a wooden trellis of red cedar, its narrow width dictated by the size of the river locks. The plan is that climbing plants can grow around the structure so that eventually the barge blends into its surroundings. This should also offer greater privacy for the occupants. Inside a central white wall separates the sleeping and kitchen area from the living space. Floor-to-ceiling windows along one side allow for natural light to pour in—an essential element for the studio—whereas on the shore side there are no windows to ensure privacy. At either end there are sliding french windows. Red cedar planks cover the ceiling, floors, and walls. Classic modern chairs and tables by the designers furnish the interiors, including Striped Sedia by Magis and Metal Side Table by Vitra.

The boat was originally constructed in Le Havre before being towed more than 93 miles upriver to Chatou. Once moored against the shore it can be reached via a wooden walkway. From inside the studio there are spectacular views over the river, the same landscape that inspired Renoir's *Le déjeuner des canotiers* (1881). The surrounding water reflects back the image of the modernist barge which at night glows like a lantern. The Bouroullecs' philosophy is, "We like to start without prejudice, with a fresh eye." They possess a strong graphic sensibility and rational approach to functionality. This is a beautiful and balanced example of their work—a floating space for contemplation.

Bouroullecs so typischen sauberen, ordentlichen Linien auszeichnet.

Mit einem sehr knappen Budget entwarfen die Brüder eine 110 Quadratmeter große Fläche, die für die Künstler und Autoren als Wohnstätte und Atelier zugleich dient. Eine 23 Meter lange und 5 Meter breite Aluminiumhülle ist mit hölzernem Flechtwerk aus roter Zeder bedeckt, wobei die geringe Breite von der Größe der Flussschleusen vorgegeben ist. Der Entwurf sieht vor, dass die Kletterpflanzen um das Bauwerk herum wachsen, so dass das Hausboot letztendlich mit seiner Umgebung verschmelzen wird. Dies bietet den Bewohnern darüber hinaus zusätzliche Privatsphäre. Innen trennt eine weiße Mauer in der Mitte den Schlaf- und Küchenbereich vom Wohnraum. Vom Boden bis zur Decke reichende Fenster entlang einer Seite des Bootes lassen natürliches Licht hineinfallen – ein für das Atelier wesentliches Element – während zur Wahrung der Privatsphäre zur Uferseite hin keine Fenster eingebaut wurden. An beiden Enden befinden sich Schiebetüren. Decke, Böden und Wände sind mit Planken aus roter Zeder bedeckt. Die Innenräume sind mit klassischen modernen Stühlen und Tischen nach einem Entwurf der Designer eingerichtet, einschließlich Striped Sedia von Magis und einem metallenen Seitentisch von Vitra.

Ursprünglich wurde das Boot in Le Havre erbaut, bevor es 150 Kilometer flussaufwärts nach Chatou geschleppt wurde. Das am Ufer befestigte Boot kann über einen hölzernen Steg erreicht werden. Das Innere des Ateliers bietet spektakuläre Ausblicke über den Fluss – über dieselbe Landschaft, die Renoir zum *Frühstück der Ruderer* (1881) inspirierte. Das umgebende Wasser spiegelt das Bild des modernistischen Bootes wider, das bei Nacht wie eine Laterne aufglüht. Die Bourroullecs stellen ihre Philosophie so dar: „Wir beginnen ohne Vorurteile, mit einem frischen Blick." Sie verfügen ein starkes grafisches Gespür und einen vernunftbetonten Ansatz zur Funktionalität. Das Hausboot ist ein schönes, ausgewogenes Beispiel ihres Werks – ein schwimmender Raum zur Kontemplation.

mètres carrés qui sert à la fois de résidence et de studio pour les artistes et auteurs. Une coquille en aluminium, de 22,8 mètres de long par 4,8 mètres de large, est recouverte d'un treillis de cèdre. Sa largeur, étroite, est dictée par la taille des écluses. Les plantes grimpantes peuvent pousser autour de la structure de manière à ce que la péniche se mêle à son environnement. Ces plantes offriront également une plus grande intimité aux occupants. À l'intérieur, un mur blanc central sépare la chambre et la cuisine du séjour. Des baies vitrées du sol au plafond d'un côté laissent entrer la lumière naturelle, un élément essentiel pour le studio - alors que l'autre côté, donnant sur la rive, n'offre aucune fenêtre pour garantir une plus grande intimité. À chaque extrémité se trouvent des portes-fenêtres coulissantes. Des panneaux de cèdre recouvrent le plafond, le sol et les murs. Des chaises et des tables modernes classiques des designers meublent l'intérieur, dont des chaises Striped Sedia par Magis et une table Metal Side Table par Vitra.

Le bateau a été construit au Havre avant d'être remorqué sur plus de 150 kilomètres à contre-courant jusqu'à Chatou. Une fois amarré, on y accède par une passerelle en bois. L'intérieur du studio offre une vue spectaculaire sur le fleuve, le même paysage que celui du Déjeuner des canotiers (1881) de Renoir. L'eau renvoie l'image de la péniche moderne, qui, la nuit, s'illumine telle une lanterne. Les Bouroullec aiment « commencer sans préjugé, avec un ?il nouveau ». Nous avons là un exemple magnifique et équilibré de leurs travaux, un espace flottant à contempler.

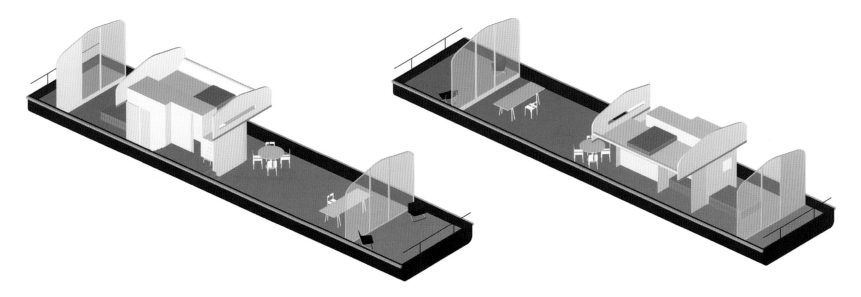

above Axonometrics showing the studio space, bedroom, and kitchen from both sides.

oben Axonometrische Darstellung des Atelierraums, Schlafzimmers und der Küche von beiden Seiten.

ci-dessus Axonométrie présentant le studio, la chambre et la cuisine des deux côtés.

left A central white wall separates the sleeping and kitchen areas from the studio space. The interior is furnished with chairs and tables designed by the Bouroullec brothers.

links Eine weiße Mauer in der Mitte trennt den Schlaf- und Küchenbereich vom Atelier-raum. Die Innenräume sind mit Stühlen und Tischen nach Entwürfen der Brüder Bouroullec möbliert.

gauche Un mur blanc central sépare la chambre et la cuisine du studio. L'intérieur est meublé de chaises et de tables conçues par les frères Bouroullec.

below The studio space with views directly onto the river. Red cedar is used throughout.

unten Der Atelierraum mit Aussichten auf den Fluss. Für den gesamten Bau wurde rotes Zedernholz verwendet.

ci-dessous Studio avec vue directement sur le fleuve. Le cèdre est employé de toutes parts.

Island Resorts and Hotels

Ferienanlagen und Hotels

Complexes hôteliers flottants

Burj Al Arab I Reethi Rah I Earth Spa I Bulgari Resort
Dellis Cay I Nurai Resort and Hotel

The growth of global tourism has led the modern traveller to search for ever more exotic holidays. Inevitably, most summer resorts are built near water, but these examples take the concept a step further creating recreational spaces on water. By using architectural devices such as pools, ponds, walkways, bridges, piers, and promenades, the architect can bring the building to the water. A towering modern hotel, an eco-spa, a clifftop retreat, and man-made paradise island offer a glimpse into the possibilities of exclusive island living. The island destinations combine contemporary architecture with dream locations, including Thailand, the Maldives, Bali, and Dubai. The final two developments, in Abu Dhabi and the Caribbean, show the future of luxury bespoke island design, with villas, hotels, and spas by well-known international architects.

previous page Imagined view out from Kengo Kuma's spa on Dellis Cay Island in the Caribbean.

vorherige Seite Möglicher Blick von Kengo Kumas Wellnessbad auf der karibischen Insel Dellis Cay.

page précédente Vue depuis le spa de Kengo Kuma sur l'île de Dellis Cay, dans les Caraïbes.

left An island bungalow on Reethi Rah, the Maldives.

links Ein Inselbungalow auf Reethi Rah auf den Malediven.

gauche Bungalow flottant sur l'île de Reethi Rah, aux Maldives.

La croissance du tourisme mondial a incité le voyageur moderne à rechercher des vacances toujours plus exotiques. La plupart des complexes hôteliers sont inévitablement construits à proximité de l'eau mais les exemples suivants vont encore plus loin: ce sont des espaces de loisirs sur l'eau. Grâce aux structures architecturales telles que les piscines, bassins, passerelles, ponts, embarcadères et fronts de mer, les architectes peuvent déplacer les bâtiments sur l'eau. Un magnifique hôtel moderne, un éco-spa, des vacances au sommet d'une falaise et une île paradisiaque artificielle sont autant de possibilités de séjour sur les îles. Ces destinations combinent architecture contemporaine et emplacements de rêve tels que la Thaïlande, les Maldives, Bali et Dubaï. Les deux derniers développements, à Abu Dhabi et aux Caraïbes, présentent l'avenir d'une architecture flottante de luxe sur mesure, avec villas, hôtels et spas, conçus par des architectes de renommée internationale.

Mit dem Anwachsen des weltweiten Tourismus macht sich der moderne Reisende auf die Suche nach immer exotischeren Urlaubserlebnissen. Die meisten Sommerferienanlagen finden sich unweigerlich am Wasser, aber die folgenden Beispiele gehen noch einen Schritt weiter: Diese Freizeiteinrichtungen wurden auf dem Wasser errichtet. Architektonische Mittel wie Becken, Teiche, Fußgängerwege, Brücken, Stege und Promenaden ermöglichten es den Architekten, das Gebäude näher ans Wasser zu bringen. Ein hoch aufragendes, modernes Hotel, ein Öko-Wellnessbad, eine Zuflucht auf einer Felsspitze und eine künstlich geschaffene Paradiesinsel bieten einen Einblick in die Möglichkeiten exklusiven Insellebens. Die Inselorte verbinden zeitgenössische Architektur mit Traumstandorten, einschließlich Thailand, den Malediven, Bali und Dubai. Die letzten beiden Bauprojekte in Abu Dhabi und in der Karibik zeigen mit Villen, Hotels und Bädern berühmter internationaler Architekten Beispiele für die Zukunft luxuriösen, maßgefertigten Inseldesigns.

Burj Al Arab

Dubai, UAE
Atkins Design Studio
1999

The Burj Al Arab hotel, 9 miles south of the city of Dubai, is probably the most luxurious hotel in the world. Completed in 1999, it quickly became an icon for Dubai, much in the same way as the Eiffel Tower symbolizes Paris and the Sydney Opera House, Australia. The architects deliberately chose a shape that they hoped would be instantly recognizable and symbolically representative of the country—a massive billowing sail as a dramatic tribute to the region's nautical heritage.

The hotel cost $650 million to build, took over five years to complete, and sits on a man-made island 820 feet from the Jumeirah Beach Resort. The island itself took longer to build than the hotel and was an extraordinary feat of engineering. First sand was reclaimed from the sea. Then 250 131-feet long concrete piles were driven into the sand (because the building is built only on sand the piles rely on friction). Finally, a surface layer of rocks was added as well as honey-combed shaped concrete armor units to protect the foundation from sea erosion. A slender, curving road bridge links the island to the shore.

The building is formed by a V-shaped steel external skeleton that encases a reinforced concrete tower superstructure that houses the lifts, escape stairs, and services. The steel frame

Das Hotel Burj Al Arab, 15 Kilometer südlich der Stadt Dubai gelegen, ist wahrscheinlich das luxuriöseste Hotel der Welt. Nach seiner Fertigstellung im Jahr 1999 wurde es schnell zum Symbol für Dubai, ebenso wie der Eiffelturm Paris und das Sydney Opera House Australien verkörpern. Die Architekten wählten bewusst eine Form, von der sie hofften, dass sie sofort erkennbar und symbolisch für das Land sei – ein massives, sich bauschendes Segel als aufsehenerregender Tribut an die Schifffahrts-tradition der Region.

Die Erbauung des Hotels kostete $650 Millionen, und die Fertigstellung nahm über fünf Jahre in Anspruch. Es steht auf einer künstlich angelegten Insel 250 Meter vom Jumeirah Beach Resort entfernt. Die Aufschüttung der Insel dauerte länger als die Erbauung des Hotels und war eine beachtliche Ingenieurleistung. Zunächst wurde Sand aus dem Meer zurück gewonnen. Dann wurden 250 vierzig Meter lange Betonpfosten in den Sand getrieben (weil das Gebäude ausschließlich auf Sand erbaut ist, sind die Pfosten auf die Reibungsberührung angewiesen). Schließlich wurden eine Ober-flächenschicht aus Felsen sowie wabenförmige Betonpanzereinheiten hinzugefügt, um die Fundamente vor einer Auswaschung durch die See zu schützen. Die Insel ist über eine

L'hôtel Burj Al Arab, à 15 km au sud de Dubaï, est certainement l'hôtel le plus luxueux au monde. Achevé en 1999, il est rapidement devenu une icone à Dubaï, de la même manière que la Tour Eiffel symbolise Paris et l'Opéra de Sydney l'Australie. Les architectes ont délibérément choisi une forme qu'ils espéraient être immédiatement reconnaissable et qui représenterait le pays, une imposante voile gonflée par le vent comme hommage spectaculaire à l'héritage nautique de la région.

La construction de l'hôtel a nécessité 650 millions de dollars et cinq années de travaux; il siège sur une île artificielle située à 250 mètres du complexe Jumeirah Beach Resort. La construction de l'île à elle-seule à pris plus de temps que celle de l'hôtel et représente un exploit extraordinaire d'ingénierie. Le sable a avant tout été récupéré dans la mer. 250 piles en béton de 40 mètres de long ont ensuite été intégrées au sable; le bâtiment étant uniquement construit sur le sable, les piles supportent le frottement. Enfin, une couche de pierres a été ajoutée ainsi qu'une armature en béton alvéolée pour protéger les fondations de l'érosion marine. L'île est reliée à la terre par une fine courbe goudronnée.

Le bâtiment est formé par un squelette externe en acier, en forme de V, qui retient une

and cross bracing across the back of the atrium are designed to help the building withstand wind and earthquake loading. Facing the land is a curved white double-skinned screen made of 0.04 in. thick glass-fiber fabric with a Teflon coat designed to stop dirt from sticking and keep direct sunlight out.

At 1,053 feet it is the tallest hotel in the world. The interior is luxurious in the extreme, featuring a 590-feet high atrium, flanked by golden columns, and a centerpiece of a water arch that shoots water 100 feet up into the air. No expense was spared with the decoration: over 30 different types of marble were used throughout and 86,000 square feet of 22 carat gold leaf. There are 202 duplex suites, each with double-height ceilings—the building itself is only 28 apartments high. At the top of the hotel—656 feet above the Persian Gulf—there are two distinct features: a helipad and a restaurant. Al Muntaha (The Highest), the restaurant, is supported by a full cantilever that extends 88.5 feet either side of the mast. Guests can also eat at Al Mahara (The Oyster), an undersea restaurant.

schlanke, bogenförmige Überführung mit dem Ufer verbunden.

Das Gebäude selbst besteht aus einem V-förmigen äußeren Stahlskelett, das einen Turmaufbau aus Stahlbeton umhüllt, in dem sich die Fahrstühle, Fluchttreppen und Dienstleistungsbereiche befinden. Der Stahlrahmen und die Querverstrebungen über der Rückseite des Atriums sollen dazu beitragen, dass das Gebäude der Belastung durch Winde und Erdbeben besser standhält. Dem Land zugewandt wurde ein gebogener, weißer und aus zwei Häuten bestehender Schirm aus 1mm dickem Glasfaserstoff mit Teflonbeschichtung errichtet, der Schmutz und direkte Sonneneinstrahlung abwehren soll.

Mit 321 Metern ist das Burj Al Arab das höchste Hotel der Welt. Das Innere ist extrem luxuriös, mit einem 180 Meter hohen, von goldenen Säulen umsäumten Atrium und einem Wasserspiel, das Wasser bis zu 32 Meter hoch in die Luft spritzt, als Herzstück. Bei der Innenausstattung wurden keinerlei Kosten gescheut: Insgesamt wurden mehr als 30 verschiedene Marmorarten und 8.000 Quadratmeter 22-karätiges Blattgold verwendet. Es sind 202 Doppelsuiten vorhanden, deren Deckenhöhe jeweils doppelt so hoch wie üblich ist – das Gebäude selbst ist nur 28 Stockwerke hoch. Im obersten Stockwerk des Hotels – 200 Meter über dem Persischen Golf – befinden sich zwei auffallende Bauelemente: ein Hubschrauberlandeplatz und ein Restaurant. Das Restaurant Al Muntaha (Das Höchste) wird von einer Auskragung getragen, die sich bis 27 Meter nach jeder Seite des Mastes erstreckt. Gäste können außerdem im Untersee-Restaurant Al Mahara (Die Auster) speisen.

superstructure en béton armé accueillant les ascenseurs, les escaliers de secours et les services. Le cadre en acier et le châssis traversant l'arrière de l'atrium permettent au bâtiment d'affronter le vent et les tremblements de terre. Face à la terre, un double écran blanc, courbé, en fibre de verre de 1mm d'épaisseur recouvert de Téflon empêche l'incrustation du sable et repousse la lumière directe du soleil.

D'une hauteur de 321 mètres, il s'agit de l'hôtel le plus haut du monde. L'intérieur est d'un luxe extrême, avec un atrium de 180 mètres de haut, encadré de colonnes dorées, et une arche d'eau qui jaillit à 32 mètres de haut. La décoration n'a pas été négligée: plus de 30 types de marbre et 8000 mètres carrés de feuilles d'or 22 carats ont été utilisés. L'hôtel compte 202 suites en duplex (le bâtiment ne compte que 28 appartements sur toute sa hauteur). Au sommet de l'hôtel, soit à 200 mètres au-dessus du Golfe persique, se trouvent un héliport et un restaurant. Le restaurant Al Muntaha, littéralement « le plus haut », se trouve sur une plate-forme en porte-à-faux qui s'étend sur 27 mètres de chaque côté du mât. Les visiteurs peuvent également se restaurer à l'Al Mahara, « l'huître », un restaurant situé sous la mer.

previous page The huge white screen is made of glass fiber fabric with a Teflon coat to prevent dirt from sticking.

vorherige Seite Der riesige, weiße Schirm besteht aus einem 1mm dicken Glasfaserstoff mit einer Teflonbeschichtung, um Schmutz abzuwehren.

page précédente L'imposant écran blanc est constitué de fibre de verre de 1mm d'épaisseur et d'un revêtement en Téflon pour empêcher l'incrustation du sable.

right Hollow concrete armor units are designed to absorb the impact of the waves without throwing water onto the island.

rechts Hohle Betonpanzereinheiten sollen den Aufprall der Wellen abfangen, ohne jedoch Wasser auf die Insel zu werfen.

droite Une armature en béton caverneux permet d'absorber l'impact des vagues et d'éviter l'eau sur l'île.

left Inspiration for the building's shape came from yacht sails.

links Die Inspiration für die Form des Bauwerks stammt von Jachtsegeln.

gauche La forme du bâtiment fait penser à une voile.

below The exoskeleton is designed to brace the building against wind and earthquakes.

unten Das äußere Skelett soll das Gebäude gegen Wind und Erdbeben schützen.

ci-dessous L'exosquelette est conçu pour affronter le vent et les tremblements de terre.

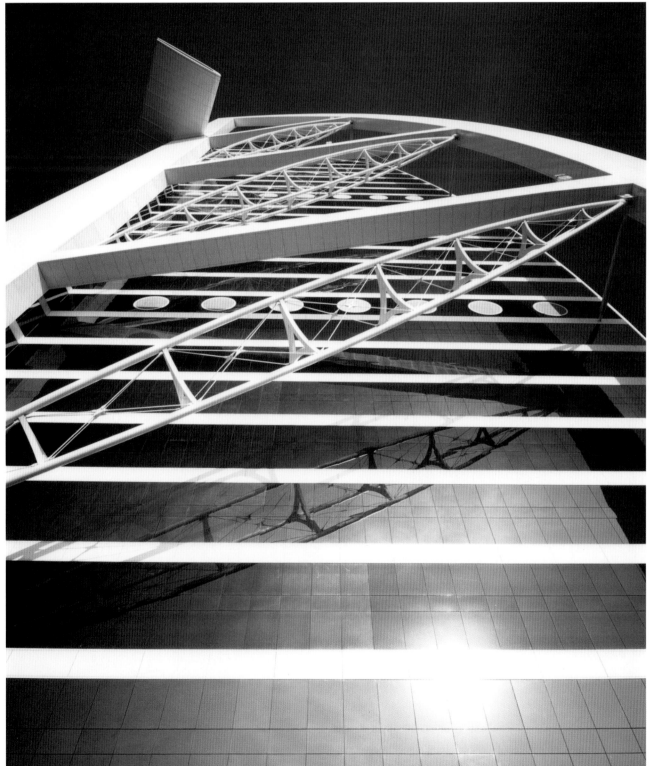

left Each of the diagonal trusses on the side of the building are as long as a soccer pitch.

links Die diagonalen Träger auf der Seite des Gebäudes sind so lang wie ein Fußballfeld.

gauche Les poutres triangulaires, posées en diagonale sur les côtés du bâtiment sont aussi longues qu'un terrain de football.

right The base of the lobby atrium with water fountain. At 590 feet it is the tallest lobby in the world.

rechts Das Fundament der Lobby mit dem Springbrunnen. Mit 150 Metern ist sie die höchste Lobby der Welt.

droite Base de l'atrium avec la fontaine. Mesurant 150 mètres, c'est le hall le plus haut du monde.

Reethi Rah

Maldive Islands

Jean-Michel Gathy, Denniston International Architects & Planners

2005

This island, in the middle of the Indian Ocean, was originally only 12.35 acres before it was reshaped and enlarged to 121 acres by relocating sand from the sea bed. Its shape was requested by the developer and is not natural to the Maldives atoll. Not only was the resort created from scratch, but also the fauna was imported—a jungle of 18,000 mature palm trees were replanted on the island. However, the architect of the project, Jean-Michel Gathy, is quick to stress that he was very careful not to affect the natural sea habitat so sand was sucked from two spots far from the reef and care was taken not to disturb the flow of the sea.

There are several building types on the island: bungalows that float on piles above the sea, villas (large and small), and the Lodge which houses bars, restaurants, kitchens, a library, and other amenities. Throughout the island, the architect used the same materials, architectural language, and shapes. The buildings are based on simple Maldivian architecture, with thatch roofs and wooden structures—the same structures that fisherman have used there for centuries. The timber used is a mixture of woods from Malaysia—balu, ramin, kapur. Typically, the floors are a mixture of balu and terrazzo designed to be very comfortable when walking barefoot, while teak

Diese Insel in der Mitte des Indischen Ozeans war ursprünglich nur fünf Hektar groß, bevor sie umgestaltet und durch Aufschüttung von Sand vom Meeresboden auf 49 Hektar vergrößert wurde. Die vom Bauunternehmer gewünschte Form ist nicht die natürliche Form des Malediventolls. Nicht nur die Ferienanlage wurde von Grund auf neu geschaffen, sondern auch die Fauna wurde importiert – ein Dschungel aus 18.000 vollentwickelten Palmen wurde auf der Insel wieder eingepflanzt. Der Architekt des Projekts, Jean-Michel Gatty, betont jedoch schnell, dass er bei der Gestaltung große Sorgfalt walten ließ, um das natürliche Meeresbiotop nicht zu beeinträchtigen. Der Sand wurde daher an zwei weit von dem Riff entfernten Stellen im Meer entnommen, und die Erbauer achteten darauf, die Meeresströmungen nicht zu stören.

Auf der Insel sind mehrere Gebäudetypen vorhanden: Bungalows, die auf Pfosten über dem Meer schwimmen, Villen (große und kleine) und die Lodge, die Bars, Restaurants, Küchen, eine Bibliothek und andere Einrichtungen beherbergt. Der Architekt verwendete auf der gesamten Insel durchweg dieselben Materialien, dieselbe architektonische Sprache und dieselben Formen. Die Gestaltung der Gebäude beruht auf der einfachen Architektur der Malediven mit Reetdächern und hölzernen Strukturen – dieselbe

À l'origine, cette île située au milieu de l'Océan indien ne s'étendait que sur cinq hectares avant d'être réaménagée et élargie à 49 hectares, grâce à du sable des fonds marins. Sa forme artificielle est différente des atolls des Maldives et a été demandée par le promoteur. Le complexe a été créé à partir de rien, la faune a été importée et une jungle de 18 000 palmiers adultes a été replantée sur l'île. L'architecte chargé du projet, Jean-Michel Gatty, s'empresse cependant d'affirmer qu'il a veillé à ne pas affecter l'habitat naturel marin. Le sable a donc été aspiré à deux emplacements, à distance du récif, et une attention particulière a été portée au courant marin.

Plusieurs types de bâtiments se côtoient sur l'île: bungalows flottant sur pilotis, villas (petites et grandes) et le Lodge, qui accueille bars, restaurants, cuisines, bibliothèque et autres espaces d'agrément. L'architecte a employé les mêmes matériaux sur toute l'île, le même langage architectural et les mêmes formes. Les bâtiments s'inspirent de l'architecture simple des Maldives, avec des toits de chaume et des structures en bois – les mêmes structures utilisées par les pêcheurs depuis des siècles. Le bois employé est un mélange de bois de Malaisie (*balu, ramin, kapur*) et les sols mêlent *balu* et terrazzo, très confortables pour marcher

cladding is used for the interiors. All the buildings are technologically simple and technically solid. Because Reethi Rah is one of the world's most prestigious resorts, aspects including insulation, stability, and waterproofing had to be of the highest standards.

The bungalows, that hover over the water, are in eight clusters of four bungalows each, about 1,000–1,300 feet apart. They are designed to not affect the sea currents, give privacy, and reduce their visual impact on the rest of the island. The villas are inland from the water's edge, deliberately set back from the sea so as to blend with the interior jungle. Each has its own infinity pool. The idea of the villas and Lodge was to create a "vibration going through the jungle." People who visit the "One and Only" development are usually looking for simplicity and that was the intention of Gathy, to create an environment that is about extreme relaxation as well as being humble in approach. A visually low-profile, luxury resort.

Bauweise, die die einheimischen Fischer seit Jahrhunderten anwendeten. Als Bauholz wurden verschiedene Hölzer aus Malaysia verwendet – *Balu, Ramin, Kapur*. Die Böden bestehen im Allgemeinen aus einer Mischung aus *Balu* und Terrazzo und sind so entworfen, dass sie sich beim Barfußlaufen sehr bequem anfühlen, während für die Innenausstattung eine Teakverkleidung Verwendung fand. Alle Gebäude sind technisch einfach und solide erbaut. Da Reethi Rath eine der prestigeträchtigsten Ferienanlagen der Welt ist, mussten Aspekte wie Isolierung, Stabilität und Wasserschutz den höchsten Leistungsanforderungen genügen.

Die über dem Wasser schwebenden Bungalows sind in acht Gruppen von je vier Gebäuden angelegt, die jeweils 300-400 Meter voneinander entfernt liegen. Sie sind so errichtet worden, dass die Meeresströmungen nicht beeinträchtigt werden, die Privatsphäre der Bewohner gewahrt bleibt und die optische Beeinträchtigung der übrigen Insel so gering wie möglich gehalten ist. Die Villen wurden weiter landeinwärts angelegt und bewusst vom Meer abgesetzt, um mit dem Dschungel im Inneren der Insel zu verschmelzen. Jede von ihnen verfügt über ihr eigenes Überlaufbecken. Durch die Idee der Villen und der Lodge sollte eine „durch den Dschungel gehende Vibration" geschaffen werden. Besucher des einzig wahren Bauprojekts sind üblicherweise auf der Suche nach Schlichtheit, und so lag es auch in der Absicht Gattys, ein Umfeld zu schaffen, bei dem es um äußerste Entspannung und einen bescheidenen Ansatz geht. Eine optisch unauffällige Luxusanlage.

pieds nus. Le teck n'est employé qu'à l'intérieur. Tous les bâtiments sont simples sur le plan technologique, et solides sur le plan technique. Reethi Rath étant l'un des complexes les plus prestigieux au monde, les aspects tels que l'isolation, la stabilité et l'étanchéité devaient être d'un niveau sans égal.

Les bungalows, qui flottent sur l'eau, sont répartis en huit groupes de quatre, séparés les uns des autres par 300 à 400 mètres. Conçus pour ne pas affecter les courants marins, ils offrent une certaine intimité et restent discrets. Les villas se trouvent à l'intérieur de l'île, volontairement en retrait de la mer pour se mêler à la jungle intérieure. Chacune possède sa propre piscine. L'idée des villas et du Lodge était de créer une « onde traversant la jungle ». Les visiteurs de ce site unique en son genre recherchent généralement la simplicité: Jean-Michel Gatty souhaitait ainsi créer un environnement humble et relaxant, un complexe luxueux mais discret.

left Tapasake Restaurant floats over the sea, a form of low-profile, but sophisticated architecture.

links Das Tapasake Restaurant schwebt über dem Meer, eine unauffällige, aber raffinierte Form der Architektur.

gauche Le restaurant Tapasake flotte sur la mer, une architecture discrète mais sophistiquée.

right Detail of one of the water villas. All structures are in timber with thatched roofs.

rechts Detail einer Wasservilla. Alle Bauwerke bestehen aus Holz mit Reetdächern.

droite Détails de l'une des villas sur l'eau. Toutes les structures sont en bois avec un toit de chaume.

left A bathroom from one of the beach villas.

links Ein Badezimmer in einer der Strandvillen

gauche Salle de bain de l'une des villas sur la plage.

above Tapasake, the over-water restaurant. The design is based on traditional Maldivian architecture.

oben Tapasake, das Restaurant über dem Meer. Der Entwurf beruht auf der traditionellen Architektur der Malediven.

ci-dessus Le Tapasake, le restaurant sur l'eau, s'inspire de l'architecture traditionnelle des Maldives.

below Each of the beach villas, which are set back in the jungle, has its own infinity pool.

unten Jede der Strandvillen, die in den Dschungel zurückgesetzt sind, verfügt über ihr eigenes Überlaufbecken.

ci-dessous Chacune des villas de la plage, retirées dans la jungle, possède sa propre piscine.

below A lap pool at the Lodge blends with the surrounding ocean.

unten Ein Sportpool in der Lodge verschmilzt mit dem umgebenden Ozean.

ci-dessous Une piscine longue et étroite située au Lodge se mêle à l'océan.

right The grand entrance to the Lodge which incorporates a restaurant, library, and bars.

rechts Der prächtige Eingang zur Lodge, die ein Restaurant, eine Bibliothek und mehrere Bars beherbergt.

droite L'entrée principale du Lodge, qui accueille restaurant, bibliothèque et bars.

left The Lodge. Buildings on the island use a mixture of Malaysian woods, including balu, ramin, and kapur.

links Die Lodge. Für die Gebäude auf der Insel wurde eine Mischung aus malaysischen Hölzern verwendet, darunter *Balu*, *Ramin* und *Kapur*.

gauche Le Lodge. Les bâtiments de l'île sont construits avec divers bois de Malaisie, dont le balu, le ramin et le kapur.

Earth Spa

Hua Hin, Thailand
DWP
2005

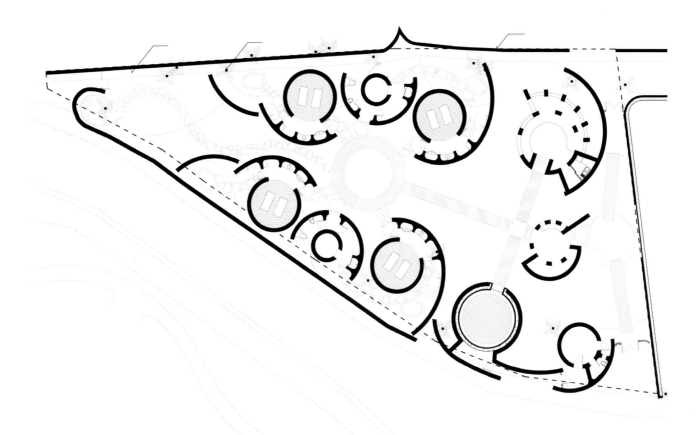

Situated 124 miles south of Bangkok on the Gulf of Thailand, the Thai seaside resort of Hua Hin developed in the 1920s when King Rama VII built a summer palace there. Today, it is a major tourist resort, a 30-minute flight from the capital.

Earth Spa was created by Design Worldwide Partnership (DWP), a multi-disciplinary studio based in Asia, for its client, Six Senses. Set over 14,920 square feet of water and landscaping, the spa was built inland, close to the sea. Nine ochre domed buildings sit on top of a lake, each one its own mini island, surrounded by water and linked by narrow interconnecting wooden walkways. Like warm caves or cocoons surrounded by reeds and lily ponds, they welcome the visitor in.

Inspired by villages in northern and northeastern Thailand, where buildings are designed to stay a comfortable temperature, even in summer, and traditional African mud buildings, the distinctive facility is the only one of its kind in the world. A search for harmony is translated into the circular layout of the property, inspired by the natural striations found in sea shells on the local beach.

DWP were mindful to use sustainable and recyclable materials—domes are built out of clay-like mud mixed with rice husks, straw, and local reused natural materials. The dome shape is ideal for dealing with heavy rainfall typical

Das 200 Kilometer südlich von Bangkok am Golf von Thailand gelegene Seebad Hua Hin entstand in den Zwanziger Jahren, als König Rama VII sich dort einen Sommerpalast erbauen ließ. Heute hat es sich zu einem bekannten Touristenort entwickelt und ist 30 Minuten mit dem Flugzeug von der Hauptstadt entfernt.

Earth Spa wurde von Design Worldwide Partnership, einem interdisziplinären Studio aus Asien, für seinen Kunden Six Senses geschaffen. Das über 1.386 Quadratmeter Wasser und Landschaftsarchitektur angelegte Bad wurde landeinwärts in unmittelbarer Nähe des Meeres erbaut. Neun von ockerfarbenen Kuppeln gekrönte Gebäude befinden sich über einem See, jeder davon bildet seine eigene Mini-Insel, von Wasser umgeben und über enge hölzerne Fußgängerstege verbunden. Wie warme Höhlen oder von Schilfröhren und Wasserlilienteichen umgebene Kokons heißen sie Besucher willkommen.

Inspiriert von Dörfern im nördlichen und nordöstlichen Thailand, wo Gebäude so geplant werden, dass sogar im Sommer eine angenehme Temperatur gewahrt bleibt, sowie von traditionellen afrikanischen Schlammbauten, ist diese außergewöhnliche Anlage weltweit die einzige ihrer Art. Die Suche nach Harmonie wird in die kreisförmige Gestaltung der Anlage

Situé à 200 kilomètres au sud de Bangkok, sur le Golfe de Thaïlande, le complexe hôtelier thaï de Hua Hin s'est développé dans les années 1920 lorsque le roi Rama VII y créa un palais d'été. C'est aujourd'hui un centre touristique important, à 30 minutes de vol de la capitale.

L'Earth Spa a été créé par Design Worldwide Partnership, un cabinet multidisciplinaire basé en Asie, pour son client Six Senses. Installé sur plus de 1386 mètres carrés d'eau et de paysage, le spa est édifié sur la terre, à proximité de la mer. Neuf bâtiments en dôme ocre siègent sur un lac, formant de minuscules îles reliées par d'étroites passerelles en bois. Tels des cavernes chaleureuses ou des cocons entourés de roseaux et de nénuphars, ils accueillent le visiteur.

Inspirés des villages du nord et du nord-est de la Thaïlande, où les maisons sont conçues pour garder une température confortable même en été, et des maisons africaines traditionnelles en terre, le complexe se distingue par son genre. La recherche d'harmonie se traduit dans la disposition circulaire des maisons, inspirées des courbes naturelles des coquillages des plages locales.

Les architectes de DWP ont veillé à utiliser des matières durables et recyclables. Les dômes sont construits avec une boue similaire à

during the monsoon season because the shape allows the water to flow down without eroding the outer surface. The tallest building, the meditation cave, is 24.5 feet tall with an internal diameter of 13.8 feet. Walls are up to 31 in. thick. Each has a low opening directly onto the water to allow for cool breezes to enter the buildings. A few small windows set in the walls ensure privacy for visitors. An opening at the top gives ventilation and lets in natural light.

The spa comprises four treatment rooms with private outdoor jacuzzi, two steam rooms, a meditation cave, a relaxing area, and the reception area. Treatments put special emphasis on "skin food" (nothing should be put on the skin that is not eaten) using coconut, rice, avocado, lime, papaya, ginger, limegrass, and cucumber. Four main elements come together in the spa: earth—the construction material; water—surrounding the domes; air—natural ventilation; and fire—used to heat stones, create steam, and in the sauna.

übersetzt, die von den natürlichen Rillen auf Seemuscheln am örtlichen Strand inspiriert wurde.

DWP achteten sorgfältig darauf, nachhaltige und wieder verwendbare Materialien zu verwenden – die Kuppeln wurden aus lehm-artigem Schlamm, Reisspelzen, Stroh und einheimischen wiederverwendeten Natur-materialien erbaut. Die Kuppelform ist ideal für die schweren Regenfälle, die während des Monsuns häufig auftreten, weil die Form es dem Wasser erlaubt, hinabzufließen, ohne die äußere Oberfläche auszuwaschen. Das größte Gebäude, die Meditationshöhle, ist 7,5 Meter hoch mit einem Innendurchmesser von 4,2 Metern. Die Wände sind bis zu 80 cm dick. Jedes Gebäude verfügt über eine unmittelbar auf das Wasser hinausgehende Öffnung, damit kühle Brisen hinein wehen können. Einige wenige kleine Fenster in den Wänden gewährleisten die Privatsphäre der Gäste. Eine Öffnung im oberen Teil sorgt für eine natürliche Belüftung und lässt natürliches Licht hinein.

Das Wellnessbad verfügt über vier Behand-lungsräume mit einem privaten Freiluft-Whirlpool, zwei Dampfräumen, einer Meditationshöhle, einem Entspannungs- und einem Empfangs-bereich. Bei den Behandlungen wird ein Schwerpunkt auf „Hautnahrung" (die Haut sollte von nichts berührt werden, dass nicht auch gegessen wird) gelegt und Kokosnuss, Reis, Avocado, Limonen, Papayas, Ingwer, Zitronengras und Gurken verwendet. Im Wellnessbad kommen vier Hauptelemente zusammen: Erde – das Baumaterial; Wasser – das die Kuppeln umge-bende Element; Luft – natürliche Belüftung; und Feuer – zur Erhitzung der Steine, Erzeugung von Dampf und in der Sauna.

l'argile, des écorces de riz, de la paille et des matières naturelles locales recyclées. La forme du dôme est idéale pour affronter les pluies diluviennes qui s'abattent durant la mousson, puisque l'eau peut s'écouler sans éroder la surface extérieure. Le bâtiment le plus haut, la grotte de méditation, mesure 7,5 mètres de haut et 4,2 mètres de diamètre. Les murs peuvent atteindre 80 cm d'épaisseur. Chacun est directement ouvert sur l'eau pour laisser la brise entrer et rafraîchir les lieux. Les rares petites fenêtres permettent aux clients de conserver leur intimité. Une ouverture au plafond joue le rôle de ventilation naturelle et laisse pénétrer la lumière naturelle.

Le spa compte quatre salles de soins, avec des jacuzzis extérieurs privés, deux saunas, une grotte de méditation, un espace de relaxation et l'accueil. Les soins mettent l'accent sur « les aliments pour la peau » et consistent donc à ne rien mettre sur la peau qui ne soit pas comestible: noix de coco, avocat, citron vert, papaye, gingembre et concombre font ainsi partie des soins. Le spa rassemble les quatre éléments: la terre (matière de la construction), l'eau (qui entoure le dôme), l'air (la ventilation naturelle) et le feu (utilisé pour chauffer les pierres et créer la vapeur dans le sauna).

right Spa domes appear to be floating on ponds. Similar types of mud-hut are found in Africa, ideal for staying cool in a hot climate.

rechts Die Kuppeln des Bads scheinen auf Teichen zu schwimmen. Ähnliche Arten von Schlammhütten finden sich in Afrika; sie sind ideal, um in einem heißen Klima Kühlung zu schaffen.

droite Les dômes du spa semblent flotter sur les bassins. On trouve des huttes similaires en Afrique, idéales pour maintenir une température agréable dans un climat chaud.

left Earth domes have entrances close to the water's edge to allow cool breezes to flow through.

links Die Erdkuppeln verfügen über Eingänge nahe am Rande des Wassers, damit kühle Brisen die Gebäude durchwehen können.

gauche L'entrée des dômes en terre est située au bord de l'eau pour laisser la brise pénétrer.

bottom left Openings at the top of each building provide natural ventilation and light.

unten links Öffnungen im oberen Teil jedes Gebäudes bieten natürliche Belüftung und Licht.

ci-desous à gauche Les ouvertures au plafond de chaque construction offrent une ventilation et une lumière naturelles.

left Steps leading down into one of the relaxation domes.

links Stufen führen hinab in eine der Entspannungskuppeln.

gauche Les escaliers mènent à l'un des dômes de relaxation.

below Interconnecting walkways over the water are made from natural materials with sensitive landscaping accenting the connection between man and the environment.

unten Miteinander verbundene Fußgängerstege über dem Wasser bestehen aus natürlichen Materialien, und eine feinfühlige Landschaftsgestaltung akzentuiert die Verbindung zwischen Mensch und Umwelt.

ci-dessous Les passerelles sur l'eau, construites avec des matériaux naturels, sont sensibles au paysage et accentuent le lien entre l'homme et l'environnement.

Bulgari Resort

Pecatu, Bali, Indonesia
Antonio Citterio and Partners
2006

above This resort is characterized by a series of bars and restaurants set on their own islands at the top of a cliff.

oben Die Ferienanlage verfügt über eine Reihe von Bars und Restaurants, die auf eigenen Inseln auf einer Klippe erbaut wurden.

ci-dessus Ce complexe se caractérise par plusieurs bars et restaurants, des îles en eux-mêmes, situés au sommet d'une falaise.

left A 1930s painting of the island of Bali by Miguel Covarrubias in the reception pavilion.

links Im Empfangspavillon hängt ein aus den 1930er Jahren stammendes Gemälde der Insel Bali von Miguel Covarrubias.

gauche Un tableau des années 1930 de l'île de Bali par Miguel Covarrubias se trouve dans le hall d'accueil.

below The open-air bar and infinity pool blend seamlessly with the ocean below.

unten Die Freiluftbar und das Überlaufbecken verschmelzen übergangslos mit dem darunter liegenden Ozean.

ci-dessous Le bar de plein air et une piscine immense se mélangent en toute transparence à l'océan situé plus bas.

above The cliff-side infinity pool overlooked by the dining and bar area. Water is a constant theme.

oben Blick aus den Speise- und Barbereichen zum Überlaufbecken auf der Klippenseite. Das Thema Wasser ist ständig präsent.

ci-dessus La piscine en bord de falaise surplombée par l'espace bar et restauration. L'eau est un thème récurrent.

right Hot and cold plunge pools overlooking the Indian Ocean.

rechts Heiße und kalte Tauchbecken mit Aussicht auf den Indischen Ozean.

droite Bassins chauds et froids surplombant l'océan Indien.

The island of Bali is one of the most popular tourist destinations in southeast Asia. In recent years, it has seen an increasing number of luxury resorts built there. Probably the most spectacular, in terms of architecture and pure luxury is the Bulgari Resort at Pecatu on the island's southwestern tip.

Designed by the Italian architects Antonio Citterio and Partners, the studio behind the first Bulgari Hotel in Milan, built in 2004, the resort is perched atop a 525-feet high cliff on the dry Bukit peninsula. The high steep slope of the promontory made it necessary to build it into sloping terraces. Although the resort is not an island, its remoteness and location—to get there from the beach it is necessary to take a private inclined elevator—make it uniquely isolated. In addition, many of the buildings are surrounded by shallow pools, designed to be islands in themselves—microcosms of the larger landscape to which they belong.

The architectural plan shows a clear division between the private and public spaces. The walled villas are grouped together on the western side of the resort, while on the other side there are restaurants, a bar, a cliff-edge swimming pool, and hot and cold plunge pools. There is a twofold spirit, on the one hand the quiet, private, and secret atmosphere of the

Die Insel Bali ist eines der beliebtesten Touristenziele in Südostasien. In den letzten Jahren wurde dort eine zunehmende Anzahl von Luxusferienanlagen erbaut. Die im Hinblick auf Architektur und reinen Luxus wahrscheinlich spektakulärste ist das Bulgari Resort in Pecatu auf der Südwestspitze der Insel.

Die von den italienischen Architekten Antonio Citterio and Partners, dem Studio hinter dem ersten, 2004 erbauten Bulgari Hotel in Mailand, entworfene Anlage wurde auf einer 60 Meter hohen Klippe der trockenen Bukit-Halbinsel errichtet. Der hohe, steile Hang des Felsvorsprungs erforderte eine Bauweise in abfallenden Terrassen. Obgleich die Ferienanlage sich nicht auf einer Insel befindet, ist sie aufgrund ihrer Abgeschiedenheit und ihrer Lage – vom Strand aus kann man sie nur mit einem privaten Fahrstuhl erreichen – auf einzigartige Weise isoliert. Darüber hinaus sind viele der Gebäude von flachen Becken umgeben, die selbst als Inseln entworfen wurden – Mikrokosmen des Gesamtbildes der Landschaft, zu der sie gehören.

Der Bauplan zeigt eine saubere Unterteilung zwischen privaten und öffentlichen Räumen. Die ummauerten Villen sind auf der Westseite der Ferienanlage zusammengefasst, während sich auf der anderen Seite Restaurants, Bars, am

Bali, l'une des destinations touristiques les plus populaires, est une île située en Asie du sud-est. Ces dernières années, un nombre croissant de complexes touristiques de luxe y ont vu le jour. Le plus spectaculaire en termes d'architecture et de luxe est sans aucun doute le complexe hôtelier Bulgari, à Pecatu, à la pointe sud-ouest de l'île.

Conçu par les architectes italiens Antonio Citterio and Partners, concepteurs du premier Hôtel Bulgari à Milan en 2004, le complexe hôtelier est perché au sommet d'une falaise de 160 mètres de haut, sur la péninsule de Bukit. La pente raide du promontoire a été nécessaire pour sa construction en terrasses. Bien que le complexe ne soit pas une île, sa distance et son emplacement en font un lieu isolé; il faut prendre un ascenseur incliné privé pour y accéder depuis la plage. Les nombreux bâtiments sont entourés de bassins peu profonds, qui en font ainsi des îles, des microcosmes du paysage plus vaste auxquels ils appartiennent.

Le plan architectural montre une nette division entre les espaces publics et privés. Les villas fermées sont regroupées du côté ouest tandis que les restaurants, les bars, la piscine en bord de falaise et les bains chauds et froids sont regroupés du côté est. Il règne un esprit double:

villas, and on the other the glamorous and busy area of the bars and restaurants.

In this luxury "village," contemporary Italian interior design mixes with traditional Balinese architecture. There are 59 ocean-view villas, each with its own plunge pool and patio with secluded tropical garden. Three larger two-bedroom villas feature a large pool as well as studio and kitchen. And the most exclusive of all is the Bulgari Villa, at an extraordinary 14,000 square feet, with four bedrooms, two living rooms, and 65-feet swimming pool. Traditionally, Balinese houses combine indoor and outdoor spaces. These villas reflect this style: the bedrooms have views across the terrace, the bathrooms floor-to-ceiling glass walls, and the living rooms are open-air pavilions.

Furthermore, local, natural materials have been used in the construction, in particular wood and stone. The resort landscape walls are of bukit, a white coral stone that turns black when wet, the garden and interior walls are made of hand-cut natural lava and *palimanan* stone, and the various pools are clad in green *subakumi* stone. A tawny type of mahogany wood from Java, called bangkiray, is used on floors and details. Roofs are mainly of palm leaf straw or *alang-alang*.

Klippenrand gelegene Schwimmbecken sowie heiße und kalte Tauchbecken befinden. So ist die Atmosphäre der Anlage zweigeteilt: auf der einen Seite die ruhige, private und zurück-gezogene Atmosphäre der Villen und auf der anderen Seite der glanzvolle, betriebsame Trubel der Bars und Restaurants.

In diesem „Luxusdorf" vereint sich zeit-genössische italienische Innenausstattung mit traditioneller balinesischer Architektur. Es umfasst 59 Villen mit Meeresblick, jede davon mit eigenem Tauchbecken und Patio mit abgeschlossenem tropischem Garten. Drei größere Zweizimmervillen verfügen über ein großes Schwimmbecken sowie Studio und Küche. Die exklusivste aller Villen ist die Bulgari Villa mit ihren unglaublichen 1.300 Quadratmetern, vier Schlafzimmern, zwei Wohnzimmern und einem 20 Meter langen Schwimmbecken. Balinesische Häuser verbinden traditionell Räume im Inneren und im Freien miteinander, und dieser Stil spiegelt sich auch in diesen Villen wider: Die Schlafzimmer bieten Ausblicke über die Terrasse, die Badezimmer haben vom Fußboden bis zur Decke durchgängig verglaste Wände und die Wohnzimmer sind Freiluftpavillons.

Darüber hinaus wurden beim Bau einheimi-sche, natürliche Materialien verwendet, insbeson-dere Holz und Stein. Die Landschaftsmauern der

d'un côté, l'ambiance intime, privée et calme des villas; d'un autre, l'espace glamour et vivant des bars et des restaurants.

Dans ce « village luxueux », le design intérieur contemporain italien se mêle à l'architecture traditionnelle balinaise. Le complexe compte 59 villas avec vue sur la mer, chacune possédant son propre bassin et sa propre cour avec jardin tropical isolé. Trois villas plus grandes, avec deux chambres doubles, sont équipées d'une grande piscine, d'un salon et d'une cuisine. Enfin, la plus spectaculaire de toute, la villa Bulgari, de 1300 mètres carrés, compte quatre chambres, deux salons et une piscine de 20 mètres carrés. Les maisons traditionnelles balinaises combinent espaces intérieurs et extérieurs. Les villas du Centre Bulgari reflètent ce style: la chambre offre une vue sur la terrasse, les salles de bain sont entourées de murs en verre, et le salon et le pavillon sont en plein air.

Des matières naturelles locales ont été utilisées pour la construction, notamment le bois et la pierre. Les murs extérieurs sont en *butik*, du corail blanc qui noircit à l'humidité. Les murs intérieurs et des jardins sont en lave naturelle taillée à la main et en pierre de *palimanan*, et les nombreux bassins sont habillés de pierre verte de *subakumi*. Un type fauve de bois d'acajou, le

The public spaces are notable for being surrounded by water. A spa incorporates a pond that features a floating wooden bridge; the lounge bar is reached by a walkway over an infinity pool; and the Italian restaurant overlooks a reflection pool. Set on the tip of Bali overlooking the Indian Ocean, the resort feels as if it is floating on water. Like Pura Luhur, the nearby Hindu Sea Temple, it is a sort of stone ship.

Ferienanlage bestehen aus *Butik*, einem weißen Korallenstein, der durch Nässe schwarz wird, der Garten und die Innenwände aus von Hand gehauener Lava und *Palimanan*-Stein, und die verschiedenen Schwimmbecken sind mit grünem *Subakumi*-Stein verkleidet. Für die Böden und verschiedene Details wurde eine gelb-braune Mahagoniart aus Java namens *Bangkiray* verwendet. Die Dächer bestehen vorwiegend aus Palmblattstroh oder *Alang-Alang*.

Bemerkenswert an den öffentlichen Räumen ist, dass sie von Wasser umgeben sind. Ein Wellnessbad umschließt einen Teich mit einer schwimmenden, hölzernen Brücke; die Lounge-Bar können Gäste über eine Fußgängerbrücke über ein Überlaufbecken erreichen und das italienische Restaurant überblickt ein Spiegelbecken. Angesichts ihrer Lage auf einem Felsvorsprung am Rande von Bali mit Blick auf den Indischen Ozean scheint die Ferienanlage auf dem Wasser zu treiben. Wie der nahege-legene Hindutempel Pura Luhur Uluwatu ist sie eine Art Schiff aus Stein.

bangkiray, a été utilisé pour le sol et les finitions. Les toits sont principalement en feuilles de palmier, l'*alang-alang*.

Les espaces publics, remarquables, sont entourés d'eau. Le spa possède un bassin avec un pont en bois flottant ; on accède au bar lounge par une passerelle qui traverse une piscine immense et le restaurant italien surplombe une piscine dans laquelle il se reflète. Situé au sommet de Bali, surplombant l'océan Indien, ce complexe hôtelier semble flotter sur l'eau. Tout comme Pura Luhur Uluwatu, le temple Hindou situé à proximité, il ressemble à une cité de pierre.

right top A floating bridge stretching over a pond leads to the spa and a Joglo house.

rechts oben Eine schwimmende Brücke erstreckt sich über einen Teich und führt zum Wellnessbad und einem Joglo-Haus.

ci-dessus à droite Un pont flottant, qui s'étend sur un bassin, conduit au spa et à un Joglo.

right bottom Hand-carved intricate designs on the teak wood Joglo house, reflections of Javanese, Chinese, Hindu, and Arabic cultures.

rechts unten Handgeschnitzte, aufwändige Designs am Teakholz des Joglo-Hauses in der Tradition der javanischen, chinesischen, hinduistischen und arabischen Kultur.

ci-dessous à droite Gravures complexes sur le Joglo en teck, reflets des cultures javanaise, chinoise, hindou et arabe.

above The enormous 14,000 square feet Bulgari Villa features a 65-foot swimming pool.

oben Die 1.300 Quadratmeter Grundfläche umfassende Bulgari Villa verfügt über ein 20 Meter langes Schwimmbecken.

ci-dessus La villa Bulgari, de 1200 mètres carrés, avec sa piscine de 20 mètres carrés.

right An entrance gate to one of the villas with lava stone walls, *alang-alang* thatch roof, and bronze lantern.

rechts Eingangstor zu einer der Villen mit Mauern aus Lavagestein, einem mit Alang-Alang gedeckten Dach und einer Bronzelaterne.

droite Une porte d'entrée de l'une des villas avec les murs en pierre volcanique, le toit en chaume d'alang-alang et une lanterne en bronze.

below The resort's villas reflect the walled indoor-outdoor nature of traditional Balinese houses.

unten Die Villen der Ferienanlage spiegeln die ummauerte Innen-Außen-Bauweise traditioneller balinesischer Häuser wider.

ci-dessous Les villas du complexe hôtelier reflètent la combinaison de l'intérieur et de l'extérieur des maisons traditionnelles balinaises.

right Bathrooms feature floor-to-ceiling glass walls. Bangkiray, a tawny mahogany from Java, is used extensively.

rechts In den Badezimmern sind die Wände vom Boden bis zur Decke verglast. Bangkiray, ein gelbbrauner Mahagoni aus Java, wird ausgiebig verwendet.

droite Les salles de bain possèdent des murs en verre. Le bangkiray, un bois d''acajou de Java, est utilisé à profusion.

Dellis Cay

Dellis Cay, Turks and Caicos Islands

Piero Lissoni, Zaha Hadid, David Chipperfield, Kengo Kuma,
Shigeru Ban, Carl Ettensperger

2010

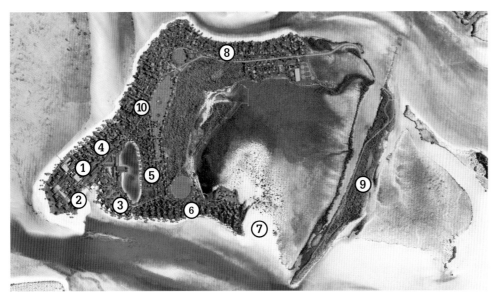

previous page External view of hotel and swimming pool, designed by Piero Lissoni.

vorherige Seite Beispiel einer möglichen Aussicht aus Kengo Kumas Wellnessbad auf Dellis Cay in der Karibik.

page précédente Le designer italien Piero Lissoni a conçu plusieurs villas de plage pour l'île.

above A beach villa by Piero Lissoni, a low, flat building with expansive open-plan interiors.

oben Eine Strandvilla von Piero Lissoni, ein niedriges, flaches Gebäude mit ausgedehnten, offen angelegten Innenräumen.

ci-dessus Villa en bord de plage conçue par Piero Lissoni, un bâtiment peu élevé avec un intérieur ouvert très spacieux.

right Interior of a hotel bedroom by Lissoni, a combination of minimalism and elegance.

rechts Inneres eines Hotelzimmers von Lissoni, eine Verbindung aus Minimalismus und Eleganz.

droite Chambre d'hôtel de Piero Lissoni, mélange de minimalisme et d'élégance.

Dellis Cay is a small, natural island that forms part of the Turks and Caicos Islands, 575 miles south of Miami. The 558-acre island paradise was bought by the Turkish developer Cem Kinay to create what he describes as a very private community. Six renowned architects have been commissioned to design 124 private villas, 154 residences, a Mandarin Oriental Hotel, marina, and spa.

The architects assembled include the Italian Piero Lissoni who will be responsible for designing the hotel, the first building visitors see when docking on the island. In addition to the hotel, consisting of 52 suites and 17 villas, he has designed 24 hotel residences and nine beach houses. His collection of contemporary architecture is both minimal and modern, with an emphasis on bringing the outside in and the inside out. As a consequence, the villas are open-plan with expansive, outdoor terraces and balconies. The three-story beach houses are positioned around a central pond, all interconnected by a series of walkways that lead to the beach.

Shigeru Ban's beach villas, to the south, will be largely prefabricated and have an emphasis on lightness and transparency. Some shaped as S's, some as H's, they will be placed along the shore with a private bridge linking the main

Dellis Cay ist eine kleine natürliche Insel, die zu den Turks- und Caicosinseln 925 Kilometer südlich von Miami gehört. Das 226 Hektar große Inselparadies wurde von dem türkischen Bau-unternehmer Cem Kinay erworben, um dort eine laut seinen Worten sehr private Gemeinschaft zu schaffen. Sieben renommierte Architekten erhiel-ten den Auftrag, 24 Privatvillen, 154 Wohnungen, ein Mandarin Oriental Hotel, einen Jachthafen und ein Wellnessbad zu entwerfen.

Zu der Gruppe von Architekten gehört der Italiener Piero Lissoni, der für den Entwurf des Hotels verantwortlich zeichnen wird – das erste Gebäude, das Besucher bei ihrer Ankunft auf der Insel sehen werden. Neben dem aus 52 Suiten und 17 Villen bestehenden Hotel hat er 24 Hotel-residenzen und neun Strandhäuser entworfen. Sein zeitgenössisches architektonisches Werk ist sowohl minimal als auch modern, mit einem Schwerpunkt auf dem Versuch, das Äußere nach Innen und das Innere nach Außen zu tragen. Infolgedessen sind seine Villen offen angelegt und verfügen über ausgedehnte Außenterrassen und Balkone. Die dreistöckigen Strandhäuser wurden um einen Teich herum errichtet und sind über eine Reihe von Gängen miteinander verbunden, die zum Strand führen.

Shigeru Bans Strandvillen im Süden werden vorwiegend aus Fertigbauteilen und mit einem

Dellis Cay est une petite île naturelle appartenant aux îles Turques et Caïques, à 925 km au sud de Miami. L'île paradisiaque de 226 hectares a été achetée par le développeur turc Cem Kinay pour créer ce qu'il décrit comme une communauté très privée. Sept architectes reconnus ont été chargés de concevoir 124 villas privées, 154 résidences, un hôtel oriental mandarin, une marina et un spa.

Parmi les architectes, Piero Lissoni est responsable de la conception de l'hôtel, le premier bâtiment qu'apercevront les touristes en posant le pied sur l'île. En plus de l'hôtel, qui comptera 52 suites et 17 villas, il a conçu 24 résidences hôtelières et 9 maisons sur la plage. Ses travaux d'architecture contemporaine sont à la fois minimalistes et modernes, et s'efforcent de mêler intérieur et extérieur. Par conséquent, les villas sont ouvertes sur de spacieuses terrasses extérieures. Les trois maisons en bord de mer se trouvent autour d'un bassin central et sont toutes reliées par plusieurs passerelles qui conduisent à la plage.

Les villas de Shigeru Ban, au sud, seront en grande partie préfabriquées et mettront l'accent sur la lumière et la transparence. En forme de S ou de H, elles seront placées le long de la rive avec un pont privé reliant les principales villas aux pavillons perchés sur la mer. Zaha Hadid,

villas to square water pavilions perched over the sea. Zaha Hadid, who is masterplanning the island, is contributing a number of villas the most impressive of which is the experimental Villa B, a glass-walled house with a geometric concrete roof. Carl Ettensperger's over-the-water villas will follow the natural curves of the southern shore offering direct contact with the sea, while David Chipperfield's villas on the north coast will attempt to elegantly blend with the dramatic surrounding landscape.

Besides the hotel, the other main structure will be the Mandarin Oriental Spa. Designed by Japanese architect Kengo Kuma, it will be hidden within a sea of mangroves in the middle of the island. When finished, it will be the largest spa in the Caribbean—a collection of pavilions and private treatment rooms that float over a lake, with a series of shallow pools and ponds acting as reflective surfaces.

Although the exclusive development (prices for residences range from $2 million to $20 million) will obviously have some effect on the natural environment which is home to many birds, the architects and developer have attempted to limit their impact on the island. The buildings tend to be small and low with a maximum height of 40 feet. Trees are used to enclose and hide buildings, and the majority of

Schwerpunkt auf Leichtigkeit und Transparenz errichtet. Einige Villen sind S-förmig, andere wiederum H-förmig; sie werden entlang dem Meeresufer angelegt, wobei die Hauptvillen über private Brücken mit quadratischen Wasserpavillons über dem Meer verbunden sind. Zaha Hadid, die die Gesamtleitung über die Planung innehat, trägt eine Reihe von Villen zur Gestaltung der Insel bei, von denen die experimentelle Villa B, ein Haus mit Glaswänden und einem geometrischen Betondach, die eindrucksvollste ist. Carl Ettenspergers Villen über dem Wasser werden den natürlichen Einbuchtungen der Südküste folgen und unmittelbaren Kontakt mit dem Meer haben, während David Chipperfields Villen an der Nordküste elegant mit der dramatischen Landschaft verschmelzen werden.

Neben dem Hotel selbst wird das Wellnessbad des Mandarin Oriental das zweite wesentliche Gebäude auf der Insel sein. Das von dem japanischen Architekten Kengo Kuma entworfene Gebäude wird in einem Meer von Mangrovenbäumen in der Mitte der Insel verborgen liegen. Nach seiner Fertigstellung wird es das größte Wellnessbad in der Karibik sein – eine Ansammlung von Pavillons und privaten Behandlungsräumen, die auf einem See treiben, mit einer Reihe flacher Becken und

responsable du plan d'ensemble de l'île, participe à certaines villas dont la plus spectaculaire est la Villa B expérimentale, une maison entièrement en verre, avec un toit géométrique en béton. Les villas sur l'eau de Carl Ettensperger suivront les courbes naturelles de la rive sud, offrant un contact direct avec la mer, tandis que les villas de David Chipperfield sur la côte nord tenteront de se mêler en toute élégance au paysage exceptionnel environnant.

À côté de l'hôtel, le spa oriental mandarin est l'autre structure principale. Conçu par l'architecte japonais Kengo Kuma, le spa sera caché dans une mer de mangroves au centre de l'île. Une fois terminé, il sera le plus grand des Caraïbes, où plusieurs pavillons et salles de soins privées flotteront sur un lac, avec plusieurs bassins peu profonds jouant le rôle de surface de réflexion.

Le développement (le prix des résidences varie entre 2 et 20 millions de dollars) aura à l'évidence des conséquences sur l'environnement naturel qui accueille de nombreux oiseaux, mais les architectes et le promoteur tentent de limiter l'impact sur l'île. Les bâtiments sont plutôt petits et d'une hauteur maximale de 12 mètres.

Les arbres entourent et cachent les bâtiments et la plupart des maisons sont situées

left and above The centerpiece on the island is a spa by Kengo Kuma, set on its own lake.

links und oben Das Herzstück der Insel ist ein von Kengo Kuma entworfenes Wellnessbad, das in einem eigenen See errichtet wurde.

ci-dessus et gauche La pièce maîtresse de l'île, le spa de Kengo Kuma, posé sur son propre lac.

the villas are situated along the seashore at intervals. The designs themselves, although thoroughly modern, use transparency to bring the natural beauty of the island into the homes and impose as little as possible on the landscape.

Teiche, die als spiegelnde Oberflächen dienen.

Obgleich dieses exklusive Bauprojekt (die Preise für die Residenzen variieren von $2 Millionen bis zu $20 Millionen) ganz sicher eine gewisse Auswirkung auf die Umwelt haben wird, die vielen Vogelarten ein Zuhause bietet, waren die Architekten und der Bauherr bestrebt, die Folgen für die Insel in Grenzen zu halten. Die Bauten sind mit einer maximalen Höhe von 12 Metern eher klein und niedrig. Es werden Bäume verwendet, um die Gebäude zu umrahmen und zu verbergen, und die Mehrheit der Villen wurde in Intervallen entlang der Küste errichtet. Die Entwürfe selbst, obgleich durch und durch modern, setzen Transparenz ein, um die natürliche Schönheit der Insel in die Häuser zu tragen und die Landschaft so wenig wie möglich zu beeinträchtigen.

au bord de l'eau, à distance les unes des autres. Le design, bien que très moderne, utilise la transparence pour intégrer la beauté naturelle de l'île aux maisons et affecter le moins possible le paysage.

left Villa B by Zaha Hadid is a glass-walled house with concrete roof.

links Die Villa B von Zaha Hadid ist ein Haus mit gläsernen Wänden und einem Betondach.

gauche La villa B de Zaha Hadid est habillée de verre et d'un toit en béton.

right Roof and floor plans of Hadid's Villa B.

rechts Dach- und Grundrisse von Hadids Villa B.

droite Plan du toit et du sol de la Villa B de Hadid.

right bottom The geometric roof of Villa B with its large overhang offers shade for the pool.

rechts unten Das geometrische Dach der Villa B mit seiner großen Überkragung bietet Schatten für den Pool.

ci-dessous à droite Le toit géométrique de la villa B avec son important débord offre de l'ombre sur la piscine.

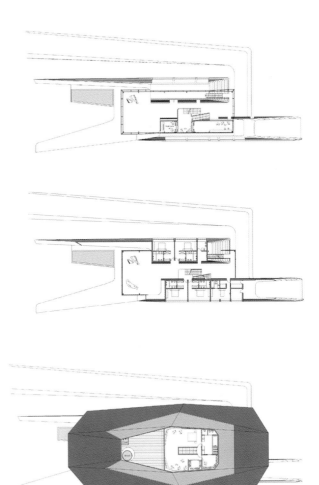

above Over-the-water guesthouses are linked to the beach, and the S House, by a wood deck bridge.

oben Die Gästehäuser über dem Wasser sind mit dem Strand verbunden, das S-Haus mit einer hölzernen Deckbrücke.

ci-dessus Les maisons au-dessus de l'eau sont reliées à la plage et à la maison en S par un pont en bois.

below Plan of H House designed by Shigeru Ban.

unten Plan eines von Shigeru Ban entworfenen H-Hauses.

ci-dessous Plan de la maison en H conçue par Shigeru Ban.

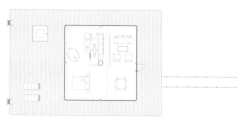

right Plan of the S House. This too has a footbridge linking it to a water guesthouse.

links Plan eines S-Hauses. Dieses Haus verfügt ebenfalls über eine Fußgängerbrücke, die es mit einem Wassergästehaus verbindet.

droite Plan de la maison en S. Un pont la relie également à une maison sur l'eau.

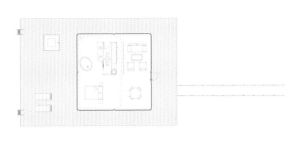

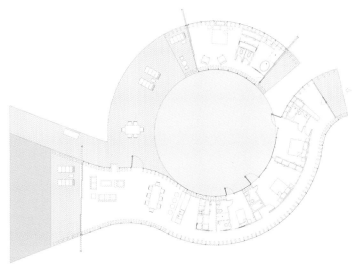

left Ban employs a combination of lightness and transparency in his H House design.

links Ban setzt in seinem Entwurf für ein H-Haus auf eine Kombination aus Leichtigkeit und Transparenz.

gauche Shigeru Ban mélange légèreté et transparence dans sa maison en H.

below Looking back to the H House from a geometric glass guesthouse.

unten Blick aus einem geometrischen, gläsernen Gästehaus auf ein H-Haus.

ci-dessous Vue sur la maison en H depuis une maison géométrique en verre.

left Detail of the Marina Villa by Zaha Hadid, a luxurious experiment in spatial design.

links Detail der von Zaha Hadid entworfenen Marina Villa, ein luxuriöses Experiment in Raumdesign.

gauche Détail de la villa Marina de Zaha Hadid, une expérience luxueuse au design spatial.

left above A villa by Carl Ettensberger, designed to blend in with the surrounding water, both man-made and natural.

rechts oben Eine von Carl Ettensberger entworfene Villa, die optisch mit den sie umgebenden – künstlich angelegten und natürlichen – Wasserflächen verschmelzen soll.

ci-dessus à gauche Villa de Carl Ettensberger, à la fois naturelle et artificielle, se mélangeant à l'eau environnante.

left The master bedroom in a villa on the north of the island by the British architect David Chipperfield.

links Das Hauptschlafzimmer in einer von dem britischen Architekten David Chipperfield entworfenen Villa im Norden der Insel.

gauche La chambre principale dans une villa au nord de l'île par l'architecte britannique David Chipperfield.

Nurai Resort and Hotel

Abu Dhabi, UAE
Studio Dror, AW2
2010

above Water villas perched over the sea are reached by boat or via wooden jetties.

oben Die über dem Meer angelegten Wasservillen können mit dem Boot oder über hölzerne Landungsstege erreicht werden.

ci-dessus Les villas sont perchées sur la mer. On y accède en bateau ou par des jetées en bois.

right New York firm Dror undertook the concept design scheme for the island, masterplanning was by AW2.

rechts Das New Yorker Unternehmen Dror entwarf das Konzept für die Insel, die Gesamtplanung lag in den Händen von AW2.

droite Le cabinet d'architectes new-yorkais Dror a entrepris le projet d'aménagement de l'île, planifié par AW2.

Nurai, derived from the Arabic word "nour" meaning light, is an untouched natural island located just northeast of Abu Dhabi. Developed by Zaya, the boutique luxury resort consists of a series of residential villas, a hotel, and marina. It can be reached in 25 minutes by boat or 5 minutes by helicopter from Abu Dhabi.

Architecture Workshop 2 (AW2), a Paris-based company, are responsible for designing the hotel and marina, while multi-disciplinary New York Studio Dror have designed all the residences on the 1-mile long island. There are two main residential building types: seaside estates and water villas. Construction will be mainly in concrete and steel, with detailing in a variety of other materials.

The estates, 13,000 square feet each, will have either five or six bedrooms. Each of the 31 residences has its own private beach, garden, infinity swimming pool, service quarters, and outdoor showers. The 36 water villas, 5,400 square feet each, offer the possibility of open-plan living over water. Built on pillars over the sea, these glass boxes are reached by wooden piers. Like tentacles on a sea creature the piers and water villas meander out to sea. They each have three bedrooms, four bathrooms, a rooftop garden, and enveloping balconies on the first floor. Because of the very hot climate, cooling is

Nurai, das sich von dem arabischen Wort „nour" ableitet und Licht bedeutet, ist eine bislang unberührte, natürliche Insel wenige Kilometer nordöstlich der Stadt Abu Dhabi. Die von Zaya entwickelte Boutique-Luxusferienanlage besteht aus einer Reihe von Privatvillen, einem Hotel und einem Jachthafen. Sie kann von Abu Dhabi aus mit dem Boot in 25 Minuten oder mit dem Hubschrauber in 5 Minuten erreicht werden.

Architecture Workshop 2 (AW2), ein in Paris ansässiges Unternehmen, ist für den Entwurf des Hotels und des Jachthafens verantwortlich, während das interdisziplinäre Studio Dror aus New York alle Privathäuser auf der 1,5 Kilometer langen Insel entworfen hat. Bei den Privat-häusern gibt es zwei Hauptbauweisen: Küstenlandsitze und Wasservillen. Sie werden hauptsächlich aus Beton und Stahl mit Details in einer Vielzahl anderer Materialien erbaut.

Die Landsitze, jeder davon 1.200 Quadratmeter groß, verfügen entweder über fünf oder über sechs Schlafzimmer. Jedes der 31 Privathäuser verfügt außerdem über einen eigenen Privat-strand, einen Garten, ein Überlaufbecken, Dienstbotenquartiere und Außenduschen. Die 36 Wasservillen von je 500 Quadratmetern Größe bieten die Möglichkeit, in einem offen angelegten Wohnraum unmittelbar über dem

Nurai, dérivé de l'arabe « nour » signifiant lumière, est une île naturelle inaltérée située au nord-est d'Abu Dhabi. Développé par Zaya, le complexe de luxe est composé de plusieurs villas résidentielles, d'un hôtel et d'une marina. On y accède en 25 minutes par bateau ou en 5 minutes par hélicoptère depuis Abu Dhabi.

Architecture Workshop 2 (AW2), un cabinet d'architectes parisien, est chargé de la conception de l'hôtel et de la marina, tandis que le cabinet new-yorkais Dror s'occupe de toutes les résiden-ces sur l'île d'1,5 kilomètre de long. Deux types de bâtiments résidentiels seront conçus: les proprié-tés en bord de mer et les villas sur l'eau. La construction se fera principalement en béton et en acier. Les finitions seront réalisées en divers autres matériaux.

Les propriétés, chacune de 1200 mètres carrés, compteront cinq ou six chambres. Chacune des 31 résidences possède une plage privée, un jardin, une grande piscine, des parties communes et des douches extérieures. Les 36 villas sur l'eau, de 500 mètres carrés chacune, offre une vue sur l'eau. Construites sur pilotis au-dessus de la mer, on accède à ces maisons de verre par des embarcadères en bois. Comme des tentacules, les embarcadères et les villas serpentent sur la mer. Chaque maison compte trois chambres, quatre salles de bain, un toit

paramount. This is achieved via cross ventilation, integrated shading devices, and the use of modern energy-efficient glass.

The most dramatic part of the design is the estates' earth roofs. Dror describe this as an "architectural carpet" that "allows every resident to be hidden under a section of land" —literally sweeping everything under the carpet. As luxury was such an important aspect of the island, building underground allows for services and circulation to be kept out of sight. The architects could play with the interesting landscape of the island and experiment with the way land and interior spaces blend together. The carpet metaphor is also relevant because the Gulf region is famous for carpet making. Indeed, traditional carpet patterns are to be designed on the ceilings of the villas on the underside of the "carpet." By camouflaging the

Wasser zu leben. Diese auf Pfeilern über dem Meer erbauten Glaskästen können über hölzerne Stege erreicht werden. Wie die Fangarme einer Spinne erstrecken sich die Stege und Wasservillen auf das Meer hinaus. Jede der Villen verfügt über drei Schlafzimmer, vier Badezimmer, einen Dachgarten und umlaufende Balkone im ersten Stockwerk. Wegen des sehr heißen Klimas ist die Kühlung der Gebäude von vorrangiger Bedeutung. Sie wird durch Querlüftung, integrierte Abschattungselemente und die Verwendung modernen energiesparenden Glases erzielt.

Der aufsehenerregendste Teil des Entwurfs sind die Erddächer der Landsitze. Dror beschreibt sie als „architektonischen Teppich", der es „jedem Bewohner erlaubt, sich unter einem Stück Land zu verbergen" – buchstäblich alles unter den Teppich zu kehren. Da Luxus auf der Insel ein derart wichtiger Aspekt ist, wurden die Dienst-

végétalisé et des balcons au premier étage. En raison du climat extrêmement chaud, il est essentiel de rafraîchir les lieux: les maisons offrent donc une ventilation transversale, des pare-soleil intégrés et sont équipés de verre écoénergétique.

Les toits en terre sont la partie la plus impressionnante des propriétés. Dror les décrit comme un « tapis architectural » qui « permet à tous les résidents de se cacher sous une couche de terre » – balayant littéralement tout ce qui se trouve sous le tapis. Le luxe étant un aspect important de l'île, les services et la circulation devaient rester invisibles, donc souterrains. Les architectes peuvent jouer avec le paysage intéressant de l'île et expérimenter la manière dont se mêlent la terre et les espaces intérieurs. La métaphore du tapis s'applique également à cette région du Golfe, célèbre pour son activité

previous page One of the seaside villas, known as Villa F, with grass roof. The "architectural carpet" helps the buildings blend with the natural environment.

vorherige Seite Eine der Küstenvillen, Villa F, mit ihrem Grasdach. Der „architektonische Teppich" lässt die Gebäude mit der natürlichen Umgebung verschmelzen.

page précédente L'une des villas en bord de mer, la Villa F, avec son toit de verdure. Le « tapis architectural » permet au bâtiment de se mêler à l'environnement naturel.

above Paris-based studio AW2 designed the island's hotel seen here with the pool.

oben Das in Paris ansässige Studio AW2 entwarf das Hotel auf der Insel, das hier mit Schwimmbecken zu sehen ist.

ci-dessus Le cabinet parisien AW2 a conçu l'hôtel de l'île, ici avec la piscine.

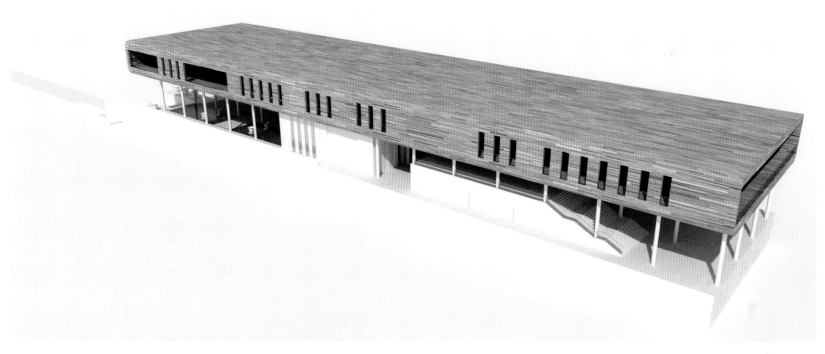

top The hotel's geometric shape is deliberately intended to contrast with the free flowing shape of the island.

oben Die geometrische Form des Hotels soll bewusst einen Gegensatz zu der in freiem Fluss befindlichen Form der Insel bilden.

haut La forme géométrique de l'hôtel contraste volontairement avec la forme plus fluide de l'île.

above left The extensive use of pools and ponds adds an ethereal layer to the hotel giving the building a sense of weightlessness.

oben links Die ausgiebige Verwendung von Becken und Teichen verleiht dem Hotel etwas Ätherisches, indem sie ihm einen Anschein von Gewichtslosigkeit verleiht.

en haut à gauche Les nombreuses piscines et bassins ajoutent une touche aérienne à l'hôtel, conférant au bâtiment une certaine légèreté.

above right A hovering structure, the hotel is designed to be read from afar as a modern ship's hull floating on water.

oben rechts Als schwebendes Bauwerk wurde das Hotel so entworfen, dass es aus der Ferne wie der Rumpf eines modernen Schiffes im Wasser aussieht.

en haut à droite Structure flottante, l'hôtel doit être vu de loin, tel la coque d'un navire sur l'eau.

above Cross ventilation, integrated shading devices, and the use of modern glass will help cool the water villas.

oben Querbelüftung, integrierte Beschattungselemente und die Verwendung modernen Glases helfen bei der Kühlung der Villen.

ci-dessus La ventilation transversale, les pare-soleil intégrés et le verre permettent de garder une température fraîche dans les villas sur l'eau.

right Another of the seaside villas, Villa B. Dror plan to provide the seaside villas with a sense of nature and privacy.

rechts Eine weitere Küstenvilla, Villa B. Dror will den Küstenvillen ein Gefühl von Natur und Privatsphäre verleihen.

droite Autre villa en bord de mer, la Villa B; Dror prévoit d'ajouter aux villas en bord de mer une aura de nature et d'intimité.

far right Interior view looking out to sea from the entrance of Villa B.

ganz rechts Innenansicht vom Eingang der Villa B hinaus auf das Meer.

au loin à droite Vue intérieure, avec vue sur la mer depuis l'entrée de la villa B.

buildings, they are given a sense of solitude and natural setting.

A combination of innovative landscape design and modern, minimalist architecture, Dror's intentions are for residents to experience nature while living in highly-designed spaces. The "paradise" island caters for everything, including three restaurants, a spa, fitness center, and private helipad.

leistungsbereiche und die Belüftung unter der Erde verborgen angelegt. Die Architekten hatten die Gelegenheit, mit der interessanten Landschaft der Insel zu spielen und mit der Verschmelzung von Land und Innenräumen zu experimentieren. Die Teppichmetapher ist außerdem von Bedeutung, weil die Golfregion für ihr Teppichhandwerk berühmt ist. So werden traditionelle Teppichmuster für die Decken der Villen auf der Unterseite des „Teppichs" entworfen. Die Tarnung der Gebäude verleiht ihnen ein Gefühl der Zurückgezogenheit in einer natürlichen Umgebung.

Dror möchte den Bewohnern durch die Verbindung aus innovativem Landschaftsdesign und moderner, minimalistischer Architektur Gelegenheit bieten, die Natur zu erfahren, und ihnen zugleich das Gefühl geben, in Räumen mit ausgefeiltem Design zu leben. Die „Paradiesinsel" bietet alle Annehmlichkeiten, einschließlich dreier Restaurants, eines Wellnessbads, eines Fitnesscenters und eines privaten Hubschrauberlandeplatzes.

de tissage. Des motifs de tapis traditionnels seront dessinés aux plafonds des villas, sur le revers du « tapis ». En camouflant les bâtiments, on leur confère une aura de solitude et de naturel.

Combinaison d'aménagement paysager et d'architecture minimaliste, les intentions de Dror sont de faire connaître la nature aux résidents, tout en profitant d'espaces modernes. « L'île paradisiaque » s'occupe de tout: trois restaurants, un spa, un centre de fitness et un héliport privé sont à la disposition des visiteurs.

Artificial Islands
Künstliche Inseln
Îles artificielles

Kansai International Airport I Central Park Grin Grin I The Palm Jumeirah
Sanya Phoenix Island I Federation Island

Artificial, or man-made, islands are nothing new. In Ireland and Scotland in prehistoric times there were *crannógs*—small, circular lake islands; much of Venice was expanded using timber rafts and wooden piles; and the Dutch developed polders—square pieces of land protected from the water by means of dikes. However, in the 21st century the reasons for building new islands have changed. Today, architects are commissioned to construct airports, hotels, and holiday resorts at sea. In countries like Japan, where much of the country is either built-up or mountainous, building in the sea is a necessary alternative. In Dubai, where most of the land is desert, creating new cities on water has obvious appeal. For the engineer, the challenge is to create islands that can withstand earthquakes, sea erosion, subsidence, and even typhoons. For the architect, it is to build something spectacular.

previous page The Palm Jumeirah before building construction began.

vorherige Seite Das Palm Jumeirah vor der Bauausführung.

page précédente Le Palmier de Jumeirah avant le commencement de la construction.

left Kansai International Airport, designed by Renzo Piano, sits on a man-made island.

links Der von Renzo Piano entworfene Internationale Flughafen von Kansai sitzt auf einer künstlich angelegten Insel.

gauche L'aéroport international de Kansai, conçu par Renzo Piano, se trouve sur une île artificielle.

Les îles artificielles, ou créées par l'homme, ne sont pas nouvelles: en Irlande et en Écosse, aux temps préhistoriques, on trouvait des crannógs, petites îles circulaires sur des lacs; Venise était étendue par des radeaux et des piliers de bois; et les Néerlandais ont développé les polders, des étendues de terre protégées de l'eau par des digues. Cependant, au XXIe siècle, les raisons de construire de nouvelles îles ont changé. Aujourd'hui, les architectes sont chargés de concevoir des aéroports, des hôtels et des centres de vacances en bord de mer. Dans des pays tels que le Japon, où la plupart du territoire est construit en hauteur ou constitué de montagnes, les constructions flottantes sont une alternative nécessaire. À Dubaï, où le désert couvre une grande partie du territoire, la construction de nouvelles villes sur l'eau a un attrait évident. Pour l'ingénieur, le défi consiste à créer des îles pouvant supporter les tremblements de terre, l'érosion de la mer, l'affaissement et les typhons. Pour l'architecte, le défi est de créer un édifice spectaculaire.

Künstliche oder von Menschenhand angelegte Inseln sind nichts Neues. In Irland und Schottland gab es bereits in prähistorischer Zeit sogenannte Crannógs – kleine, in Seen gelegene runde Inseln; ein Großteil von Venedig wurde mit Hilfe hölzerner Fundamente und Pfosten erbaut, und die Niederländer entwickelten Polder – quadratische Grundstücke, die mit Deichen vor dem Wasser geschützt wurden. Im 21. Jahrhundert haben sich jedoch die Gründe für die Anlegung neuer Inseln geändert. Heute werden Architekten beauftragt, Flughäfen, Hotels und Ferienanlagen im Meer zu entwerfen. In Ländern wie Japan, wo ein Großteil des verfügbaren Bodens entweder bebaut oder bergig ist, wird das Bauen im Meer zur notwendigen Alternative. In Dubai, das zu einem großen Teil aus Wüste besteht, hat die Schaffung neuer Städte auf dem Wasser einen offensichtlichen Reiz. Für den Ingenieur besteht die Herausforderung darin, Inseln zu schaffen, die Erdbeben, Erosion durch das Meer, Bodensenkungen und sogar Taifunen widerstehen können; für den Architekten besteht sie darin, etwas Spektakuläres zu bauen.

Kansai
International Airport

Kansai, Japan
Renzo Piano Building Workshop
1994

The Kansai International Airport, which was completed in 1994 after 7 years of construction, is one of the world's most extraordinary examples of civil engineering. When it was finished, it became only the second man-made artefact visible from space, along with the Great Wall of China. Consisting of an artificial island, airport passenger terminal, and a double-level bridge to the mainland it cost an estimated $20 billion.

The first part of the project was to build an artificial island in the middle of Osaka Bay. The region around Osaka is heavily built up or mountainous so there was no obvious location for a new international airport. It was therefore decided to build it on a new island, sited so that planes would take off and land over the sea. Both the building and island had to be built to last as earthquakes and typhoons are common in the area.

Located 3 miles offshore, the 1,262-acre island is 59-65 feet deep and was built on 65 feet of soft clay that had to be compacted in order to create a firm foundation. This was achieved by using 1 million sand piles on top of which 3.28 feet of sand were placed. Earth was placed on top of this, the weight of which squeezed the water out of the clay below. The perimeter of the islands was created using steel caisons sunk into the sea bed. Finally, crushed

Der Internationale Flughafen von Kansai, der 1994 nach sieben Jahren Bauzeit fertig gestellt wurde, ist eines der außergewöhnlichsten Beispiele des Bauingenieurwesens weltweit. Bei seiner Fertigstellung war er neben der Chinesischen Mauer das einzige andere von Menschenhand geschaffene Artefakt, das aus dem Weltall sichtbar war. Die aus einer künstlichen Insel, dem Passagierterminal des Flughafens und einer zweistöckigen Brücke zum Festland bestehende Anlage kostete schätzungsweise $20 Milliarden Dollar.

Der erste Teil des Projekts bestand darin, in der Mitte der Bucht von Osaka eine künstliche Insel zu schaffen. Die Gegend um Osaka ist stark bebaut oder bergig, so dass kein offensichtlicher Standort für den neuen Internationalen Flughafen vorhanden war. Deshalb wurde beschlossen, den Flughafen auf einer neuen Insel zu bauen, so dass die Flugzeuge über dem Meer starten und landen würden. Sowohl die Gebäude als auch die Insel mussten auf lange Sicht beständig gebaut werden, da in dieser Gegend häufig Erdbeben und Taifune auftreten.

Die 5 Kilometer vom Festland entfernte, 511 Hektar große Insel ist 18-20 Meter tief und wurde auf 20 Metern weichen Lehms erbaut, der gepresst werden musste, um ein festes

L'aéroport international de Kansai, achevé en 1994 après 7 ans de construction, est l'un des exemples d'ingénierie civile les plus spectaculaires au monde. Lorsque sa construction fut terminée, il est devenu la deuxième création humaine visible depuis l'espace, avec la Grande Muraille de Chine. L'île artificielle, le terminal passagers de l'aéroport et un double pont le reliant à la terre ont coûté près de 20 milliards de dollars.

La première partie du projet consistait à créer une île artificielle au milieu de la baie d'Osaka. La région d'Osaka a pour caractéristique d'être déjà densément bâtie et très montagneuse. Il n'y avait donc pas d'emplacement approprié pour un nouvel aéroport international. Il a donc été décidé de le construire sur une nouvelle île, positionnée de manière à ce que les avions puissent y décoller et atterrir. L'aéroport et l'île devaient tous deux être construits en tenant compte des tremblements de terre et des typhons relativement fréquents dans la région.

Située à 5 km au large des côtes, l'île de 511 hectares et de 18-20 mètres de profondeur a été construite sur 20 mètres d'argile souple ayant dû être compactée pour obtenir des fondations solides. Un million de tas de sable ont dû être utilisés, surmontés d'un mètre supplémentaire. L'ajout de terre a permis à l'eau

left Great glazed gable wall at one end of the terminal building.

oben Große verglaste Giebelwand an einem Ende des Terminalgebäudes.

gauche L'immense mur pignon vitré à une extrémité du terminal.

above View showing the curving roof, designed to follow the flow of air.

oben Ansicht des gebogenen Daches, das den Luftströmungen folgen soll.

ci-dessus Vue du toit courbé, conçu pour suivre le flux d'air.

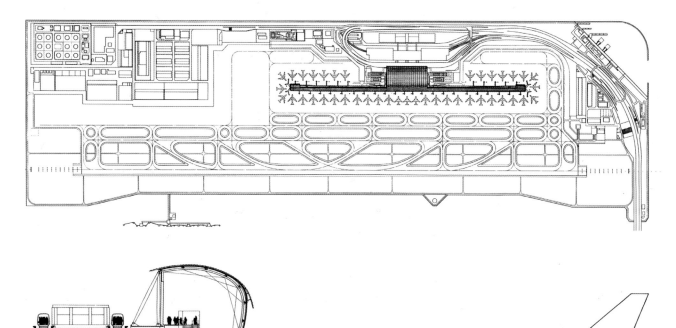

rock (three mountains were raised in the process) was used for landfill.

The airport itself was designed as a hub for Southeast Asia and Australasia serving 25 million passengers a year. It consists of one runway, 1 mile long, and a dramatic sweeping terminal building. The multi-floor terminal has three main levels, international departures on top, domestic flights in the middle, and international arrivals at the bottom. Domestic flights use the central portion and international flights the wings. An open-plan design was employed for a number of reasons: it allows for transparency; it was a way to dramatically expose the structural elements; and it helps passengers quickly orientate themselves. The main walls are glazed and the massive silver curving roof is constructed of steel panels. Using a toroidal curved shape, the roof is designed to follow the natural curve of decelerating air, thereby avoiding the use of air conditioning. Designed to be seen from the air, it looks like a giant glider.

Although thoroughly modern in its design and materials, the building has traditional elements: the exposed roof structure has strong links with traditional Japanese temples and the exposed roof trusses and props and lofty ceilings are reminiscent of medieval architecture. Nature is an important influence

Fundament zu schaffen. Dies wurde mit Hilfe von 1 Million Sandpfeiler erreicht, auf die eine Schicht von 1 Meter Sand aufgeschüttet wurde. Darüber wurde Erde geschichtet, deren Gewicht das Wasser aus dem darunter liegenden Lehm quetschte. Der Umriss der Insel wurde mit Hilfe von Senkkästen aus Stahl geschaffen, die in den Meeresboden eingelassen wurden. Schließlich wurden gebrochene Felsen zur Aufschüttung verwendet (bei dem Verfahren wurden drei Berge abgetragen).

Der Flughafen selbst wurde als Drehscheibe für Südostasien und Australasien mit einer geplanten Passagierzahl von 25 Millionen pro Jahr entworfen. Er besteht aus einer 1,7 Kilometer langen Landebahn und einem spektakulären, weitläufigen Terminalgebäude. Das mehrstöckige Terminal verfügt über drei Ebenen: internationale Abflüge im obersten Stockwerk, Inlandsflüge in der Mitte und internationale Ankünfte im untersten Stockwerk. Für die Inlandsflüge wird der mittlere Abschnitt verwendet und für die internationalen Flüge die Seitenflügel. Aus mehrerlei Gründen wurde ein offen angelegter Entwurf bevorzugt: Er ermöglicht Transparenz, bietet die Möglichkeit, die auffälligen Strukturelemente offen zu legen, und hilft den Passagieren, sich schnell zu orientieren. Die wichtigsten Wände sind verglast

de l'argile des couches inférieures de ressortir, sous l'effet de masse. Des caissons en acier plongés dans le fond marin délimitent le périmètre de l'île et le terrain a été comblé par de la pierre concassée (trois montagnes ont été élevées durant le processus).

L'aéroport en lui-même a été conçu comme une plaque tournante pour l'Asie du Sud-est et l'Australasie, desservant 25 millions de passagers par an. Il est constitué d'une piste d'1,7 km de long et d'un terminal spectaculairement étendu comptant trois niveaux. Les départs internationaux se font au dernier étage, les vols intérieurs au milieu et les arrivées internationales en bas. Les vols intérieurs occupent la partie centrale et les vols internationaux les ailes. Pour de nombreuses raisons, la construction est ouverte: elle permet de laisser entrer la lumière, d'exposer les éléments structurels et de faciliter l'orientation des passagers. Les principales cloisons sont vitrées et l'imposant toit courbé argenté est constitué de panneaux en acier. La courbe toroïdale du toit suit la courbe naturelle de l'air de décélération, évitant ainsi d'équiper l'aéroport de climatisation. Vue de haut, la construction ressemble à un planeur géant.

Malgré la modernité du design et des matières, l'ouvrage est constitué d'éléments

above The man-made island is linked to the mainland by a double level bridge.

oben Die künstlich angelegte Insel ist über eine zweistöckige Brücke mit dem Festland verbunden.

ci-dessus L'île artificielle est reliée à la terre par un double pont.

right The central main terminal roof sweeps into the boarding wings.

rechts Das geschwungene Dach des zentralen Haupt-terminals zieht sich bis zu den Flügeln des Abfluggebäudes hin.

droite Le terminal central principal s'étend dans l'aile d'embarquement.

left Massive structural elements, including roof trusses and props, are left exposed both outside and inside to give the building a sense on monumentality.

links Massive strukturelle Elemente, einschließlich der Dachbinder und Stützen, liegen sowohl außen als auch innen frei, um dem Gebäude ein Gefühl von Monumentalität zu verleihen.

gauche Des éléments de structure massifs, dont les poutres de la toiture et les piliers, sont exposés à l'extérieur comme à l'intérieur pour conférer à la structure un sens de monumentalité.

too—the interior is like a huge skeleton, its white arches like the ribs of a dinosaur. From above, its flowing silvery roof blends in with the surrounding environment of the water, waves, and wind.

und das massive gebogene silberfarbene Dach besteht aus Stahlplatten. Die ringförmig gebogene Form des Daches sollte der natürlichen Verlangsamung der Luftströme folgen, so dass die Verwendung einer Klimaanlage vermieden werden konnte. Von der Luft aus gesehen sieht der Flughafen wie ein gigantisches Segel-flugzeug aus.

Obgleich in Entwurf und Materialien durch und durch modern, verfügt das Gebäude auch über traditionelle Elemente: Die freigelegte Dachstruktur hat Gemeinsamkeiten mit traditionellen japanischen Tempeln, und die Dachträger und -stützen und die luftigen Decken erinnern an mittelalterliche Architektur. Auch die Natur übt einen bedeutenden Einfluss aus: Das Innere wirkt wie ein riesiges Skelett, seine weißen Bögen wie die Rippen eines Dinosauriers. Von oben verschmilzt das fließende, silbrige Dach mit der umgebenden Landschaft aus Wasser, Wellen und Wind.

traditionnels: la structure exposée de la toiture rappelle fortement les temples japonais, tandis que les fermes, piliers et hauts plafonds rappellent l'architecture médiévale. La nature a également influencé la conception: l'intérieur s'apparente à un squelette géant, ses arches blanches imitant les côtes d'un dinosaure. Vu du ciel, le toit argenté ondulé se fond avec l'environnement, l'eau, les vagues et le vent.

Central Park Grin Grin

Fukuoka, Japan
Toyo Ito & Associates Architects
2007

below Islands on an island. Three curving mounds seem to grow out of the landscape.

unten Inseln auf einer Insel. Drei bogenförmige Hügel scheinen aus der Landschaft zu wachsen.

ci-dessous Des îles sur une île. Trois monticules semblent pousser dans le paysage.

right Aerial view showing man-made Island City.

rechts Luftbild der künstlich angelegten Island City.

droite Vue aérienne d'Island City, une ville flottante artificielle.

below Each area can be walked over, under, and through.

unten Besucher können über, unter und durch jeden Bereich hindurch laufen.

ci-dessous Il est possible de grimper, de passer en dessous et de traverser chaque monticule.

right Model of three interconnected spaces and artificial lake in front.

rechts Modell der drei miteinander verbundenen Räume und des künstlichen Sees im Vordergrund.

droite Maquette de trois espaces interconnectés et du lac artificiel au premier plan.

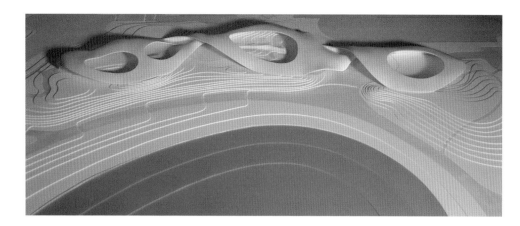

Central Park Grin Grin is situated on Island City, an artificial island in Hakata Bay in the Kyushu region of Japan. The island itself is a 988-acre platform of reclaimed land that began development in 1994. It was designed to accommodate a business park, a residential area, and 37 acres of environmentally friendly green spaces next to the port of Fukouka.

In 2002, Japanese architect Toyo Ito won a competition to build Grin Grin as part of the development of the park area. Ito is world-renowned for his innovative architecture. However, his work is typically more rigid than this building. For example, the Sendai Mediatheque and Tod's store, both in Tokyo, are wonderfully inventive but very linear. In contrast, this project is a series of sinuous and curving buildings, highly biomorphic in shape.

Three covered areas enclosing botanical gardens sit next to an artificial lake. From a distance the building looks like giant green waves flowing across the landscape. It seems to grow out of the lake shore, its huge craters and mounds reflected in the lake's water. From above, they look like three interconnected islands.

Grass and vegetation cover the outside of the domes and a complex series of wooden walkways weave over the roofs allowing visitors

Central Park Grin Grin befindet sich auf Island City, einer künstlich angelegten Insel in der Bucht von Hakata auf der japanischen Insel Kyushu. Die Insel selbst ist eine 400 Hektar große Plattform aus dem Meer gewonnenen Landes, mit deren Bebauung im Jahr 1994 begonnen wurde. Sie sollte ein Gewerbegebiet, ein Wohngebiet und ein 15 Hektar großes Gebiet mit umweltfreundlichen Grünflächen neben dem Hafen von Fukuoka beherbergen.

2002 gewann der japanische Architekt Toyo Ito den Wettbewerb zur Erbauung von Grin Grin als Teil der Entwicklung des Parklandes. Ito ist weltbekannt für seine innovative Architektur. Normalerweise sind seine Entwürfe jedoch strenger und geradliniger als dieses Gebäude. Die Sendai-Mediathek und Tods Kaufhaus, beide in Tokio, sind auf wundervolle Weise innovativ, aber sehr linear. Im Gegensatz dazu besteht dieses Bauprojekt aus einer Reihe wellen-förmiger und gebogener Gebäude, die in ihrer Form höchst biomorph sind.

Neben einem künstlich angelegten See befinden sich drei überdachte Bereiche mit botanischen Gärten. Aus der Ferne sehen die Gebäude aus wie gigantische grüne Wellen, die über die Landschaft fluten. Sie scheinen aus dem Seeufer herauszuwachsen, ihre riesigen Krater und Hügel spiegeln sich im Wasser des

Le Parc Grin Grin se trouve sur Island City, une île artificielle située dans la baie de Hakata, dans la région de Kyushu au Japon. L'île en elle-même est une plate-forme de 400 hectares de terre dont le développement a commencé en 1994. Elle a été conçue pour accueillir un centre d'affaires, une zone résidentielle et 15 hectares d'espaces verts écologiques à côté du port de Fukuoka.

En 2002, l'architecte japonais Toyo Ito a remporté le concours pour construire le parc Grin Grin au sein du projet. Toyo Ito est reconnu dans le monde entier pour son architecture innovante mais son travail est généralement plus rigide que ses ouvrages. La Médiathèque de Sendai et le magasin Tod par exemple, tous deux à Tokyo, sont magnifiquement inventifs mais très linéaires. Par opposition, le projet est une série de bâtiments sinueux et incurvés, de forme extrêmement biomorphiques. Trois zones couvertes comprenant des jardins botaniques sont juxtaposées à un lac artificiel. À distance, les bâtiments ressemblent à une vague verte géante qui traverse le paysage. Elle semble sortir du lac, ses cratères et monticules géants se reflétant dans l'eau. Vus de haut, ils ressemblent à trois îles interconnectées.

L'herbe et la végétation recouvrent l'extérieur des dômes et une série complexe de passerelles en bois passe sur les toits permettant aux

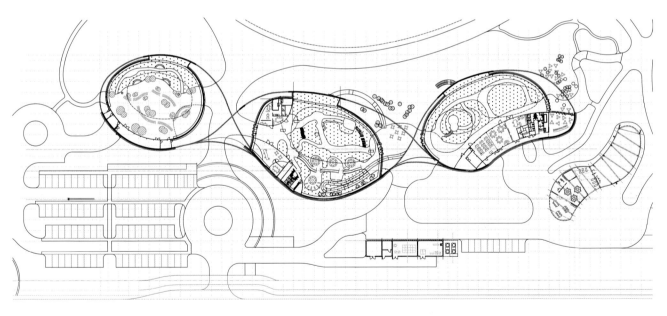

left The domes are designed as spaces for reading, eating, and relaxing in a "green" environment.

links Die Kuppeln wurden als Räume zum Lesen, Essen und Entspannen in einer „grünen" Umgebung entworfen.

gauche Les dômes sont des espaces de lecture, de restauration et de repos dans un environnement écologique.

to walk up, over, and underneath the structures. Parts of the structure cantilever to provide shelter and shade, as well as entrances and seating areas. The main structure is a series of undulating forms covered in FRP (Fiberglass Reinforced Plastic) and a 15.7-in. thick skin of reinforced concrete. Cleverly, there are no joints or seams in the smooth surface of the cement. Inserted into the roofs are glass skylights which allow natural light to flood into the greenhouses below and which can be opened for ventilation.

Inside the park, paths meander through the vegetation of the greenhouses. Each greenhouse has a different plant cultivation theme, botanical displays of the region's flora. However, the zones are intended as more than just places to appreciate plants—around each exhibit are spaces for reading books, eating lunch, or growing your own plants. These are calm oases for learning, resting, and eating.

This building is technically very complex, but the way the intersecting spaces blend with the

Sees. Von oben sehen sie wie drei miteinander verbundene Inseln aus.

Die Kuppeln sind von außen mit Gras und Vegetation bedeckt und über die Dächer zieht sich ein komplexes Netz aus hölzernen Stegen, die es Besuchern ermöglichen, auf, über und unter den Strukturen her zu laufen. Einzelne Teile des Bauwerks sind freitragend und bieten Schutz und Schatten sowie Platz für Eingänge und Sitzbereiche. Das Hauptgebäude besteht aus einer Reihe wellenförmiger Elemente, die mit FVK (Faserverbundkunststoff) und einer 40 cm dicken Schicht aus Stahlbeton bedeckt sind. Intelligenterweise befinden sich in der glatten Oberfläche des Zements keine Verbindungsstellen und Nähte. In die Dächer sind Oberlichter aus Glas eingelassen, die natürliches Licht in die darunter liegenden Gewächshäuser fluten lassen und zur besseren Belüftung geöffnet werden können.

Innerhalb des Parks winden sich Pfade durch die Vegetation der Gewächshäuser. Jedes

visiteurs de grimper, de passer sur ou sous les structures.

Certaines parties de la structure sont en porte-à-faux pour fournir un abri et de l'ombre, ainsi que des entrées et des espaces d'attente. La structure principale est constituée de plusieurs formes ondoyantes couvertes de PRV (plastique renforcé de fibres de verre) et d'une couche de 40 cm de béton. Aucun joint ni raccord n'apparaît sur la surface lisse cimentée. Des lucarnes laissent entrer la lumière dans les serres et peuvent être ouvertes pour l'aération.

À l'intérieur du parc, des chemins serpentent à travers la végétation des serres. Chaque serre offre un thème de culture différent, une vitrine botanique de la région. Ces zones ont cependant un rôle plus étendu. Autour de chaque exposition sont installés des espaces de lecture, de restauration ou de culture, où il est possible de faire pousser ses propres plantes. Ce sont des oasis de sérénité pour apprendre, se détendre et se restaurer.

left The smooth surface of the reinforced concrete exterior.

links Die glatte Oberfläche der äußeren Stahlbetonwände.

gauche Surface extérieure lisse, en béton armé.

above Entrance to one of the domes. Glass sunlights can be opened.

oben Eingang in eine der Kuppeln. Die Oberlichter aus Glas können geöffnet werden.

ci-dessus Entrée de l'un des dômes. Les panneaux en verre au plafond peuvent être ouverts.

right Plants inside one of the greenhouses.

rechts Pflanzen in einem der Gewächshäuser.

droite Les serres abritent des plantes.

below By covering the domes in grass and vegetation it allows them to blend in and seem less artificial.

unten Die Bepflanzung der Kuppeln mit Gras und Vegetation lässt sie mit der Umgebung verschmelzen und weniger künstlich wirken.

ci-dessous En recouvrant les dômes d'herbe et de végétation, ils se fondent et semblent plus naturels.

right Parts of the building are cantilevered to provide shelter and shade, as well as entrances.

rechts Teile des Gebäudes sind freitragend und bieten Schutz und Schatten sowie Eingangsmöglichkeiten.

droite Certaines parties de la construction sont en porte-à-faux pour fournir un abri, de l'ombre, et servir d'entrée.

landscape make it look simple. Computer simulation allowed Ito to work out a structurally optimal shape when bending the original shapes. The result is a set of free-form, organic shapes. This concept of an "emerging grid" is described by the architect himself as a "transformation of standardized rigidity into fluid organic space… that signals endless new possibilities interrelating architecture and people."

Gewächshaus ist mit einer thematisch anderen Pflanzenkultur bepflanzt, jede eine botanische Darstellung der einheimischen Flora. Die einzelnen Zonen sollen jedoch mehr als nur Orte sein, an denen Besucher Pflanzen betrachten können – um jedes Exponat herum sind Flächen zum Lesen, für Picknicks oder für den Anbau eigener Pflanzen angelegt. Es sind ruhige Oasen zum Lernen, Ausspannen und Essen.

Technisch sind die Gebäude sehr komplex, aber die Art, in der die sich überschneidenden Räume mit der Landschaft verschmelzen, lässt sie schlicht aussehen. Eine Computersimulation erlaubte es Ito, eine bautechnisch optimale Form zu finden, als er die ursprünglichen Formen biegen ließ. Das Ergebnis ist eine Reihe frei geformter, organischer Formen. Dieses Konzept eines „entstehenden Netzes" ist laut dem Architekten selbst „eine Umwandlung einer standardisierten Starrheit in einen flüssigen, organischen Raum… die unendliche neue Möglichkeiten in der Beziehung von Architektur und Mensch verspricht."

Cet ouvrage est très complexe d'un point de vue technique mais la manière dont les différents espaces se fondent dans le paysage le rend très simple. La simulation sur ordinateur a permis à Toyo Ito de trouver une forme optimale sur le plan structurel en travaillant les formes d'origine : il en résulte des formes organiques. L'architecte décrit ce concept de « quadrillage émergent » comme une « transformation de la rigidité standardisée en espace naturel fluide qui indique des possibilités infinies de lier l'architecture et les personnes. »

The Palm Jumeirah

Dubai, UAE

Atkins Design Studio

2006–2012

left Looking back toward the shore with villas to the left and right.

links Blick zum Ufer mit Villen auf der linken und rechten Seite.

gauche Vue vers la côte et villas à gauche et à droite.

right top Satellite view of the Dubai coastline. Jumeirah is the middle palm island.

rechts oben Satellitenbild der Küste von Dubai. Jumeirah ist die mittlere Palmeninsel.

ci-dessus à droite Vue satellite de la côte de Dubaï. Jumeirah est l'île en forme de palmier située au centre.

right bottom Rendering of the island showing Trump Tower in foreground and Atlantis Hotel on breakwater.

rechts unten Wiedergabe der Insel mit dem Trump Tower im Vordergrund und dem Atlantis Hotel auf dem Wellenbrecher.

ci-dessous à droite Image numérique de l'île avec la Tour Trump au premier plan et l'hôtel Atlantis en brise-lames.

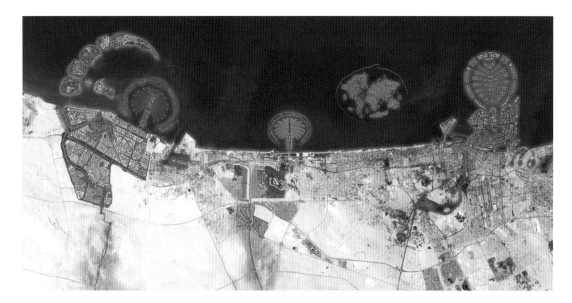

The Palm Jumeirah is probably the most remarkable man-made island ever built. Just off the coast of Jumeirah, the 1,359-acre island has been developed by Nakheel, and is designed in the shape of a date palm, the national plant of the United Arab Emirates. Although there are two other artificial palm-shaped islands nearby—The Palm Jebel Ali and The Palm Deira—both of which are bigger, the Jumeirah was the first to be built on.

Land reclamation began in 2001 and in 2006 the first residential units were handed over. The engineering task was massive. More than 3,300 million cubic meters of sand and 7 million tons of rock were used in the construction of the island, and over 40,000 workers were involved. Sand was dredged from the bottom of the sea to create the islands and the crescent breakwater was built using rocks in order to create a natural reef. The crescent has two breaks either side to allow for natural tidal flow in order to prevent the seawater becoming stagnant.

There are three parts to the island—the trunk linking the island to the shore; the fronds, 17 in total including the spine, branching out from the trunk; and the encircling crescent that forms the curved breakwater. High-rise apartments, hotels, and shopping malls are located along the trunk known as the Palm

The Palm Jumeirah ist vermutlich die außergewöhnlichste Insel, die je von Menschenhand angelegt wurde. Die 560 Hektar große, unmittelbar vor der Küste von Jumeirah gelegene Insel wurde von Nakheel erschlossen und in der Form einer Dattelpalme gestaltet, der Nationalpflanze der Vereinigten Arabischen Emirate. Obwohl sich in der Nähe zwei weitere künstliche Inseln in Palmenform befinden – The Palm Jebel Ali und The Palm Deira, die beide größer sind – war Jumeirah die erste.

Die Bodengewinnung begann im Jahr 2001 und schon im Jahr 2006 waren die ersten Wohneinheiten fertig gestellt. Die Aufgabe der Bauingenieure war gigantisch. 95 Millionen Kubikmeter Sand und 7 Millionen Tonnen Felsen wurden für die Aufschüttung der Insel verwendet, über 40.000 Arbeiter waren daran beteiligt. Bei der Aufschüttung der Insel wurde Sand vom Grund des Meeres ausgebaggert, und der mondsichelförmige Wellenbrecher wurde mit Hilfe von Felsen angelegt, um ein natürliches Riff zu schaffen. Die Mondsichel verfügt über zwei Einschnitte auf jeder Seite, um einen natürlichen Gezeitenstrom zu ermöglichen und einen Stillstand des Meerwassers zu vermeiden.

Die Insel besteht aus drei Teilen – dem Stamm, der die Insel mit dem Ufer verbindet, den einschließlich des Dorns insgesamt 17 Palmen-

Le Palmier de Jumeirah est probablement l'île artificielle la plus remarquable jamais construite. A courte distance au large de Jumeirah, l'île de 560 hectares a été développée par Nakheel et créée en forme de palmier, l'arbre national des Émirats arabes unis. Bien que deux autres îles artificielles en forme de palmier se trouvent à proximité, le Palmier de Jebel Ali et le Palmier de Deira, par ailleurs plus grandes, le Palmier de Jumeirah a été la première île.

Le remblai a débuté en 2001 et en 2006, les premières résidences étaient disponibles. Le travail technique a été considérable et la construction de l'île a nécessité quatre-vingt-quinze millions de mètres de cubes de sable, sept millions de tonnes de pierres et 40 000 ouvriers. Le sable a été dragué du fond de la mer pour créer l'île et les brise-lames ont été construits avec des rochers, afin de créer un récif naturel. Le croissant est interrompu de chaque côté pour laisser les vagues pénétrer et empêcher la stagnation de l'eau.

L'île comprend trois parties: le tronc, qui relie l'île à la côte; les frondes, 17 au total, dont l'épine poursuit la lancée du tronc; et le croissant qui encercle le tout en formant le brise-lames. Des tours d'appartements, des hôtels et des centres commerciaux sont placés

Golden Mile. In contrast, 8,000 low-rise holiday villas, each with its own private garden and access to the water, are built in neat rows along the fronds. More hotels, including the Atlantis, and luxury villas are to be found on the crescent. A high level monorail runs along the length of the trunk connecting the island to the mainland over a 984-foot bridge, and a six-lane tunnel, 82 feet below sea level, links the spine to the crescent.

From an architectural point of view, the most innovative building on the island is the Trump International Hotel and Tower, located in the middle of the Golden Mile. The stone, steel and glass façaded tower is the work of the British firm Atkins, who are best known for the Burj Al Arab Hotel further along the coast. The building climbs to over 820 feet, two high-rise towers, 50 and 61 stories respectively, 85 feet apart at their closest. The enormous space—approximately 2 million square feet—contains a hotel, apartments, boutique offices, a resort spa, swimming pool, health club, restaurants, business center, and parking facilities for 1,200 cars. At the bottom the towers stand on a four-story bisected podium structure with the monorail running underneath the lobby. The towers then split again only to reconnect at level 39 giving the structure its unique design—

wedeln, die sich vom Stamm fächerförmig ausbreiten, und der diese kreisförmig umgebenden Mondsichel, die den gekrümmten Wellenbrecher bildet. Entlang des Stamms befinden sich Hochhausapartments, Hotels und Einkaufszentren, die als Goldene Meile der Palm bezeichnet werden. Im Gegensatz dazu wurden auf den Palmenwedeln in ordentlichen Reihen 8.000 Urlaubsvillen von geringer Höhe erbaut, die jeweils über ihren eigenen privaten Garten und Zugang zum Wasser verfügen. Weitere Hotels, einschließlich des Atlantis, und Luxusvillen befinden sich auf der Mondsichel. Eine erhöhte Monorail-Bahn verläuft entlang des gesamten Stamms und verbindet die Insel über eine 300 Meter lange Brücke mit dem Festland. Ein sechsspuriger Tunnel 25 Meter unter dem Meeresboden verbindet den Dorn mit dem Sichelmond.

Das vom architektonischen Standpunkt aus gesehen innovativste Gebäude auf der Insel ist der Trump Tower in der Mitte der Goldenen Meile. Der aus Stein, Stahl und Glas erbaute Turm ist das Werk des britischen Architektur-büros Atkins, das für das Burj Al Arab Hotel etwas weiter entlang der Küste wohl am bekanntesten ist. Das Gebäude erhebt sich bis auf über 250 Meter Höhe und umfasst zwei Hochhaustürme mit 50 bzw. 61 Stockwerken,

le long du tronc, dénommé le Palm Golden Mile. 8 000 maisons de vacances, chacune avec jardin privé et accès à la mer, sont construites en lignes étroites le long des frondes. D'autres hôtels, dont l'Atlantis, et villas luxueuses se trouvent sur le croissant. Un monorail surélevé descend le long du tronc, reliant l'île à la terre par un pont de 300 mètres. Un tunnel à six voies, situé à 25 mètres sous le niveau de la mer, relie l'épine au croissant.

D'un point de vue architectural, l'ouvrage le plus innovant de l'île est la Tour Trump, située au milieu du Golden Mile. La tour en pierre, en acier et en verre est le travail du cabinet britannique Atkins, plus connu pour son hôtel Burj Al Arab, sur la côte. L'édifice, avec deux tours de 50 et 61 étages et distantes de 26 mètres à certains endroits, s'élève à plus de 250 mètres. L'espace immense, d'environ 200 000 mètres carrés, contient un hôtel, des appartements, des bureaux, un spa, une piscine, un club de sport, des restaurants, un centre d'affaires et un parking de 1 200 places. Les tours s'élèvent sur une plate-forme de quatre étages scindée en deux, le monorail passant sous le hall. Elles sont de nouveau séparées et se rejoignent au quarantième étage pour former ce design unique – la

above Surrounding breakwater has gaps to allow water currents in and out of the island.

oben Der umgebende Wellenbrecher verfügt über Öffnungen, um Wasserströme in und aus der Insel fließen zu lassen.

ci-dessus Le brise-lames comporte des ouvertures pour laisser les courants marins entrer et sortir de l'île.

left Construction of the Palm Golden Mile with high-rise apartments, hotels, and malls going up.

links Erbauung der Goldenen Meile der Palm mit den dort entstehenden Hochhaus-apartments, Hotels und Ein-kaufszentren.

gauche Construction du Palm Golden Mile avec les immenses appartements, hôtels et centres commerciaux.

above The Atlantis Hotel is situated on the breakwater directly opposite the Golden Mile.

oben Das Hotel Atlantis befindet sich auf dem Wellenbrecher unmittelbar gegenüber der Goldenen Meile.

ci-dessus L'hôtel Atlantis est placé sur le brise-lames, juste en face du Golden Mile.

right Computer rendering of the Palm Mall on the island. A monorail, above the road, links it to the mainland.

rechts Computerwiedergabe der Palm Mall auf der Insel. Eine Monorail-Bahn über der Straße verbindet die Insel mit dem Ufer.

droite Simulation par ordinateur du Palm Mall. Un monorail, au-dessus de la route, relie l'île à la terre.

288

the connecting structure is mainly made of steel to make it as light as possible. At the very top the "diamond-shaped pinnacle" is the most expensive penthouse in Dubai.

die am engsten Punkt nur 26 Meter voneinander entfernt sind. Das gewaltige Gebäude beherbergt auf etwa 200.000 Quadratmetern Fläche ein Hotel, Apartments, kleine, elegante Büros, ein Wellnessbad, ein Schwimmbecken, einen Fitnessclub, Restaurants, ein Geschäftszentrum und Parkmöglichkeiten für 1.200 Fahrzeuge. Das untere Ende der Hochhaustürme steht auf einer vierstöckigen, halbierten Podiumsstruktur, unter deren Lobby die Monorail-Bahn verläuft. Die Türme trennen sich dann erneut, um sich im 39. Stockwerk wieder zu vereinigen und geben dem Bauwerk sein einzigartiges Aussehen – die verbindende Struktur besteht hauptsächlich aus Stahl, um sie so leicht wie möglich zu halten. Die „diamantenförmige Turmspitze" ist das teuerste Penthouse in Dubai.

structure de connexion est principalement en acier, choisi pour sa légèreté. Au sommet, le « pinacle du bâtiment » en forme de losange abrite l'appartement le plus cher de Dubaï.

left Trump Tower designed by Atkins. Another of their buildings, the Burj Al Arab, can be seen in the distance.

links Der von Atkins entworfene Trump Tower. In der Ferne ist ein weiteres, von dem Architekturbüro entworfenes Gebäude, das Burj Al Arab, zu sehen.

gauche Tour Trump, conçue par Atkins. On distingue au loin un autre ouvrage des architectes, le Burj Al Arab.

below The steel and glass Trump Tower splits at the bottom before rejoining on level 39.

unten Der Trump Tower aus Glas und Stahl trennt sich im unteren Teil, bevor er sich auf Höhe des 39. Stockwerks wieder vereint.

ci-dessous La Tour Trump, en acier et en verre, est scindée à la base pour se réunifier au quarantième étage.

Sanya Phoenix Island

Sanya, China
MAD
2012

Sanya is the southernmost city in the Hainan Province, an area notable for its tropical coastline and many islands. It shares the same geographical latitude and climate as Miami and is a fashionable tourist resort for both Chinese and foreigners, in particular Russians.

Sanya Phoenix Island is a new man-made island built on a huge reef plate in Sanya Bay. The island has a total area of over 3 million square feet, and is 0.78 miles long by 1,150 feet wide. Masterplanned by Beijing-based architects MAD, whose ambition is to "examine and develop a unique concept of futurism," it will feature a variety of building types, including luxury housing, shops, a hotel, restaurants, port, yacht club, and convention center.

The plan is to create a new luxury harbor and tourist destination. A curving, donut-shaped high-rise hotel will be the centerpiece, a symbol of Sanya Phoenix Island. Next to it, there will be five smaller, but similarly shaped towers with luxury apartments. All six towers will dominate the skyline—the main tower will reach a height of 590 feet, while the smaller towers will be 325 feet high. Their organic elliptical shapes refer to waves from the sea or tropical plants.

Ten-thousand-ton luxury cruise liners will be able to dock at the west of the island in the new International Cruise Terminal. This is set to

Sanya ist die am weitesten südlich gelegene Stadt in der chinesischen Provinz Hainan, einer Gegend, die für ihre tropische Küste und ihre vielen Inseln bekannt ist. Sie liegt auf demselben geografischen Breitengrad wie Miami, hat dasselbe Klima und ist ein modischer Urlaubsort für Chinesen wie Ausländer, insbesondere Russen.

Sanya Phoenix Island ist eine neue, künstlich angelegte Insel auf einer riesigen Riffplatte in der Bucht von Sanya. Die Gesamtfläche der Insel beträgt 360.000 Quadratmeter; sie ist 1,25 Kilometer lang und 350 Meter breit. Die Gesamtplanung lag in den Händen des in Peking ansässigen Architekturbüros MAD, deren Anspruch es ist, „ein einzigartiges Konzept des Futurismus zu untersuchen und zu entwickeln". Die Insel wird eine Vielfalt von Gebäudetypen beherbergen, darunter Luxuswohnungen, Läden, ein Hotel, Restaurants, ein Hafen, einen Jachtklub und ein Tagungszentrum.

Der Plan sieht die Errichtung eines neuen Luxushafens und eines Touristenzentrums vor. Ein gebogenes Hotelhochhaus in Form eines Doughnuts wird den Mittelpunkt und das Wahrzeichen von Sanya Phoenix Island bilden. Daneben werden fünf kleinere, aber ähnlich geformte Hochhaustürme mit Luxusapartments entstehen. Die sechs Türme werden die

Sanya est la ville la plus au sud de la province de Hainan, une région connue pour sa côte tropicale et ses nombreuses îles. Elle partage la même latitude géographique et le même climat que Miami. C'est une station touristique en vogue pour les Chinois et les étrangers, notamment les Russes.

L'Île Phoenix est une île artificielle construite sur un immense plateau en relief dans la Baie de Sanya. Sa surface totale est de 360 000 mètres carrés. Elle mesure 1,25 kilomètre de long et 350 mètres de large. Le plan directeur a été réalisé par le cabinet d'architectes MAD, basé à Pékin, dont l'ambition est « d'examiner et de développer un concept unique de futurisme ». L'ouvrage comprendra différents types de bâtiments, dont des logements de luxe, des boutiques, un hôtel, des restaurants, un port, un club de yacht et un palais des congrès.

L'objectif est de créer un nouveau port de luxe et une nouvelle destination touristique. Un hôtel immense en forme d'anneau sera la pièce centrale, le symbole de l'île Phoenix. À côté, cinq autres hôtels, plus petits mais de forme similaire, offriront des appartements de luxe et les six tours domineront l'horizon. La tour principale atteindra 180 mètres de haut et la plus petite 99 mètres. Leurs formes elliptiques rappellent les vagues de la mer ou les plantes

become Asia's largest mother port for cruise liners serving hundreds of thousands of tourists. A yacht club and marina are planned for the other end of the island, on the northeastern shore, with berths for 150–300 yachts. Here the design is far more modest in scale. The club itself is a flowing organically-shaped low-rise building with skylights and encircling glass façades.

MAD's ambition is to do away with linear, cubic buildings and to create instead fluid designs (MAD's founder, Yansong Ma, worked for Zaha Hadid before forming his own studio in 2004). As Ma puts it, "I like floating. I like the unstable feeling. I like the curve."

Silhouette der Insel dominieren – der Hauptturm wird eine Höhe von 180 Metern erreichen, während die kleineren Türme 90 Meter hoch sein werden. Ihre organische Ellipsenform soll an die Wellen des Meeres oder an tropische Pflanzen erinnern.

Luxuskreuzfahrtschiffe mit einem Gewicht von 10.000 Tonnen werden an dem neuen Internationalen Kreuzfahrtterminal im Westen der Insel festmachen können. Damit steht schon fest, dass die Insel der größte asiatische Heimat-hafen für Kreuzfahrtschiffe werden wird, der den Anforderungen Hunderttausender von Touristen gerecht werden kann.

Für das andere Ende der Insel sind am Nordostufer ein Jachtklub und ein Jachthafen mit Ankerplätzen für 150-300 Boote geplant. Das Design ist hier viel bescheidener. Der Klub selbst ist ein fließendes, organisch geformtes niedriges Gebäude mit Oberlichtern und umgebenden Glasfassaden.

MADs Anspruch ist es, lineare, würfelförmige Gebäude zu vermeiden und stattdessen flüssige Bauwerke zu schaffen (bevor Yansong Ma im Jahre 2004 sein eigenes Studio gründete, arbeitete er für Zaha Hadid). Ma beschreibt seine Vorstellungen wie folgt: „Ich liebe Schwebendes. Ich liebe das Gefühl der Instabilität. Ich liebe Kurven."

tropicales. Des paquebots de croisière de dix milles tonnes pourront s'amarrer à l'ouest de l'île au nouveau Terminal international, qui devrait devenir le port le plus important d'Asie pour les paquebots de croisière, transportant des centaines de milliers de touristes. Un yacht club et une marina sont prévus à l'autre extrémité de l'île, sur la côte nord-est, grâce à des emplacements pour 150 à 300 yachts. Ici, le design est beaucoup plus modeste en termes d'échelle. Le club en lui-même est un bâtiment peu élevé, de forme organique, avec des lucarnes et des façades de verre.

L'ambition de MAD est de supprimer les bâtiments linéaires, cubiques et de créer des ouvrages fluides (le fondateur de MAD, Yansong Ma, a travaillé pour Zaha Hadid avant d'ouvrir son propre cabinet en 2004). Comme l'explique Yansong Ma, « J'aime la sensation d'instabilité. J'aime les courbes. »

previous page Computer drawing showing the hotel (right) and one of the apartment towers.

vorherige Seite Computerzeichnung mit Ansicht des Hotels (rechts) und eines der Apartmentblöcke.

page précédente Image numérique présentant l'hôtel (à droite) et l'une des tours d'appartements.

left A yacht club is at one end of the island, with tower apartments and hotel at the other.

links Auf der einen Seite der Insel befindet sich ein Jachtklub, während auf der anderen Seite Hochhausapartments und ein Hotel errichtet werden.

gauche Un yacht club se trouve à une extrémité de l'île, un hôtel est situé à l'autre.

above Chinese studio MAD's designs are typically organic and fluid.

oben Die Entwürfe des chinesischen Architekturstudios MAD sind üblicherweise organisch und flüssig.

ci-dessus Les travaux du cabinet d'architectes chinois MAD sont généralement fluides et organiques.

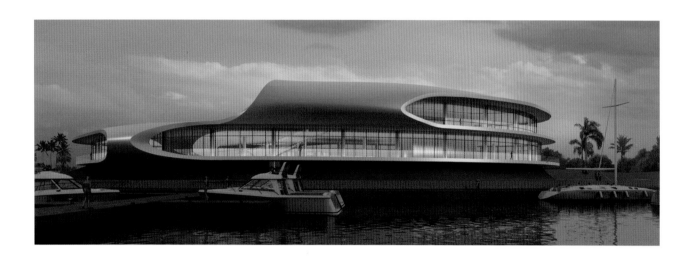

right The yacht club and marina.

rechts Der Jachtklub und der Jachthafen.

droite Le yacht club et la marina.

left Encircling glass façades on the yacht club will offer night views of the marina.

links Die kreisförmigen Glasfassaden des Jachtklubs bieten nächtliche Ausblicke auf den Hafen.

gauche Les façades en verre entourent le yacht club et offrent une vue sur la marina la nuit.

left Buildings on the northeast end of the island are low-lying in direct contrast to the towers at the other end.

links Die Gebäude auf der nordöstlichen Seite der Insel sind niedrig und bilden damit einen unmittelbaren Gegensatz zu den Hochhaustürmen am anderen Ende.

gauche Les bâtiments à l'extrémité nord-est de l'île sont relativement peu élevés par rapport aux tours situées à l'autre extrémité.

Federation Island

Sochi, Russia

Erick van Egeraat associated architects

2014

Erick van Egeraat was one of the founders of the renowned Dutch architecture studio Mecanoo, famous for its very inventive and playful designs. In 1997, Van Egeraat left to set up his own studio, EEA (Erick van Egeraat associated architects). They have described their style as "warm, inviting architecture" compared to what they consider the neo-modern style of Mecanoo.

In 2007, EEA presented their plans for Federation Island to the then President of the Russian Federation, Vladimir Putin. EEA had been commissioned to design and build a new series of islands off the Black Sea coast very near the town of Sochi. Sochi has won the right to host the 2014 Winter Olympics and Federation Island is planned to open at the same time. Although Russia has a vast coastline, very little is suitable for outdoor living. However, the climate at Sochi—hot summers and mild winters—is ideal for a holiday development.

Consisting of seven main islands, three breakwater islands, and many smaller ones, the miniature archipelago will be in the shape of the map of the Russian Federation. The waterways will mirror Russia's river network, while Russia's mountains will be reflected in miniature on the islands. It will become a luxury resort offering housing, shopping, and holiday facilities for 30,000 people. A four-lane bridge and two

Erick van Egeraat war einer der Begründer des berühmten niederländischen Architekturstudios Mecanoo, das für seine äußerst erfinderischen und spielerischen Entwürfe bekannt wurde. Im Jahr 1997 verließ Van Egeraat Mecanoo, um sein eigenes Studio zu gründen (Erick van Egeraat Associated Architects). Die Architekten beschreiben ihren Stil als „warme, einladende Architektur", um sich von dem abzugrenzen, was sie als den neo-modernistischen Stil von Mecanoo ansehen.

2007 legten EEA dem Präsidenten der Russischen Föderation, Wladimir Putin, ihre Pläne für die Föderationsinsel vor. EEA erhielt den Auftrag, nahe bei der Stadt Sotschi vor der Küste des Schwarzen Meeres eine Reihe neuer Inseln zu entwerfen und anzulegen. Sotschi hatte den Zuschlag für die Ausrichtung der Olympischen Winterspiele des Jahres 2014 erhalten und die Föderationsinsel soll zur gleichen Zeit eröffnet werden. Obwohl Russland über eine ausgedehnte Küste verfügt, sind nur wenige Orte zum Leben im Freien geeignet. Das Klima in Sotschi – heiße Sommer und milde Winter – ist jedoch ideal für die Errichtung einer Ferienanlage.

Das aus sieben Hauptinseln, drei Wellen-brechern und vielen kleineren Insel bestehende Miniatur-Archipel soll die Form der Russischen Föderation widerspiegeln. Die Wasserwege

Erick van Egeraat était l'un des fondateurs du célèbre cabinet d'architectes néerlandais Mecanoo, connu pour ses ouvrages très inventifs et gais. En 1997, Erik Van Egeraat a fondé son propre cabinet, EEA (Erick van Egeraat Associated Architects). Leur style revisite une « architecture chaude et accueillante » par rapport au style néo-moderne de Mecanoo.

En 2007, EEA a présenté à Vladimir Poutine, Président de la Fédération de Russie, ses plans pour l'Île de la Fédération. EEA a été chargé de concevoir et de construire une nouvelle série d'îles au large de la côte de la Mer Noire, à proximité de la ville de Sochi. Sochi hébergera les Jeux Olympiques d'hiver de 2014 et l'Île de la Fédération devrait ouvrir en même temps. Bien que la Russie soit dotée d'une côte très étendue, la plupart reste climatiquement inadaptée à l'habitation. Cependant, à Sochi, le climat (étés chauds et hivers modérés) est idéal pour développer un centre touristique.

Constitué de sept îles principales, de trois îles brise-lames et de nombreuses autres plus petites, l'archipel miniature aura la forme de la carte de la Fédération de Russie. Les voies navigables imiteront les cours d'eau russes tandis que les montagnes seront représentées en miniature sur les îles. Cet archipel deviendra un complexe de luxe offrant hébergements, boutiques et centre

left Federation Island is designed to mimic the shape of Russia's rivers, islands, and mountains.

links Die Föderationsinsel soll die Formen der russischen Flüsse, Inseln und Berge nachahmen.

gauche L'Île de la Fédération imite la forme des cours d'eau russes, des îles et des montagnes.

right Seen from above, the islands will appear like a map of the Russian Federation.

rechts Von oben werden die Inseln wie eine Karte der Russischen Föderation aussehen.

droite Vues de haut, les îles ressembleront à la carte de la Fédération de Russie.

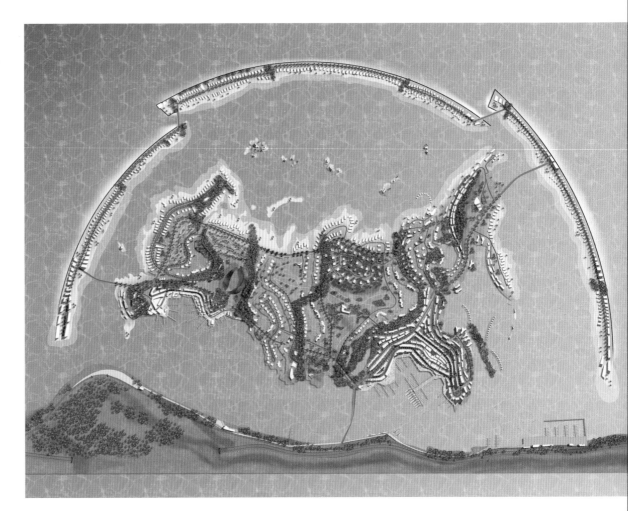

right above Sochi, on the Black Sea, has mild winters and hot summers and is ideal for resort development.

rechts oben In der Stadt Sotschi am Schwarzen Meer sind die Winter mild und die Sommer heiß; sie ist damit ideal für die Errichtung einer Ferienanlage.

ci-dessus à droite À Sochi, sur la Mer Noire, les hivers sont modérés et les étés sont chauds, ce qui en fait un lieu idéal pour développer un centre touristique.

right below Breakwaters surround and protect the central islands from erosion.

rechts unten Wellenbrecher umgeben und schützen die Inseln in der Mitte vor Erosion.

ci-dessous à droite Les brise-lames entourent et protègent les îles centrales de l'érosion.

tunnels will connect the island to the mainland 300 yards away.

The technical side is being developed by the Dutch engineering firm Witteveen + Bos who have been involved in similar projects in Dubai, notably the Palm and World Islands. They plan to reclaim 864 acres of land that will allow for 585 acres of buildings. The islands will be made either using natural underwater slopes or rock bunds. For the three breakwaters, a rubble mound structure will be used together with caisson structures. Consideration will have to be taken for the deep water (up to 98 feet), very soft subsoils, high waves, and earthquakes. In addition, many of the materials will have to be transported a distance of over 120 miles.

werden das russische Flussnetzwerk nachbilden, und auch die russischen Berge werden in Miniaturform auf der Insel wiedergegeben. Die Inseln sollen als Luxus-Ferienanlage mit Wohn- und Einkaufsbereichen und Urlaubseinrichtungen für 30.000 Menschen dienen. Eine vierspurige Brücke und mehrere Tunnel werden die Insel mit dem 275 Meter entfernten Festland verbinden.

Die technische Seite wird von dem niederlän-dischen Ingenieurbüro Witteveen + Bos entwickelt, das an ähnlichen Projekten in Dubai mitgearbeitet hat, darunter auch den Palm- und World-Inseln. Das Büro plant die Neugewinnung von 350 Hektar Land, um 237 Hektar davon zu bebauen. Die Inseln werden entweder mit Hilfe natürlicher Unterwasserabhänge oder von Felsendämmen aufgeschüttet. Für die drei Wellenbrecher wird eine Hügelstruktur aus Bruchsteinen zusammen mit Senkkästen errichtet. Besonders sorgfältig wird auf die Gefahr der tiefen Wasser (bis zu 30 Meter), sehr weichen Unterböden, hohen Wellen und Erdbeben zu achten sein. Außerdem werden viele Materialien über fast 200 Kilometer zu der Insel transportiert werden müssen.

touristique pour 30 000 personnes. Un pont à quatre voies et deux tunnels relieront l'île à la terre 300 mètres plus loin.

L'entreprise néerlandaise d'ingénierie, Witteveen + Bos se chargera de l'aspect technique. Ils se sont occupés de projets similaires à Dubaï, notamment sur les Palmiers et World Island. Ils prévoient de ramener 350 hectares de terre qui permettront de bâtir sur 237 hectares. Les îles seront créées en utilisant les pentes naturelles sous l'eau ou les digues en rochers. Pour les trois brise-lames, une structure en monticules de gravats sera combinée à des structures en caisson. La profondeur de l'eau (jusqu'à 30 mètres), les sous-sols très meubles, la hauteur des vagues et les tremblements de terre devront être pris en considération. De plus, la plupart des matériaux devront être transportés sur plus de 190 kilomètres.

Urban Islands
Städtische Inseln
Villes flottantes

New Holland Island l Waterfront City Island l Crystal Island
Zorrozaurre l Treasure Island

As the world becomes increasingly urban and populations rise so the need for new cities gets greater and greater. One way to meet this demand is to build new urban islands, or create masterplans for abandoned islands. Whereas in the past islands near or in cities were used as naval bases, shipyards, docks, or prisons, those made today have a focus on leisure and living, with malls, theaters, apartments, and parks. These new cities look at rivers or canals as part of that new experience, actively encouraging residents to see water as something recreational, through devices such as bridges, waterfronts, piers, and even ice rinks. The five projects presented here, two in Russia, one in the United States, one in Spain, and one in Dubai, offer a glimpse into the possible future city. They show how new island developments can regenerate cities and offer new ways of living.

Avec l'urbanisation du monde et la croissance de la population, le besoin en nouvelles villes augmente. Une des réponses à cette demande consiste à construire de nouvelles villes flottantes ou aménager des îles abandonnées. Alors que dans le passé les îles à proximité ou au sein des villes servaient de bases ou de chantiers navals, de quais ou de prisons, les îles créées aujourd'hui sont destinées à l'hébergement, aux loisirs, aux boutiques, aux théâtres, aux appartements et aux parcs. Dans ces nouvelles villes, les fleuves et les canaux ont une place à part entière et encouragent les résidents à considérer l'eau comme un loisir grâce aux dispositifs tels que les ponts, les fronts de mer, les embarcadères, parfois même les patinoires. Les cinq projets présentés dans cette partie, dont deux en Russie, un aux États-Unis, un en Espagne et un à Dubaï, offrent un aperçu d'éventuelles villes futures. Ces projets montrent comment les nouveaux développements peuvent régénérer des villes en offrant de nouveaux styles de vie.

Da die Welt zunehmend städtischer wird und die Bevölkerung stetig ansteigt, besteht erhöhter Bedarf nach neuen Städten. Eine Möglichkeit, diese Nachfrage zu decken, ist die Erbauung neuer städtischer Inseln oder die Erstellung von Masterplänen für verlassene Inseln. Während in der Vergangenheit Inseln neben oder in Städten als Marinestützpunkte, Werften, Docks oder Gefängnisse genutzt wurden, wird der Schwerpunkt heute mit Einkaufszentren, Theatern, Apartments und Parks eher auf Freizeit und Wohnen gelegt. Diese neuen Städte betrachten Flüsse oder Kanäle als Teil dieser neuen Erfahrung und ermutigen ihre Anwohner mit Elementen wie Brücken, Uferpromenaden, Piers und sogar Eislaufhallen aktiv, Wasser als erholende Freizeitmöglichkeit zu verstehen. Die fünf hier vorgestellten Projekte, zwei in Russland, eines in den USA, eines in Spanien und eines in Dubai bieten einen Vorgeschmack auf die mögliche Stadt der Zukunft. Sie zeigen, wie neue Inselbauprojekte Städte regenerieren und neue Arten des Wohnens bieten können.

New Holland Island

St. Petersburg, Russia
Foster + Partners
2010

New Holland, a man-made island in St. Petersburg, was created during the reign of Peter the Great when the Kryukov and Admiralteisky canals were dug linking the Moika River with the Neva. During the 18th century, it was used mainly as a timber depot for shipbuilding, and in the 19th century a naval prison and basin for naval architects were built there. In Soviet times, it accommodated high-security naval and military facilities. The military left the island in 2004 after it was decided that it should be developed into a modern cultural and commercial area.

Foster + Partners won the competition to design the 19-acre masterplan, after an earlier design by Los Angeles based firm Eric Owen Moss was rejected for being too radical. Foster's solution includes cultural and exhibition spaces, luxury hotels, offices, serviced apartments, underground parking, shops, and entertainment areas. The existing 18th- and 19th-century brick warehouses around the edge of the island will be renovated and adapted for modern use, and a new office complex will complete the missing side of the triangle. An historic rotunda will be adapted to create a 400-seat theater for traditional forms of theater, dance, and opera. The circular glass ceiling is strongly reminiscent of the one in the British Museum also designed by Foster.

Neu-Holland, eine künstliche Insel im russischen St. Petersburg, wurde während der Regentschaft Peters des Großen angelegt, als die Krjukow- und Admiralteisky-Kanäle gegraben wurden, um die Moika mit der Newa zu verbinden. Während des 18. Jahrhunderts wurde sie vor allem als Holzdepot für den Schiffbau verwendet und im 19. Jahrhundert wurden hier ein Marinegefängnis und ein Hafenbecken für Marinearchitekten errichtet. In den Zeiten der Sowjetunion beherbergte die Insel Hochsicherheitseinrichtungen der Marine und des Militärs. Das Militär verließ die Insel im Jahre 2004, nachdem der Beschluss gefasst worden war, die Insel in ein modernes Kultur- und Gewerbeviertel umzuwandeln.

Foster + Partners gewannen den Wettbewerb um den Entwurf des 7,6 Hektar umfassenden Masterplans, nachdem ein früherer Entwurf des in Los Angeles ansässigen Architekturbüros Eric Owen Moss als zu radikal zurückgewiesen worden war. Fosters Lösung umfasst Kultur- und Ausstellungsräume, Luxushotels, Büros, voll ausgestattete Apartments mit Personal, Tiefgaragen, Läden und Unterhaltungsbereiche. Die vorhandenen Warenhäuser aus Ziegelstein aus dem 18. und 19. Jahrhundert an den Rändern der Insel sollen renoviert und für den modernen Gebrauch umgestaltet werden und

New Holland, une île artificielle située à Saint-Pétersbourg, a été créée pendant le règne de Pierre le Grand lorsque le canal Kryukov et le canal Admiralteisky ont été creusés, reliant la Moïka à la Neva. Au XVIIIᵉ siècle, cette île était principalement utilisée pour entreposer le bois destiné à la construction navale. Au XIXᵉ siècle, une prison navale et un bassin pour les architectes navals y ont été construits. À l'époque soviétique, l'île accueillait les installations navales et militaires haute sécurité. Les militaires ont quitté l'île en 2004 après une décision qui allait la transformer en centre culturel et commercial.

Foster + Partners ont remporté le concours pour la conception d'un projet de 7,6 hectares, après que le plan précédent du cabinet Eric Owen Moss de Los Angeles fut rejeté pour être trop radical. La solution de Foster comprend des espaces culturels et d'exposition, des hôtels de luxe, un parking souterrain, des boutiques et des espaces de loisirs. Les entrepôts en briques datant du XVIIIᵉ et du XIXᵉ siècles sur les rives de l'île seront rénovés et adaptés à un usage moderne et un nouveau complexe de bureaux complètera le côté manquant du triangle. Une rotonde historique sera transformée en théâtre de 400 places pour recevoir des pièces de théâtre traditionnelles, des ballets et des opéras. Le plafond circulaire en verre

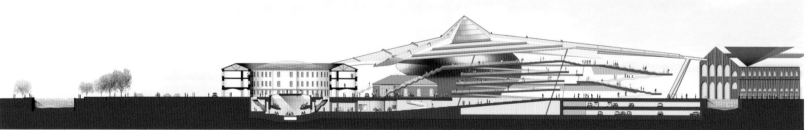

previous page The island will feature a circular theater, a performance hall, and artificial lake in the middle.

vorherige Seite Die Insel wird ein kreisförmiges Theater, einen Aufführungssaal und einen künstlichen See in der Mitte enthalten.

page précédente L'île accueillera en son centre un théâtre circulaire, une salle de concert et un lac artificiel

top By adding more bridges, the island is better linked to the rest of the city.

ganz oben Durch die Hinzufügung von weiteren Brücken wird die Insel besser mit dem Rest der Stadt verbunden.

haut En ajoutant des ponts, l'île est plus proche du reste de la ville.

above Cross section of performance hall showing the theater rotunda to the left.

oben Querschnitt des Aufführungssaals mit Ansicht der Theaterrotunde zur Linken.

ci-dessus Coupe de la salle de concert présentant le théâtre circulaire à gauche.

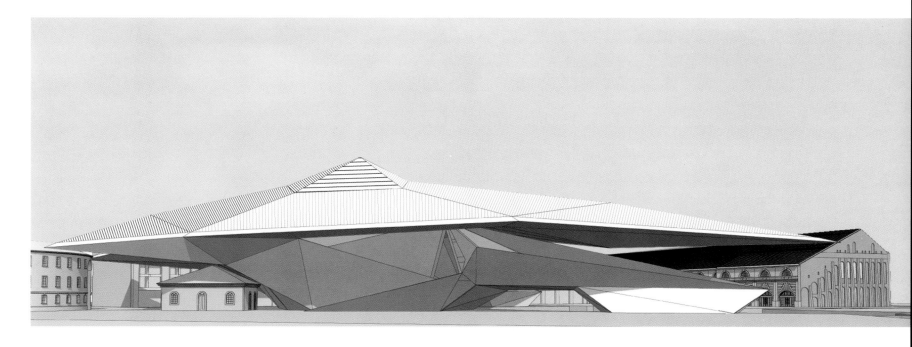

above Elevation of the performance hall which will include a 2,000-seat theater.

oben Ansicht des Aufführungssaals, der ein Theater mit 2.000 Sitzen enthalten wird.

ci-dessus Élévation de la salle de concert qui accueille un théâtre de 2 000 places.

The island's centerpiece will be the 75-feet high, star-shaped performance hall with 2,000 seats known as the Palace of Festivals. Its massive roof, with its straight lines and sharp edges, could have been inspired by "folded paper" design. Outside the hall, the old naval basin will be turned into an internal lake surrounded by a 3,000-seat outdoor arena. The basin can be flooded for regattas, or frozen over in winter to form an ice rink. A floating stage will sit in the middle. At basement level an art gallery will link the three performance venues.

Originally, there were just two bridges to the island, but Foster proposed to add another five thus integrating the complex with the rest of the city. The main entrance will be from the major city artery, Nevskiy Prospect. Plans are to make the island energy-efficient and sustainable, using the insulating properties of snow and the cooling potential of the surrounding canals.

ein neuer Bürokomplex wird die fehlende Seite des Dreiecks vervollständigen. Eine historische Rotunde wird zu einem Theater mit 400 Sitzplätzen umgewandelt, in dem traditionelle Stücke, Tanz und Opern aufgeführt werden können. Die kreisförmige Glasdecke erinnert stark an diejenige des British Museum, die ebenfalls von Foster entworfen wurde.

Der Mittelpunkt der Insel wird ein 23 Meter hoher, sternförmiger Aufführungssaal mit 2.000 Sitzplätzen sein, auch bekannt als Palast der Festivals. Die Inspiration für das massive Dach mit seinen geraden Linien und scharfen Kanten könnte von „gefaltetem Papier" stammen. Außerhalb des Saals wird das alte Hafenbecken der Marine in einen von einem Freiluftstadium mit 3.000 Sitzen umgebenen See umgewandelt. Das Becken kann für Regatten geflutet werden und das Wasser kann im Winter gefroren werden, um als Eislaufbahn zu dienen. In der Mitte wird eine schwimmende Bühne angelegt. Im Untergeschoss sind alle drei Veranstaltungsorte über eine Kunstgalerie verbunden.

Ursprünglich waren nur zwei Brücken auf der Insel vorgesehen, Foster schlug jedoch den Bau von fünf weiteren Brücken vor, um den Komplex besser in den Rest der Stadt zu integrieren. Der Haupteingang befindet sich auf der Hauptverkehrsader der Stadt, dem Newski Prospekt. Es bestehen Pläne, die Insel mit Hilfe der isolierenden Eigenschaften von Schnee und dem kühlenden Potenzial der umgebenden Kanäle energiesparender und nachhaltiger zu machen.

rappelle fortement un musée britannique également conçu par Foster.

La pièce centrale de l'île sera le Palais du Festival, une salle de concert de 23 mètres de haut pouvant accueillir 2 000 personnes. Son toit massif, aux lignes droites et aux arêtes effilées, rappelle les « origamis ». À l'extérieur de la salle, l'ancien bassin naval sera transformé en lac intérieur, entouré par une arène extérieure de 3 000 places. Le bassin peut accueillir des régates ou être gelé en hiver pour se transformer en patinoire. Une scène flottera en son milieu et au sous-sol, une galerie d'art reliera les trois salles de concert.

À l'origine, l'île n'était reliée que par deux ponts, mais Foster proposa d'en ajouter cinq, intégrant ainsi le complexe au reste de la ville. L'entrée principale se fera par l'artère principale de la ville, Nervskiy Prospect. Les plans doivent rendre l'île écoénergétique et durable grâce aux propriétés isolantes de la neige et au potentiel de refroidissement des canaux environnants.

Waterfront City Island

Dubai, UAE
OMA
2012

above A purpose-built square island—a new Manhattan in the Gulf.

oben Eine geplante quadratische Insel – ein neues Manhattan im Golf.

ci-dessus Une île carrée pour un objectif précis – un nouveau Manhattan dans le Golfe.

right Imagined aerial view of the new island city. It will form a small part of the much bigger Waterfront City development.

rechts Beispiel eines Luftbilds der neuen Inselstadt. Sie wird einen kleinen Teil des erheblich größeren Bauprojekts Waterfront City bilden.

droite Vue aérienne de la future nouvelle ville flottante. Elle fera partie d'une petite partie du plus grand développement de Waterfront City.

below At night the new island city will offer a spectacular skyline.

unten Bei Nacht wird die neue Inselstadt Besuchern mit ihrer Skyline eine spektakuläre Ansicht bieten.

ci-dessous La nuit, la nouvelle ville flottant offre une vue spectaculaire.

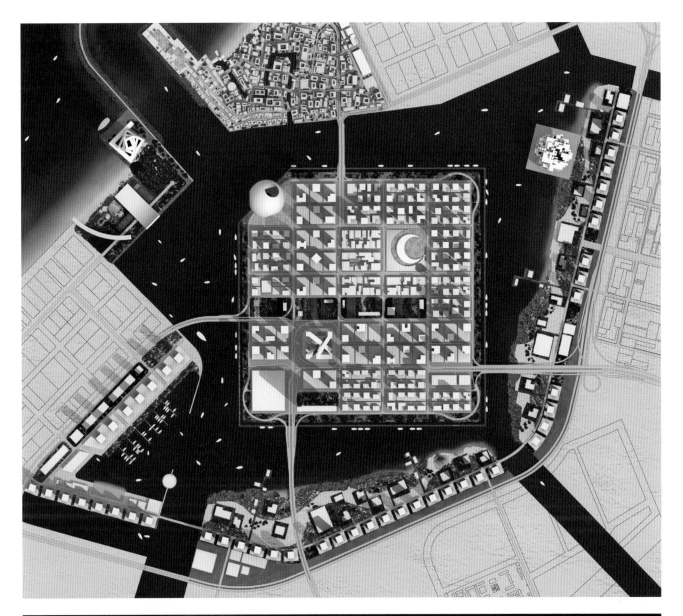

Rem Koolhaas's Dutch-based studio Office for Metropolitan Architecture (OMA) has created a masterplan for a new island city in Dubai. The island will form part of an urban development called Waterfront, situated next to Palm Jebel Ali, covering 1,500 million square feet and housing 1.5 million people. Waterfront will consist of five different districts with the island acting as the downtown and central business area.

Waterfront City, an artificial square island 4,297 feet by 4,297 feet, will be created by channeling water from the sea into canals on all sides. Flooding will take place in stages to allow for construction on the island itself. OMA have adopted a grid system of five streets by five streets containing 25 identical blocks with alternating tall and short buildings making for very high density living—a sort of Manhattan Island in the Persian Gulf. The taller and larger buildings are situated along the south side to give shade. There will be equal amounts of office space and residences to encourage people to live and work on the island and so reduce traffic.

Boulevard Park, a thin strip of green running through the center, contrasts to the more rational building elsewhere. The park will offer a soft transition from land to water through beaches, mangroves, and piers. These piers will encourage

Rem Koolhaas in den Niederlanden ansässiges Studio Office for Metropolitan Architecture (OMA) hat den Masterplan für eine neue Inselstadt in Dubai entworfen. Die Insel wird Teil eines städtischen Entwurfs namens Waterfront neben Palm Jebel Ali sein, soll 140 Millionen Quadratmeter bedecken und Wohnraum für 1,5 Millionen Menschen bieten. Waterfront besteht aus fünf verschiedenen Vierteln, wobei die Insel als Stadtzentrum und zentrales Geschäftsviertel dienen wird.

Waterfront City, eine künstliche quadratische Insel mit einer Größe von 1.310 x 1.310 Metern, wird geschaffen, indem Wasser aus dem Meer auf allen Seiten in Kanäle geleitet wird. Die Flutung wird schrittweise erfolgen, damit die Insel selbst aufgeschüttet werden kann. OMA haben ein Gitternetzsystem aus fünf Mal fünf Straßen entworfen, die 25 identische Häuserblocks mit abwechselnd hohen und niedrigen Gebäuden für eine hohe Bevölkerungsdichte schaffen – eine Art Manhattan im Persischen Golf. Die höheren und größeren Gebäude befinden sich auf der Südseite der Insel, um Schatten zu erzeugen. Auf der Insel werden in gleichem Maße Büros und Wohnflächen erbaut, um die Menschen dazu zu ermuntern, auf der Insel zu arbeiten und zu leben und so das Verkehrsaufkommen zu verringern.

Le cabinet d'architectes Office for Metropolitan Architecture (OMA) de Rem Koolhaas a créé le plan directeur d'une nouvelle ville flottante à Dubaï. L'île fera partie d'un plan urbain appelé Waterfront, situé à côté du Palmier de Jebel Ali, couvrant 140 millions de mètres carrés et pouvant accueillir 1,5 million de personnes. Waterfront sera constitué de cinq quartiers différents, l'île étant le centre urbain et d'affaires.

Waterfront City, une île artificielle carrée de 1 310 mètres de côté, sera entourée de de canaux utilisant l'eau de mer. Ce processus opéré en plusieurs étapes permettra la construction de l'île elle-même. OMA a adopté un système de quartiers de cinq rues par cinq, contenant 25 blocs identiques, en alternant les bâtiments élevés et peu élevés permettant une forte densité de population, une sorte de Manhattan dans le Golfe persique. Les bâtiments les plus hauts et les plus vastes seront situés sur le côté sud pour apporter de l'ombre. Bureaux et résidences seront construits en quantités identiques afin d'encourager les habitants à travailler et à vivre sur l'île et réduire ainsi le trafic.

Boulevard Park, la bande de verdure qui traverse le centre, contraste avec les bâtiments. Le parc offrira une légère transition de la terre à l'eau grâce à l'installation de plages, de

left The new city will house 1.5 million people.

links Die neue Stadt soll 1,5 Millionen Menschen beherbergen.

gauche La nouvelle ville pourra accueillir 1,5 million de personnes.

below A spiral tower (foreground) sits opposite a 44-story silver sphere.

unten Ein spiralförmiger Turm (Vordergrund) wird gegenüber einer silbernen Kugel mit 44 Stockwerken erbaut.

ci-dessous Une tour en spirale (premier plan) fait face à une sphère argentée de 44 étages.

right The sphere, perched on the edge of the island, will be a self-contained neighborhood.

rechts Die Kugel am Rand der Insel wird Mittelpunkt einer eigenständigen Wohngegend sein.

droite La sphère, perchée au bord de l'île, sera un quartier indépendant.

the use of water taxis to and from the island, although there will be four slender bridges, one on each side, linking the island to the mainland. Other open spaces include shaded sidewalk arcades and a waterfront boardwalk running around the outside of the island.

Besides the regular buildings there will be signature mixed-use buildings, including an 82-story spiral tower inspired by the minaret of the 9th-century Great Mosque of Samarra in Iraq and a 44-story silver sphere. The sphere is intentionally perched on the edge of the island in order for "the building to attract attention through its design cleverness, rather than by its size." It is designed as a self-contained neighborhood, with public institutions around the outside and smaller residential spheres on the inside, all linked by escalators.

The plan is highly ambitious. As the architects put it, "A square piece of city surrounded by water on all sides stands out like an icon, it allows for a rational and efficient design approach for what is perhaps one of the most complex design tasks conceivable."

Boulevard Park, ein dünner, quer durch die Mitte verlaufender Grünstreifen, bildet einen Gegensatz zu den eher vernünftig geplanten Bauten an anderer Stelle. Der Park bildet durch Strände, Mangroven und Piers einen sanften Übergang vom Land zum Wasser. Die Piers sollen die Verwendung von Wassertaxis zu und von der Insel fördern, obwohl die Insel auch über vier schlanke Brücken – einer auf jeder Seite – mit dem Festland verbunden wird. Weitere Freiluftbereiche umfassen schattige Fußgängerarkaden und eine Uferpromenade um den Rand der Insel.

Neben den normalen Wohngebäuden werden einige ikonische Gebäude für Mischzwecke errichtet, einschließlich eines spiralenförmigen Turms mit 82 Stockwerken, der vom Minarett der Großen Moschee im irakischen Samarra aus dem 9. Jahrhundert inspiriert wurde, und einer silbernen Kugel mit 44 Stockwerken. Die Kugel wird mit voller Absicht am Rand der Insel errichtet, damit „das Gebäude durch die Intelligenz seines Entwurfs anstatt durch seine Größe Aufmerksamkeit auf sich zieht". Sie ist als eigenständige Wohngegend entworfen, mit öffentlichen Einrichtungen um ihr Äußeres und kleineren Wohnkugeln im Inneren, die untereinander mit Rolltreppen verbunden sind.

Der Entwurf ist sehr ehrgeizig. Die Architekten selbst sagen darüber: „Ein quadratisches Stück Stadt, das auf allen Seiten von Wasser umgeben ist, hebt sich ab wie ein Wahrzeichen, es ermöglicht einen rationalen und effizienten Design-ansatz für vielleicht eine der komplexesten Entwurfsaufgaben, die überhaupt denkbar sind."

mangroves et d'embarcadères. Ces embarcadères encourageront l'utilisation des taxis sur l'eau pour se rendre sur l'île et quitter l'île, bien que quatre ponts très fins, un de chaque côté, relieront l'île à la terre. D'autres espaces ouverts seront créés comme des arcades ombragées et une promenade au bord de l'eau qui longera le tour extérieur de l'île.

À côté des bâtiments rectangulaires se trouveront des bâtiments à usage diversifié, dont une tour en spirale inspirée par le minaret de la Grande Mosquée du IXe siècle de Samarra en Irak et une sphère argenté de 44 étages. La sphère sera volontairement perchée au bord de l'île afin « d'attirer l'attention par l'intelligence de son design plutôt que par sa taille ». Elle est conçue comme un quartier autonome avec ses institutions publiques à l'extérieur et des sphères résidentielles plus petites à l'intérieur, toutes reliées par des escalators.

Le projet est extrêmement ambitieux. Comme l'explique l'architecte, « Un carré de ville entouré d'eau de tous côtés s'impose tel une icône; il permet une approche architecturale efficace et logique pour ce qui s'avère l'une des constructions probablement les plus complexes du monde du design. »

left Four slender bridges, one on each side, link to the island.

links Vier schlanke Brücken, eine auf jeder Seite, verbinden die Insel mit dem Festland.

gauche Quatre ponts très fins, de chaque côté, relient l'île.

right Waterfront boardwalks are an important part of the design.

rechts Uferpromenaden sind ein wesentlicher Teil des Entwurfs.

droite Les promenades au bord de l'eau sont un élément important de la conception.

Crystal Island

Moscow, Russia
Foster + Partners
2014

Crystal Island will be located just over 3 miles from the Kremlin on the Nagatino Peninsula, a spur of land surrounded by the Moscow River. Architects Foster + Partners have devised an incredibly ambitious scheme—a £2 billion "city within a city." This enormous tower will be one of the largest buildings ever built, enclosing the largest volume on the planet. At 1,475 feet tall and covering an area of almost 5.4 million square feet it will contain a total floor area of 27 million square feet. It will be twice as wide as the London Millennium Dome and four times the size of the Pentagon in Washington D.C.

The building will feature 900 serviced apartments, 3,000 hotel rooms, a school for 500 pupils, a cinema, theater, shops, and a sports complex. Two viewing platforms, one at 492 feet and another at 984 feet, will offer panoramic views of Moscow. There will be 16,500 spaces for underground parking. Residents will be able to live and work within the planned area as every amenity will be within walking distance.

The tower's spiraling tent-like form rises out of a landscaped park, its triangulated steel mega frame encased in glass. A Russian engineer, Vladimir Shukhov (1853–1939), first pioneered the use of the hyperboloid structure in architecture so it seems appropriate that Foster chose this structure for their new building.

Die Kristallinsel befindet sich nur etwas über 6 Kilometer vom Kreml entfernt auf der Nagatino-Halbinsel, einem von der Moskwa umgebenen Landvorsprung. Das Architekturbüro Foster + Partners hat sich ein unglaublich ehrgeiziges Ziel gesteckt – die Erbauung „einer Stadt in der Stadt" für 2 Milliarden Pfund. Der gewaltige Turm wird eines der größten jemals erbauten Gebäude sein und den größten Baukörper unseres Planeten umgeben. Mit einer Höhe von 450 Metern und einer Fläche von fast einer halben Million Quadratmetern wird er eine Bodenfläche von insgesamt 2,5 Millionen Quadratmetern umfassen. Er soll doppelt so breit wie der Millenium Dome in London und viermal so groß wie das Pentagon in Washington D.C. sein.

Das Gebäude wird 900 voll ausgestattete Apartments mit Personal, 3.000 Hotelzimmer, eine Schule für 500 Schüler, ein Kino, ein Theater, Läden und einen Sportkomplex enthalten. Zwei Aussichtsplattformen, die eine auf 150 Metern Höhe, die andere auf 300 Metern Höhe, werden Panoramablicke über Moskau freigeben. Außerdem verfügt das Gebäude über 16.500 Tiefgaragenplätze. Bewohner werden innerhalb des geplanten Bereichs leben und arbeiten können, da alle Einrichtungen gut zu Fuß zu erreichen sein werden.

Crystal Island se trouvera à 6 kilomètres à peine du Kremlin, sur la péninsule de Nagatino, un bout de terre entouré par le fleuve Moscou. Les architectes Foster + Partners ont élaboré un projet incroyablement ambitieux, « une ville au sein de la ville » d'une valeur de 2 milliards livres Sterling. Cette tour immense au volume inégalé sera l'une des plus grandes constructions au monde. D'une hauteur de 450 mètres et couvrant une surface approximative de cinquante hectares, elle contiendra une surface habitable de 250 hectares. Elle sera deux fois plus large que le Millenium Dome de Londres et quatre fois plus grande que le Pentagone de Washington.

La construction comptera 900 appartements meublés, 3 000 chambres d'hôtel, une école pouvant accueillir 500 élèves, un cinéma, un théâtre, des boutiques et un complexe sportif. Deux plates-formes, l'une à 150 mètres et l'autre à 300 mètres, offriront des vues panoramiques de Moscou. 16 500 places de parking souterrain seront disponibles et les résidents pourront y vivre et travailler puisque tous les services seront disponibles à proximité.

La tour, en forme de chapiteau, s'élève d'un parc de verdure. Son cadre triangulaire géant en acier est emboîté dans le verre. Un ingénieur russe, Vladimir Shuknov (1853 - 1939) est le premier à avoir utilisé la structure hyperboloïde

above A spiralling glass tent rises from the banks of the Moscow River.

oben Ein spiralförmiges Glaszelt erhebt sich von den Ufern der Moskwa.

ci-dessus Vue du chapiteau de verre en spirale depuis les rives du fleuve Moscou.

right A vast new island city in the middle of Moscow will include 900 apartments, 3,000 hotel rooms, a school, cinema, and shops.

rechts Eine riesige neue Inselstadt in der Mitte von Moskau wird 900 Apartments, 3.000 Hotelzimmer, eine Schule, ein Kino und Läden beherbergen.

droite Une immense ville flottante au milieu de Moscou, comptant 900 appartements, 3 000 chambres d'hôtels, une école, un cinéma et des boutiques.

Hyperboloid structures—buildings using hyperboloid geometry—tend to be both strong and decorative.

Sustainable features include solar panels in the exterior façade and wind turbines to generate electricity. Ventilation will be encouraged through strategically placed large atriums. Crystal Island's outer layer acts as a second skin and a thermal buffer to the extreme Moscow climate. Enclosure panels slotted into the external structural framing will be closed in winter for extra warmth and opened in summer to allow in natural light and ventilation.

Die spiralförmige, zeltähnliche Form des Turms erhebt sich aus einem landschaftlich gestalteten Park, wobei der dreieckige Riesenrahmen aus Stahl in Glas eingefasst ist. Ein russischer Ingenieur namens Wladimir Schuchow (1853-1939) leistete mit der Einführung dieser Hyperboloid-Struktur in der Architektur Pionierarbeit, daher scheint es angemessen, dass Foster die Struktur für sein neues Bauwerk übernahm. Hyperboloid-Strukturen – mit Hilfe von hyperboloider Geometrie errichtete Gebäude – sind tendenziell sowohl solide als auch dekorativ.

Zu den nachhaltigen Elementen gehören Solarzellen in der äußeren Fassade und Windturbinen zur Erzeugung von Elektrizität. Die Belüftung wird durch strategisch angelegte große Atrien gefördert. Die äußere Schicht der Kristallinsel dient als zweite Haut und als Wärmepuffer gegen das extreme Moskauer Klima. In den äußeren Strukturrahmen eingelassene Schutzplatten werden im Winter geschlossen, um zusätzliche Wärme zu bieten, und im Sommer geöffnet, um natürliches Licht und Luft in das Gebäude zu lassen.

en architecture. Il semble donc approprié que Foster l'ait choisie pour son nouvel ouvrage. Les structures utilisant la géométrie hyperboloïde sont généralement solides et esthétiques.

Le bâtiment sera caractérisé par des panneaux solaires sur la façade extérieure et des éoliennes, pour générer de l'électricité. L'aération sera encouragée par de larges atriums positionnés de manière stratégique. Le revêtement extérieur de Crystal Island joue un rôle de seconde peau et de tampon thermique pour affronter le climat extrême de Moscou. Des panneaux encastrés dans l'armature de la structure externe seront fermés en hiver pour réchauffer l'intérieur et ouverts en été pour laisser entrer l'air et la lumière naturelle.

Zorrozaurre

Bilbao, Spain
Zaha Hadid Architects
2020

above The north end of the island which is conceived as an urban "barrio."

oben Das nördliche Ende der Insel, das als städtisches „Barrio" entworfen wurde.

ci-dessus L'extrémité nord de l'île est un quartier urbain.

Zorrozaurre is a 3-mile long peninsula in Bilbao surrounded on one side by the Deusto Canal and on the other by the Nervion River. In the 1960s, it was used for maritime and port activities, but after the economic crisis of the 1970s the area went into decline. It was therefore decided that a masterplan was needed for redeveloping the peninsula; the Iraqi-born architect Zaha Hadid won the commission.

Hadid plans to open the Deusto Canal to the east turning Zorrozaurre into an island. Historic buildings will be restored and groups of new buildings orientated toward the water to offer views and sunlight will be built. Greater access to the island will come through a series of new bridges and an extension of the existing tram network down the central axis. This central avenue will be crossed by local roads and pedestrian walks. There will be green spaces at either end of the island as well as a large park in the center. On the river side, there will be a higher concentration of buildings and small streets, in contrast to the softer canal side with open spaces, ponds, and steps down to the water.

The island will be divided into three districts—South, Center, and North. The South District, close to centers of learning, medicine, business, and engineering, will have more

Zorrozaurre ist eine fünf Kilometer lange Halbinsel im spanischen Bilbao, die auf der einen Seite vom Deusto-Kanal und auf der anderen Seite von einem Fluss, dem Nervión, umgeben ist. In den Sechziger Jahren wurde sie für die Schifffahrt und als Hafen verwendet, nach der Wirtschaftskrise in den Siebziger Jahren verfiel die Gegend jedoch zusehends. Deshalb wurde der Beschluss gefasst, dass ein Masterplan zur Neugestaltung der Halbinsel erforderlich sei, und die irakische Architektin Zaha Hadid gewann den Wettbewerb um dessen Ausführung.

Hadid plant die Öffnung des Deusto-Kanals nach Osten hin, um Zorrozaurre in eine Insel zu verwandeln. Historische Gebäude werden restauriert und Gruppen neuer Gebäude werden auf das Wasser hin ausgerichtet, um schönere Aussichten und Sonneneinfall zuzulassen. Über eine Reihe neuer Brücken und eine Erweiterung des vorhandenen Straßenbahnnetzwerks entlang der Zentralachse wird ein besserer Zugang zur Insel geschaffen. Die zentrale Achse wird von örtlichen Straßen und Fußgängerwegen gekreuzt. An beiden Enden der Insel werden Grünflächen angelegt und in der Mitte ist ein großer Park vorgesehen. Die Konzentration von Gebäuden und kleinen Straßen wird auf der Flussseite größer sein, die sanftere Kanalseite

Zorrozaurre est une péninsule de cinq kilomètres de long située à Bilbao. Elle est entourée du canal Duesto d'un côté et du fleuve Nervion de l'autre. Dans les années 1960, cette péninsule accueillait des activités portuaires et maritimes, mais après la crise économique des années 70, la zone a connu un déclin. Il a donc été décidé de créer un plan directeur de redéveloppement de la péninsule et l'architecte d'origine irakienne Zaha Hadid a remporté le concours.

Zaha Hadid prévoit d'ouvrir le canal Duesto à l'est en transformant la péninsule de Zorrozaurre en île. Les bâtiments historiques seront restaurés et les nouvelles constructions seront orientées vers la mer pour offrir des vues magnifiques et la lumière du soleil. Un meilleur accès à l'île est également prévu grâce à la création de nouveaux ponts et d'une extension du réseau tramway le long de l'axe central. Cette avenue est traversée par des routes et rues piétonnes. On trouvera également des espaces verts à chaque extrémité de l'île et un immense parc en son centre. La rive accueillera une plus grande concentration de bâtiments et de ruelles, contrastant avec le côté plus doux du canal et ses espaces ouverts, ses bassins et ses escaliers conduisant à l'eau.

L'île sera divisée en trois districts, Sud, Centre et Nord. Le district Sud, proche des

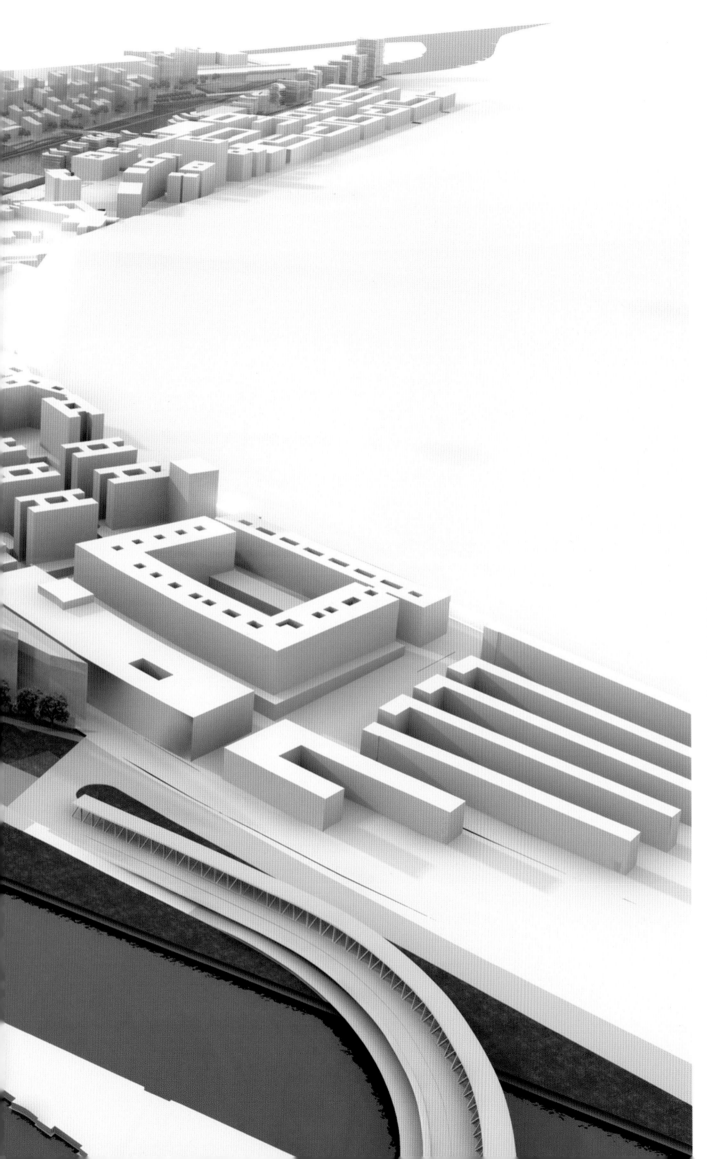

left In Hadid's plan, the canal will be opened up to the east, joining the river and creating an island.

links Laut Hadids Plan wird der Kanal nach Osten hin geöffnet, um eine Verbindung mit dem Fluss zu schaffen und eine Insel zu bilden.

gauche Selon les plans de Zaha Hadid, le canal sera ouvert à l'est, rejoignant le fleuve et formant ainsi une île.

intensive building with a mix of offices and residences. The Central District is designed to act as a reflection of the Sarriko Park on the other side of the canal and will be more open. It is seen as a center for the arts, sports, and science, connected by a "green bridge" to the university. Interesting industrial buildings will be preserved and converted into studios, workshops, and classrooms. The North District is conceived as an urban "barrio" to support the regeneration of small businesses and will have close links to the water through bridges, moorings, wooden walkways over the water, and waterside bars.

The idea is to promote a place that is "for life and work" and an "island of knowledge." With plans to build over 5,000 dwellings, for both public and private use, it will become home to nearly 15,000 new residents.

wird im Gegensatz dazu offene Räume, Teiche und Stufen zum Wasser erhalten.

Die Insel wird in drei Viertel unterteilt, den Süden, die Mitte und den Norden. Das südliche Viertel, das sich nahe an den wichtigsten Institutionen für Lehre, Medizin, Wirtschaft und Ingenieurwesen befindet, wird mit einer Mischung aus Büros und Wohngebäuden dichter bebaut sein. Die Mitte soll Spiegelbild des Sarriko-Parks auf der anderen Seite des Kanals sein und wird etwas offener sein. Hier soll ein Zentrum für Künste, Sport und Wissenschaften entstehen, das über eine „grüne Brücke" mit der Universität verbunden wird. Interessante industrielle Gebäude werden erhalten und in Studios, Werkstätten und Klassenzimmer umgewandelt. Das nördliche Viertel ist als städtisches „Barrio" vorgesehen, um die Regeneration kleiner Unternehmen zu fördern, und wird über Brücken, Ankerplätze, hölzerne Stege über dem Wasser und Bars am Ufer eine enge Verbindung mit dem Wasser aufweisen.

Die Idee besteht in der Förderung eines Ortes, der „zum Leben und Arbeiten" und als „Insel des Wissens" gedacht ist. Mit Plänen zur Erbauung von über 5.000 Unterkünften für den öffentlichen und privaten Gebrauch wird die Insel fast 15.000 neuen Bewohnern eine neue Heimat bieten.

centres de formation, de médecine, d'affaires et techniques, comptera davantage de bâtiments dynamiques, avec un mélange de bureaux et de résidences. Le district du Centre sera le reflet du Parc Sarriko de l'autre côté du canal et sera plus ouvert. Ce sera un centre pour les arts, le sport et la science, connecté par un « pont écologique » à l'université. D'intéressants bâtiments industriels seront conservés et transformés en studios, ateliers et salles de classe. Le district Nord sera un quartier urbain pour supporter la régénération des petites entreprises. Il sera étroitement lié à l'eau par les ponts, les amarrages, les passerelles en bois et les bars sur la rive.

L'idée est de promouvoir un « lieu de vie et de travail » et une « île de connaissances ». Avec ses 5 000 logements prévus, destinés à un usage public et privé, l'île accueillera presque 15 000 nouveaux habitants.

left The south end will have a massive concentration of offices and residences.

links Das südliche Ende wird eine dichte Konzentration von Büros und Wohngebäuden beherbergen.

gauche L'extrémité sud accueillera une forte concentration de bureaux et de résidences.

below Having close links to the water, via bridges, promenades, and parks, is a key part of the masterplan.

unten Die engen Verbindungen mit dem Wasser über Brücken, Promenaden und Parks sind wesentlicher Bestandteil des Masterplans.

ci-dessous Le lien étroit avec l'eau, par la création de ponts, de promenades et de parcs, est un élément essentiel des plans.

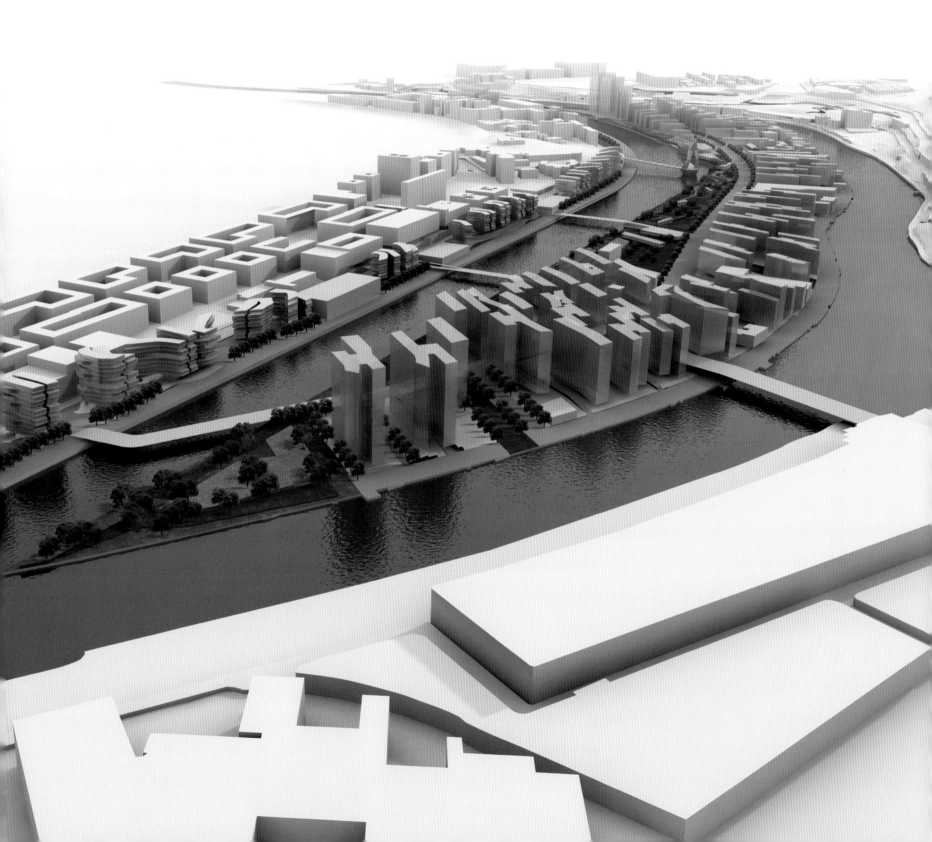

Treasure Island

San Franscisco, USA

Skidmore, Owings & Merrill

2022

left Treasure Island was originally built in 1936, and is part of Yerba Buena Island.

links Treasure Island wurde ursprünglich bereits 1936 angelegt und ist Teil der Insel Yerba Buena.

gauche Treasure Island a été construite en 1936 et est reliée à l'île de Yerba Buena.

right The island's canted grid plan is designed to take account of wind patterns.

rechts Der abgeschrägte Gitternetzplan der Insel wurde unter Berücksichtigung des Windeinfalls entworfen.

droite Le plan architectural de l'île prend en compte le régime des vents.

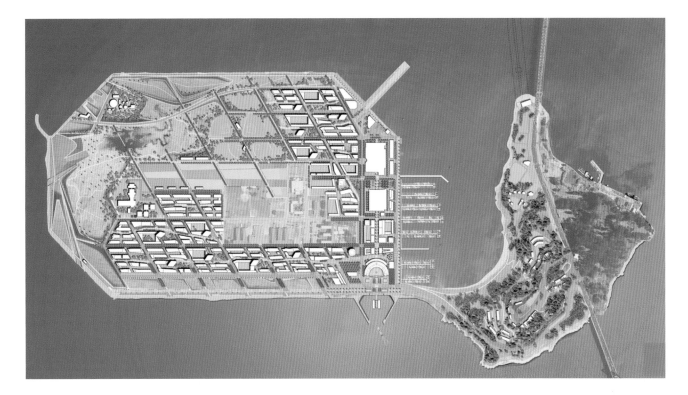

Treasure Island is a manmade extension of Yerba Buena Island in the middle of the San Fransico–Oakland Bay Bridge. It was created in 1936–37 using fill dredged from the bay and first used for the 1939 Golden Gate International Exposition. During World War II, it was used by the US Navy. In 1997, the naval station closed and it was decided to turn the island into a new city.

SOM San Francisco have designed a model for a sustainable community. In creating a new city from scratch, the architects have had to take many factors into consideration. First of all, the location in the middle of the bay means that the city will be exposed to extremes of weather, including fog, wind, and sunshine. Second, because the island is built on landfill, the risk of liquefaction is very high during an earthquake. The architects also wanted to create a place where there are few cars, which is compact and walkable. Therefore, they have designed a city that combines access to mass transit (on and off the island), urban amenities on the one hand and open spaces on the other.

To achieve this, low-rise buildings are interwoven with high-rise structures, alongside pedestrian areas and open spaces. The grid plan is at an angle to take account of the winds and buildings are positioned to create sheltered

Treasure Island ist eine künstlich angelegte Erweiterung der Insel Yerba Buena in der Mitte der Brücke von San Francisco nach Oakland. Sie wurde 1936-37 unter Verwendung von aus der Bucht ausgebaggerter Füllmasse angelegt und erstmals im Jahre 1939 für die Golden Gate International-Ausstellung verwendet. Während des Zweiten Weltkriegs wurde sie von der US Navy verwendet. Als die Marinestation 1997 aufgegeben wurde, wurde der Beschluss gefasst, die Insel in eine neue Stadt umzuwandeln.

SOM San Francisco haben ein Modell für eine nachhaltige Gemeinschaft entworfen. Aufgrund des Plans zur Gestaltung einer von Grund auf neuen Stadt mussten die Architekten viele Faktoren in Betracht ziehen. Erstens bedeutet die Lage in der Mitte der Bucht, dass die Stadt den Extremen des Wetters ausgesetzt sein wird, einschließlich Nebel, Wind und Sonneneinstrahlung. Zweitens ist das Risiko der Verflüssigung während eines Erdbebens sehr hoch, weil die Insel auf einer Bodenaufschüttung angelegt wurde. Die Architekten wollten außerdem einen Ort mit sehr wenigen Autos schaffen, der kompakt und zu Fuß begehbar ist. Deshalb haben sie eine Stadt entworfen, die Zugang zu Massen-durchgangsverkehr (von und zur Insel) mit städtischen Einrichtungen auf der einen Seite

Treasure Island est une extension artificielle de l'île de Yerba Buena, située au milieu du pont San Francisco-Oakland Bay. Créée en 1936-37 avec des remblais dragués de la baie, elle a été ouverte en 1939 pour l'exposition internationale du Golden Gate. Durant la Seconde Guerre mondiale, elle accueillait la marine américaine. En 1997, la station navale a fermé ses portes et il a été décidé de transformer l'île en nouvelle ville.

SOM San Francisco a conçu un modèle de communauté durable. En construisant une nouvelle ville à partir de rien, les architectes ont dû prendre en considération plusieurs facteurs. Le premier, l'emplacement de l'île, au milieu de la baie, signifie que la ville sera exposée aux temps extrêmes, dont le gel, le vent et le soleil. Deuxiè-mement, étant donné que l'île est construite sur du remblai, les risques de liquéfaction sont très élevés durant un tremblement de terre. Les architectes souhaitaient également créer un lieu à faible trafic et favorisant la marche à pied. Ils ont donc conçu une ville qui combine un accès aux transports en commun (pour se rendre et quitter l'île), des installations urbaines d'un côté et des espaces ouverts de l'autre.

Dans cet objectif, des bâtiments peu élevés sont entrelacés avec des structures plus hautes, le long des zones piétonnes et des espaces ouverts. Le plan quadrillé prend en compte les

left There will be four skyscrapers, each designed to cope with winds, allow in maximum sunlight, and create sheltered areas at ground level.

links Auf der Insel werden vier Hochhäuser entstehen. Jedes davon wurde so entworfen, dass es den Winden standhalten kann, dass ein Maximum an Sonnenlicht ins Gebäude fallen kann und auf Höhe des Erdgeschosses geschützte Bereiche entstehen.

gauche L'île comptera quatre tours, chacune conçue pour affronter les vents, laisser entrer un maximum de lumière et créer des abris au niveau du sol.

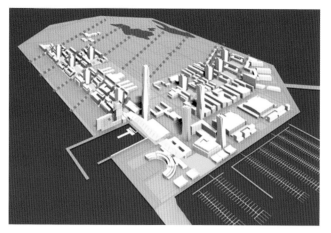

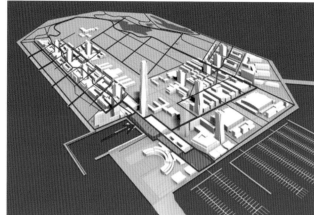

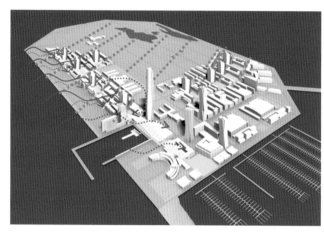

areas. There are five skyscrapers, four of 40-stories and one of 60-stories. Each one will be shaped to convey an organic aesthetic and use a great deal of glass to let in light. Mid-rise buildings, positioned to the north and west of the parks, will be lozenge shaped to reduce wind effect. Low-rise buildings are designed to shelter public spaces.

The island will also include an organic farm, wind farm, parkland, and new ferry terminal. Residential neighborhoods are positioned within a ten-minute walk to the ferry terminal to encourage car-free living. The first residents will be able to move to the island in 2013 and final completion is expected in 2022.

und offenen Räumen auf der anderen Seite vereint.

Um dieses Ziel zu erreichen, sind niedrige Gebäude mit Hochhäusern verwoben, daneben finden sich Fußgängerzonen und offene Räume. Der gitterförmige Grundriss ist unter Berücksichtigung des Windeinfalls schräg angelegt und die Gebäude sollen so errichtet werden, dass geschützte Bereiche entstehen. Auf der Insel werden fünf Hochhäuser entstehen, vier mit vierzig und eines mit sechzig Stockwerken. Jedes wird so geformt, dass es eine organische Ästhetik vermittelt, und zu einem großen Teil aus Glas erbaut sein, um Licht hinein zu lassen. Gebäude von mittlerer Größe im Norden und Westen des Parks werden eine Rautenform erhalten, um den Effekt der Winde zu verringern. Niedrige Gebäude sind so entworfen, dass sie öffentlichen Bereichen Schutz gewähren.

Die Insel wird außerdem über eine Biofarm, einen Windenergiepark, Parks und ein neues Fährterminal verfügen. Die Wohnviertel liegen alle höchstens zehn Minuten von dem Fähr-terminal entfernt, um autofreies Wohnen zu fördern. Die ersten Bewohner sollen 2013 auf die Insel ziehen können und die endgültige Fertigstellung ist für 2022 geplant.

vents et les bâtiments sont positionnés pour servir de protection. L'île compte cinq tours, quatre de 40 étages et une de 60. Par leur forme, chacune transmettra une esthétique organique et sera essentiellement constituée de verre pour laisser entrer la lumière. Les bâtiments moyennement élevés, situés au nord et à l'ouest des parcs, seront en forme de losange pour réduire l'effet du vent. Les bâtiments peu élevés serviront d'abri aux espaces publics.

L'île comprendra également une ferme biologique, un parc éolien, un espace vert et un nouveau terminal de ferry. Les résidences voisines se trouveront à 10 minutes à pied du terminal de ferry pour encourager un mode de vie sans voiture. Les premiers habitants pourront aménager su l'île en 2013. Le projet devrait être achevé dans son intégralité en 2022.

above Imagined view from the mainland to the island, lit up at dusk.

oben Beispiel für eine Aussicht vom Festland aus auf die in der Abenddämmerung erleuchtete Insel.

ci-dessus Image numérique de l'île depuis la terre, éclairée au coucher du soleil.

Floating Future
Schwimmende Zukunft
Un futur flottant

Cruiseterminal I No Man's Land I Performing Arts Center

Lilypad Project

Global warming and consequential rising sea levels mean that architects are increasingly exploring the possibility of building on water. Whether they are floating on top, hovering over, or submerged beneath the water, the examples presented here offer inventive solutions for the future. The Dutch architects Waterstudio.NL specialize in building structures that float. Indeed, their motto is "The future is wet, the future is ours!" Their ambitious plans include a floating mosque, ferry terminal, and rotating hotel. The Dead Sea project by architect Phu Hoang focuses on the socioeconomic significance of water showing how islands can be used for creating energy and purifying water. Vito Acconci's plan for a floating performance center in South Korea envisages an island that can be flooded. Finally, the Lilypad project imagines ecocities for climate refugees floating around the world's oceans.

previous page Imagined aerial view of the Maldive islands with Vincent Callebaut's floating Lilypads.

vorherige Seite Beispiel eines Luftbilds der Malediven mit Vincent Callebauts schwimmenden Lilypads.

page précédente Vue aérienne des Maldives avec les nénuphars de Callebaut.

left Waterstudio.NL's drawing of their floating ferry terminal.

links Zeichnung des schwimmenden Fährterminals von Waterstudio.NL.

gauche Dessin de Waterstudio.NL du terminal ferry flottant.

En raison du réchauffement climatique et de l'augmentation conséquente du niveau de la mer, les architectes recherchent de plus en plus de possibilités de constructions sur l'eau. Qu'ils flottent, soient suspendus ou immergés dans l'eau, les exemples présentés dans cette partie offrent des solutions innovantes pour l'avenir. Les architectes néerlandais Waterstudio.NL sont spécialisés dans les structures flottantes et ont pour slogan « L'avenir est humide, l'avenir est à nous ! » Leurs plans ambitieux sur l'eau comprennent notamment une mosquée, un terminal de ferry et un hôtel rotatif. Le projet sur la mer Morte par l'architecte Phu Hoang se concentre sur l'importance socio-économique de l'eau et étudie la manière dont les îles peuvent être utilisées pour créer de l'énergie et purifier l'eau. Le projet du Centre des arts scéniques de Vito Acconci en Corée du Sud envisage une île pouvant être immergée. Enfin, le projet Nénuphar imagine des éco-villes dans les océans du monde entier pour les réfugiés climatiques.

Die globale Erderwärmung und die daraus folgende Erhöhung der Meeresspiegel bedeuten, dass Architekten zunehmend über die Möglichkeit nachdenken, auf Wasser zu bauen. Ob auf dem Wasser schwimmend, über dem Wasser schwebend oder ganz unter Wasser erbaut, die hier vorgestellten Beispiele schlagen originelle Lösungen für die Zukunft vor. Die niederländischen Architekten von Waterstudio.NL haben sich auf schwimmende Bauwerke spezialisiert. Ihr Motto ist dementsprechend: „Die Zukunft ist nass, unsere Zukunft!" Ihre ehrgeizigen Entwürfe beinhalten eine schwimmende Moschee, ein Fährterminal und ein rotierendes Hotel. Das Tote-Meer-Projekt des Architekten Phu Hoang legt den Schwerpunkt auf die sozioökonomische Bedeutung des Wassers und zeigt, wie Inseln zur Erzeugung von Energie und zur Aufbereitung von Wasser eingesetzt werden können. Vito Acconcis Entwurf für ein schwimmendes Zentrum für Darstellende Künste sieht eine Insel vor, die geflutet werden kann. Das Lilypad Project schließlich entwirft eine Ökostadt für Klimaflüchtlinge, die auf den Ozeanen der Welt treibt.

Cruiseterminal

Dubai, UAE
Waterstudio.NL

left A combination of shape, size, and surface give the terminal stability.

links Eine Kombination aus Form, Größe und Oberfläche verleihen dem Terminal Stabilität.

gauche Une combinaison de formes, de tailles et de surfaces donne au terminal sa stabilité.

right Masterplan. The terminal will include a hotel, conference center, and shops.

rechts Masterplan. Das Terminal wird ein Hotel, ein Tagungszentrum und Läden enthalten.

droite Plan directeur. Le terminal comprendra un hôtel, un centre de conférences et des boutiques.

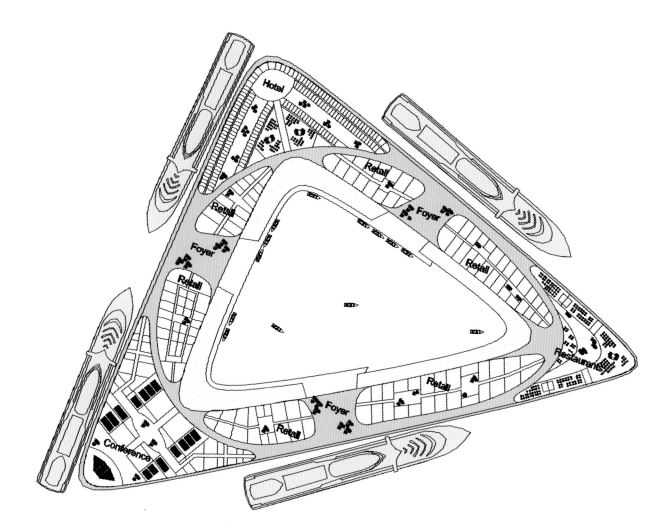

Dutch company Waterstudio are unique for working entirely on buildings on water. One of their most ambitious projects is an enormous floating cruise-ship terminal destined for the Persian Gulf.

Their revolutionary design consists of a floating triangle with an upturned corner. Measuring 2,300 by 2,300 feet, it will be large enough to allow three cruise liners to dock on its outside. Smaller boats will be able to sail under the spectacular entrance arch into the harbor. It will be located far enough out to sea to allow enough draught for even the biggest ships to moor. Water taxis and ferries will transport people to and from the shore.

Construction will be in lightweight material with the arch cantilevered from the main base. Stability has been achieved through a combination of shape, size, and surface; the structure is rigged to a foundation in the seabed via anchoring cables with dampers to allow it to move up and down, but not from side to side. The exterior surface will be clad in aluminum with about 10 percent given to PV-cells to generate electricity on the island.

Due to is vast size, the terminal will have many uses. The corners of the triangle accommodate three large functions—a 180-room hotel, a conference center, and, in the

Das niederländische Unternehmen Waterstudio ist einzigartig, weil es ausschließlich an Gebäuden auf Wasser arbeitet. Eines ihrer ehrgeizigsten Projekte ist ein gigantisches Terminal für Kreuzfahrtschiffe im Persischen Golf.

Der revolutionäre Entwurf besteht aus einem schwimmenden Dreieck mit einer nach oben gewandten Ecke. Mit seiner Fläche (700 x 700 Meter) wird es groß genug sein, um drei Kreuzfahrtschiffe an seinen Außenseiten anlegen zu lassen. Kleinere Boote können unter dem spektakulären Eingangsbogen hindurch in den Hafen fahren. Es soll weit draußen auf See errichtet werden, um selbst Schiffen mit dem größten Tiefgang einen Ankerplatz zu bieten. Wassertaxis und Fähren werden die Passagiere zwischen Terminal und Ufer hin- und hertransportieren.

Der Bau wird mit leichtgewichtigen Materialien erfolgen, wobei der Bogen sich von der Hauptbasis frei erheben soll. Stabilität wird durch die Kombination aus Form, Größe und Oberfläche erzielt; das Bauwerk ist über mit Dämpfern versehenen Ankerkabeln mit einem Fundament auf dem Meeresgrund verzurrt, damit es sich zwar hinauf und hinunter, jedoch nicht seitwärts bewegen kann. Die äußere Oberfläche wird mit Aluminium verkleidet, wobei etwa zehn Prozent der Fläche mit photovoltaischen Zellen ausgestattet sind, um auf der Insel Elektrizität zu erzeugen.

Le cabinet d'architectes néerlandais Waterstudio est unique en son genre car il ne conçoit que des constructions flottantes. L'un de leurs projets les plus ambitieux est un immense terminal ferry-croisière flottant dans le golfe Persique.

Leur projet révolutionnaire est un triangle flottant dont un angle est surélevé. Mesurant 700 mètres sur 700, il sera suffisamment grand pour aligner trois paquebots de croisière à quai. Les bateaux plus petits pourront naviguer sous l'entrée spectaculaire en forme d'arche et se rendre au port. L'île sera placée suffisamment au large pour permettre aux plus gros paquebots de s'amarrer et laisser un tirant suffisant. Des navettes et des ferries transporteront les visiteurs.

La construction comportera des matériaux légers et l'arche sera située en porte-à-faux de la base principale. La stabilité a pu être obtenue grâce à une combinaison de formes, de tailles et de surfaces; la structure est gréée aux fondations dans le fond marin par des câbles d'ancrage avec des amortisseurs pour pouvoir se soulever et s'abaisser sans bouger latéralement. L'extérieur sera revêtu d'aluminium et environ 10% de l'espace sera réservé aux cellules photovoltaïques pour générer l'électricité sur l'île.

En raison de sa taille importante, le terminal aura plusieurs fonctions. Les angles du triangle

above A restaurant will be located in the raised point of the triangle.

oben In dem angehobenen Ende des Dreiecks wird ein Restaurant eingerichtet.

ci-dessus Le sommet du triangle accueillera le restaurant.

right The massive floating terminal is big enough to moor several cruise liners.

rechts Das gewaltige schwimmende Terminal ist groß genug für mehrere Kreuzfahrtschiffe.

droite Le terminal flottant est suffisamment grand pour amarrer plusieurs paquebots de croisière.

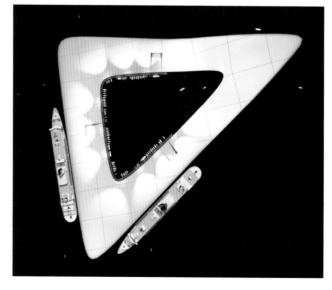

raised point, a 130,000 square foot restaurant with spectacular views over the harbor below. Over half a million square feet of retail space are located inside the structure and visitors will travel around via a circular people mover. At night the terminal will be lit up in blue light.

Aufgrund seiner gewaltigen Größe wird das Terminal vielfache Verwendungszwecke haben. Die Ecken des Dreiecks sollen drei Anlagen beherbergen – ein Hotel mit 180 Räumen, ein Tagungszentrum und an dem angehobenen Ende ein Restaurant mit 12.000 Quadratmetern Fläche und spektakulären Aussichten über den darunter liegenden Hafen. Außerdem sollen in dem Bauwerk über 50.000 Quadratmeter Einzelhandelsflächen angelegt werden und Reisende können sich in einem kreisförmigen Beförderungsmittel fortbewegen. Nachts wird das Terminal blau erleuchtet sein.

accueilleront un hôtel de 180 chambres, un centre de conférences et au sommet, un restaurant de 12 000 mètres carrés avec vue spectaculaire sur le port situé plus bas. Plus de 50 000 mètres carrés de commerces occuperont la structure et les visiteurs pourront se déplacer grâce à une navette circulaire. La nuit, le terminal sera éclairé d'une lumière bleue.

above and above right Small boats can sail under the raised arch to moor on the inside.

oben und oben rechts Kleine Boote können unter dem angehobenen Bogen hindurch fahren, um im Inneren des Terminals anzulegen.

ci-dessus et ci-dessus à droite Les petits bateaux pourront passer sous l'arche pour s'amarrer à l'intérieur.

No Man's Land

Dead Sea Region
Phu Hoang Office

Phu Hoang is a Vietnamese-born architect who founded his own studio in New York in 2004, after having worked with Michael Hopkins and Bernard Tschumi. His "No Man's Land" project has attracted a great deal of attention and been shortlisted for numerous environment prizes.

The studio makes a point of stressing that their work "explores the often overlooked intersections between culture and geopolitics." This hypothetical study looks at how architecture can resolve the problem of a rapidly receding sea and the effect this will have on tourist resorts. Their solution is to create a network of artificial islands moored in the Dead Sea. As the water recedes this area is destined to become a "no man's region" as the old boundaries will no longer be applicable.

The idea is that the islands will provide tourist facilities, water collection, and renewable energy production. One set of islands, for tourists, will create different climate zones—dry forest, arid desert, and humid tropical—all floating on a large structure. A second will be used to create energy through a solar pond and an energy downdraft tower. The third will be a water island where water molecules from the humid air above the water will be extracted. The proposal suggests the shifting of water supply conditions in the region, thereby providing conditions for political change.

Phu Hoang ist ein aus Vietnam stammender Architekt, der 2004 in New York sein eigenes Büro gründete, nachdem er mit Michael Hopkins und Bernard Tschumi zusammengearbeitet hatte. Sein Projekt „No Man's Land" hat große Aufmerksamkeit erregt und wurde für zahlreiche Umweltpreise nominiert.

Sein Studio legt Wert darauf zu betonen, dass seine Arbeit „die häufig übersehenen Schnittstellen zwischen Kultur und Geopolitik erkundet". Die hypothetische Studie erforscht, wie Architektur das Problem eines schnell sinkenden Meeresspiegels und dessen Auswirkungen auf Ferienorte für Touristen lösen kann. Die Lösung sieht die Schaffung eines Netzwerks von künstlichen, im Toten Meer verankerten Inseln vor. Angesichts des schwindenden Wassers ist die Region dazu bestimmt, zum „Niemandsland" zu werden, da die alten Grenzen nicht länger gültig sein werden.

Seine Vorstellung beinhaltet, dass die Inseln Einrichtungen für Touristen, zur Sammlung von Wasser und zur Erzeugung von Energie enthalten sollen. Eine Gruppe von Inseln für Touristen wird verschiedene Klimazonen nachbilden – ein trockenes Waldgebiet, eine ausgedörrte Wüste und feuchte Tropen – und jede davon soll auf einer großen Struktur schwimmen. Eine zweite Gruppe wird zur Erzeugung von Energie durch einen Solarteich und einen Energieabwindturm dienen. Bei der dritten handelt es sich um eine Wasserinsel, die der feuchten Luft über dem Wasser Wassermoleküle entziehen soll. Der Entwurf sieht vor, die Wasserversorgungsbedingungen in der Region zu verändern und dadurch Voraussetzungen für politische Veränderungen zu schaffen.

Phu Hoang, architecte d'origine japonaise, a ouvert son propre cabinet en 2004, après avoir travaillé avec Michael Hopkins et Bernard Tschumi. Son projet « No Man's Land » a fait l'objet d'un grand intérêt et a été sélectionné pour de nombreux prix environnementaux.

Les architectes du cabinet soulignent que leur travail « explore les intersections souvent ignorées entre culture et géopolitique ». Cette étude conceptuelle observe la manière dont l'architecture peut résoudre le problème d'une mer qui s'éloigne rapidement et l'impact sur les complexes touristiques. Leur solution consiste à créer un réseau d'îles artificielles amarré dans la mer Morte. Comme l'eau tend à y disparaître, cette région est destinée à devenir une « no man's region », puisque les anciennes frontières ne seront plus applicables.

L'idée consiste à offrir des installations touristiques, des systèmes de récupération des eaux et de production d'énergie renouvelable sur ces îles. Un premier groupe destiné aux touristes offrira différentes zones climatiques – une forêt sèche, un désert aride, et des tropiques humides. Tous les îlots flotteront sur une large structure. Un second groupe sera utilisé pour créer de l'énergie grâce à un bassin solaire et une tour énergétique. Le troisième sera consacré à l'eau et extraira les molécules d'eau contenues dans l'air chargé d'humidité. Le projet propose le changement des conditions d'approvisionnement en eau dans la région et offre ainsi des conditions au changement politique.

left A network of artificial islands moored in the Dead Sea.

links Ein Netzwerk künstlicher, im Toten Meer verankerter Inseln.

gauche Un réseau d'îles artificielles amarré dans la mer Morte.

right Some islands will be used as holiday resorts, others to generate energy or purify water.

rechts Einige Inseln finden als Ferienanlagen Verwendung, andere zur Erzeugung von Energie oder zur Wasseraufbereitung.

droite Certaines îles accueilleront des complexes touristiques, d'autres seront destinées à la production d'énergie ou à la purification de l'eau.

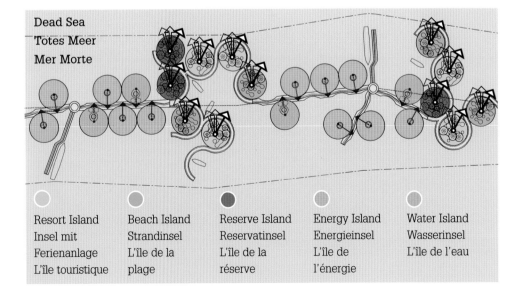

Dead Sea
Totes Meer
Mer Morte

Resort Island	Beach Island	Reserve Island	Energy Island	Water Island
Insel mit Ferienanlage	Strandinsel	Reservatinsel	Energieinsel	Wasserinsel
L'île touristique	L'île de la plage	L'île de la réserve	L'île de l'énergie	L'île de l'eau

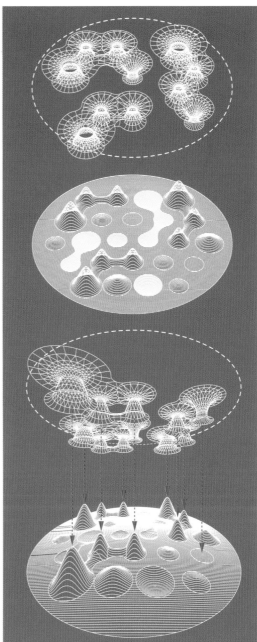

above An ambition is to develop building technology which extracts water molecules from the humid air above the sea.

oben Ein Anspruch besteht darin, eine Bautechnik zu entwickeln, die der feuchten Luft über dem Meer Wassermoleküle entzieht.

ci-dessus Un des projets consiste à développer une technologie capable d'extraire les molécules d'eau de l'air humide en suspension au-dessus de la mer.

left An imagined rendering of a resort island—there will be different climates in each dome.

links Beispiel einer Darstellung für eine Insel mit einer Ferienanlage – unter jeder Kuppel soll ein unterschiedliches Klima herrschen.

gauche Image numérique d'une île touristique. Chaque dôme aura un climat différent.

Performing Arts Center

Seoul, Korea
Acconci Studio

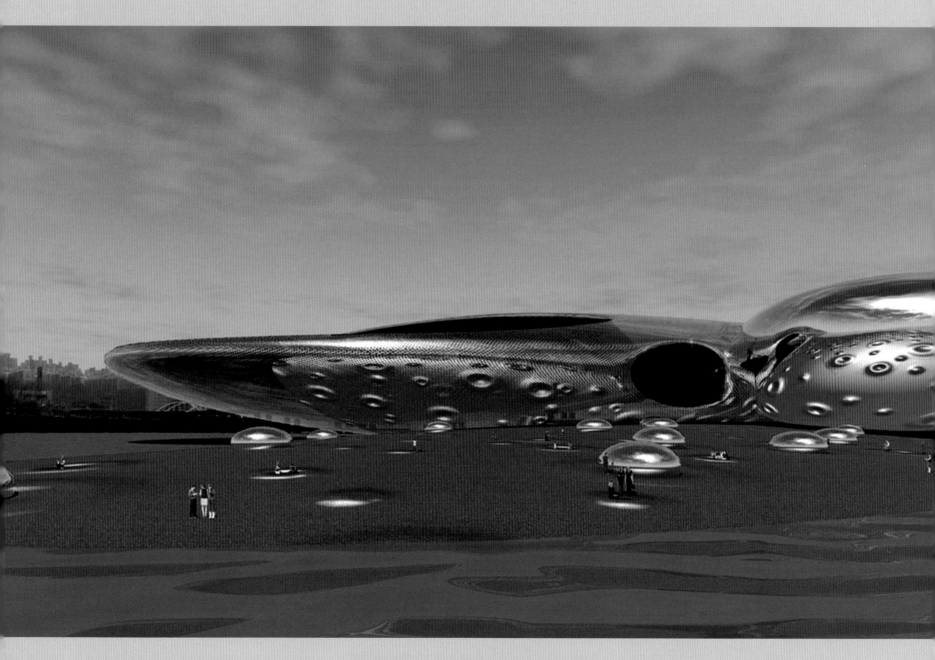

above The island's surface has neither vegetation nor buildings in order to make it floodable.

oben Ansicht des flutbaren Fundaments der Insel unter der Wasseroberfläche. Auf der linken Seite sind kleine, schwimmende Hotelkapseln sichtbar.

ci-dessus La surface de l'île ne comporte ni végétation ni constructions, afin de pouvoir être immergée.

below Showing the floodable island base below water level. Small hotel pods can be seen floating to the left.

unten Das flutbare Fundament der Insel über der Wasseroberfläche.

ci-dessous Base de l'île immersible. On aperçoit les petits dômes des hôtels à gauche.

below right The floodable island base above water level.

unten rechts Eine Brücke führt durch die Mitte des Kunstzentrums.

ci-dessous à droite La base de l'île immersible, ici au-dessus du niveau de la mer.

Vito Acconci has a reputation for coming up with truly outlandish designs. With his background in conceptual art, his architecture plays with the idea of "dissolving barriers." Although few of his designs actually have been made—his most famous to date is Mur Island (see page 36)—his ideas are always worth considering.

This design from 2005 for a Performing Arts Center in Korea is the stuff of science fiction. The arts center—an organically-shaped, mirrored "spaceship"—is cantilevered off a floodable island base, hovering above the Aangyang River. A bridge is sucked through the middle of the island building.

The island's surface is totally barren, like an alien planet, the color changing with its contours, from red to pink to purple. People can walk in and out of its crevices or sit in its craters. When the river floods, the floodable part of the island is unaffected as there are neither buildings nor greenery to wash away. Around the base, individual hotel capsules—little glass domes—are tethered to the ground by pistons which float up when the water rises.

Vito Acconci hat einen Ruf für wirklich ausgefallene Entwürfe. Mit seinem Hintergrund in konzeptioneller Kunst spielt seine Architektur mit der Idee, „Barrieren aufzulösen". Obwohl nur wenige seiner Entwürfe tatsächlich ausgeführt wurden – sein wohl berühmtester ist die Insel in der Mur (vgl. Seite 36) – sind seine Ideen immer beachtenswert.

Dieser Entwurf für ein Zentrum für Darstellende Künste in Korea aus dem Jahr 2005 ist aus dem Stoff gemacht, aus dem Science-Fiction-Romane entstehen. Das Kunstzentrum – ein organisch geformtes verspiegeltes „Raumschiff" – ist eine Auskragung über einem flutbaren Inselfundament über dem Fluss Hangang. Eine Brücke wird durch die Mitte des Gebäudes eingesaugt.

Die Oberfläche der Insel ist vollkommen unwirtlich, wie ein fremder Planet; die Farbe ändert sich mit ihren Konturen, von rot zu rosa zu purpurn. Besucher können aus ihren Spalten hinaus- und wieder hineingehen oder in ihren Kratern sitzen. Wenn der Fluss Hochwasser führt, ist der flutbare Teil der Insel davon nicht betroffen, da dort keine Vegetation vorhanden ist, die fortgespült werden könnte. Um das Fundament herum sind einzelne Hotelkapseln wie Glaskuppeln mit Kolben am Boden angebunden, die aufsteigen, sobald das Wasser ansteigt.

Vito Acconci est réputé pour ses ouvrages souvent étranges. Avec son expérience en art conceptuel, son architecture joue avec l'idée de « dissolution des barrières ». Bien que peu de ses conceptions aient été construites, sa plus célèbre à ce jour étant l'Île de la Mur (voir page 36), ses idées valent toujours d'être étudiées.

Cette conception de 2005 pour un Centre des arts scéniques en Corée s'apparente à de la science-fiction. Le Centre des arts, un « vaisseau spatial » de forme organique avec un revêtement miroir, est mis en porte-à-faux sur une base flottante immersible, au-dessus du fleuve Aangyang. Un pont traverse le centre du bâtiment flottant.

La surface de l'île est entièrement nue, telle une planète étrangère; sa couleur vire du rouge au rose, en passant par le violet. Les visiteurs peuvent entrer et sortir de ses fissures ou s'asseoir dans les cratères et lorsque le fleuve monte, la partie inférieure de l'île est immergée. La construction, ne comportant ni bâtiment ni végétation, n'en est pas affectée. Autour de la base, des capsules individuelles (de petits dômes en verre) sont reliés au sol par des pistons, qui remontent en même temps que l'eau.

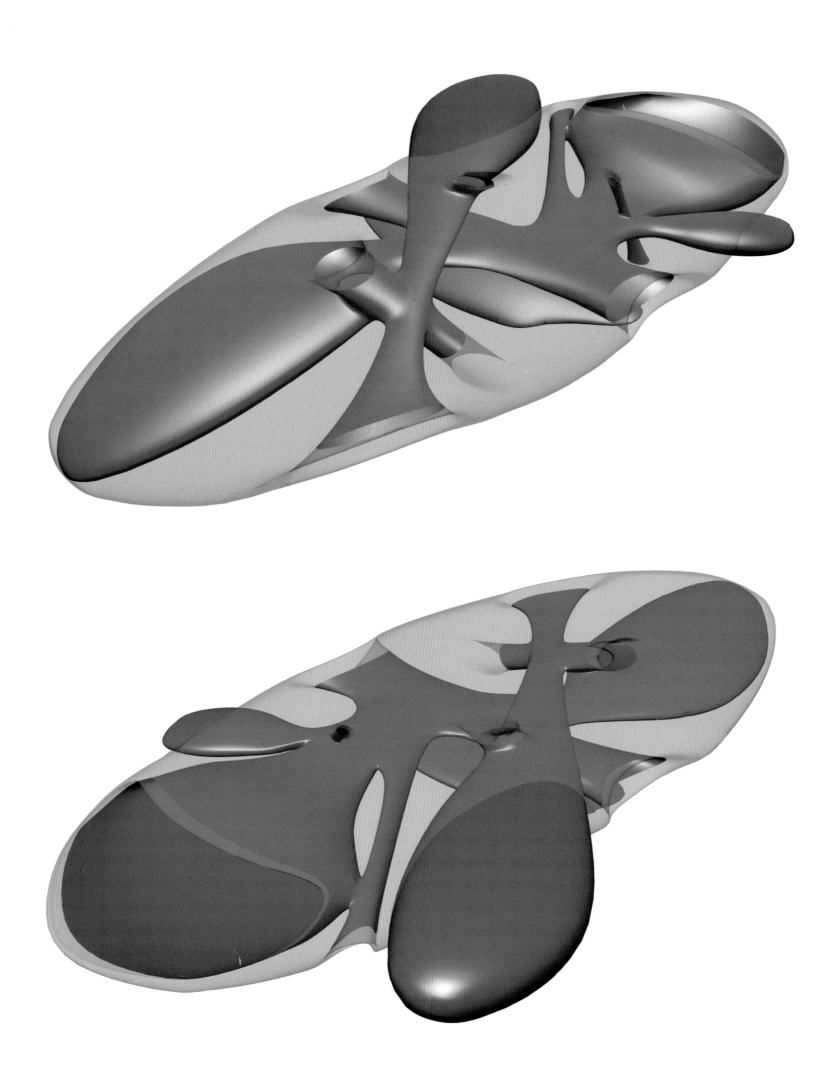

left The shape of the center is inspired by natural organs, illustrated by these computer-generated images.

links Die Form des Zentrums ist von natürlichen Organen inspiriert, wie diese mit dem Computer erzeugten Bilder zeigen.

ci-dessous à droite Un pont traverse le Centre des arts scéniques.

above Natural vegetation, such as trees, will be grown inside, rather than outside, the performing arts center.

oben Statt außen wird im Inneren des Zentrums für Darstellende Künste natürliche Vegetation, wie etwa Bäume, angepflanzt.

page suivante La surface de l'île ne comporte ni végétation ni construction afin de pouvoir être recouverte d'eau.

Lilypad Project

Vincent Callebaut Architectures

As water levels rise throughout the world as a consequence of global warming, relocating displaced people will become an increasing priority. Low-lying countries, such as the Netherlands, Bangladesh, and the Maldives, it is predicted, will be particularly affected losing large proportions of their land area.

One obvious solution is to reclaim land or build protective dams. Another is to build island cities. A young Belgian architect, Vincent Callebaut, has produced a series of detailed drawings of what he calls a "floating Ecopolis." These lilypad-shaped islands could be nomadic, floating from the equator to the poles following the warm Gulf Stream north or the cold Labrador Current south, or they could be moored off the coast of existing cities, such as Monaco.

Its structure, mainly steel and glass, is inspired by the Victoria Waterlily, a remarkably large and strong water plant. A double outer skin will be made of polyester fibers and titanium oxide designed to absorb carbon dioxide from the atmosphere. The idea is that the islands will be self-sustaining using a combination of renewable energies, including solar, thermal, wind, and tidal power. Rainwater will be recycled from a huge lagoon immersed below sea level in the center of the island that acts as a ballast for the structure.

Da die Wasserspiegel weltweit aufgrund der globalen Erderwärmung ansteigen, wird die Umsiedlung heimatloser Menschen zu einer zunehmenden Priorität werden. Tief liegende Länder wie die Niederlande, Bangladesh und die Malediven werden aller Voraussicht nach besonders betroffen sein und einen Großteil ihrer Bodenfläche verlieren.

Eine offensichtliche Lösung für das Problem ist die Wiedergewinnung von Land oder der Bau von Schutzdämmen. Eine weitere ist die Anlage von Inselstädten. Ein junger belgischer Architekt namens Vincent Callebaut hat eine Reihe detaillierter Zeichnungen angefertigt, die darstellen, was er eine „schwimmende Ökopolis" nennt. Diese wie die Blätter einer Wasserlilie geformten Inseln könnten nomadisch sein und vom Äquator bis zu den Polen treiben, dem warmen Golfstrom nach Norden folgen oder dem kalten Labradorstrom nach Süden. Sie könnten aber auch im Küstenbereich vor bestehenden Städten wie Monaco verankert werden.

Ihre Struktur, die hauptsächlich aus Stahl und Glas besteht, ist von der Wasserlilie Victoria inspiriert, einer bemerkenswert großen und starken Wasserpflanze. Eine doppelte äußere Haut aus Polyesterfasern und Titanoxid soll Kohlendioxid aus der Luft aufnehmen. Nach der Vorstellung des Architekten sind die Inseln so

Avec le réchauffement climatique et la montée des eaux, il deviendra urgent de se reloger. Selon les prévisions, les pays de faible altitude tels que les Pays-Bas, le Bengladesh et les Maldives, seront particulièrement touchés et perdront une part importante de leur territoire.

Une solution évidente consiste à rapporter de la terre ou à construire des barrages de protection. Une autre consiste à construire des villes flottantes. Un jeune architecte belge, Vincent Callebaut, a réalisé une série de dessins détaillés de ce qu'il appelle une « Écopolis flottante ». Ces îles en forme de nénuphars pourraient être nomades, flottant de l'équateur aux pôles, en suivant les courants chauds du Gulf Stream vers le Nord ou les eaux froides du courant du Labrador vers le Sud, où elles pourraient être amarrées au large des côtes des villes existantes, comme Monaco.

La structure, principalement en acier et en verre copie le nénuphar géant, une plante aquatique imposante et solide. Une double peau extérieure sera constituée de fibres de polyester et d'oxyde de titane, capable d'absorber le dioxyde de carbone de l'atmosphère. Les îles seraient indépendantes grâce à une combinaison d'énergies renouvelables, dont l'énergie solaire, thermique, éolienne et marémotrice. Les eaux de pluie seraient

right Floating islands could follow the ocean's currents.

rechts Schwimmende Inseln, die den Strömen des Ozeans folgen könnten.

droite Les îles flottantes pourraient suivre les courants de l'océan.

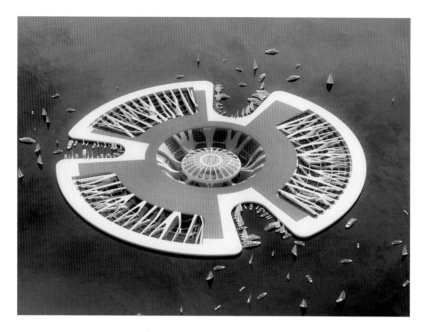

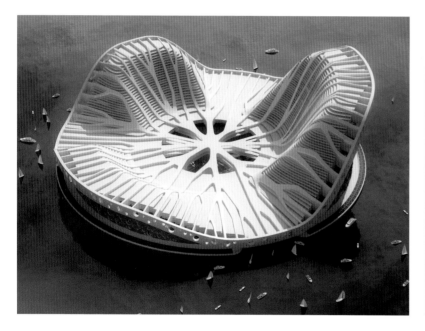

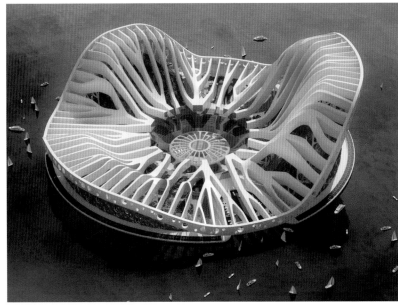

left Like a waterlily, the islands could "grow" organically, building up layer upon layer.

links Wie Wasserlilien könnten die Inseln organisch „wachsen" und Schicht über Schicht bebaut werden.

gauche Comme des nénuphars, les îles pourraient « pousser » de manière organique, les couches se créant les unes sur les autres.

right Imagined night view of the floating Ecopolis off the coast of Monaco.

rechts Beispiel einer Nacht-ansicht der schwimmenden Ecopolis vor der Küste Monacos.

droite Image numérique d'une vue de nuit de l'Ecopolis flottante, au large de Monaco.

below These floating islands could be moored to existing ports to allow for city expansion.

unten Die schwimmenden Inseln könnten an vorhandenen Häfen verankert werden, um die Erweiterung bestehender Städte zu ermöglichen.

ci-dessous Ces îles flottantes pourraient être amarrées aux ports existants pour permettre aux villes de s'étendre.

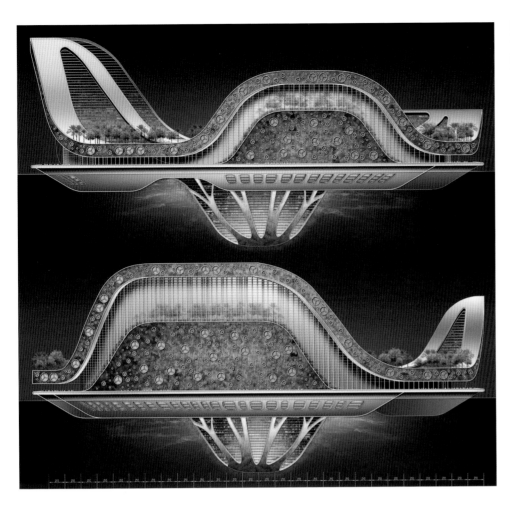

The same underwater glass bowl could be used for commercial and leisure areas, while above sea level a layer of housing with hanging gardens will be criss-crossed with streets and alleyways. Each island will have three marinas and three mountain ridges and will be able to accommodate as many as 50,000 people with offices, residences, shops, and entertainment areas. Clearly, the work of science fiction, Callebaut's vision does, nonetheless, offer a possible glimpse into the far future of island architecture.

angelegt, dass sie sich mit Hilfe einer Kombination erneuerbarer Energien wie Sonne, Wärme, Wind und Gezeiten selbst versorgen können. Aus einer riesigen, unter dem Meeresspiegel liegenden Lagune in der Mitte der Insel, die außerdem als Ballast für das Bauwerk dient, wird Regenwasser aufbereitet.

Die gleiche Unterwasser-Glasschüssel könnte außerdem für Gewerbe- und Freizeitzwecke genutzt werden, während über dem Meeresspiegel eine Schicht von Wohnhäusern mit hängenden Gärten kreuz und quer von Straßen und Gassen durchzogen wird. Jede Insel wird über drei Häfen und drei Bergzüge verfügen und bis zu 50.000 Menschen sowie Büros, Wohngebäude, Läden und Unterhaltungsbereiche aufnehmen können. Obgleich ganz eindeutig ein Werk aus dem Bereich Science Fiction, bietet Callebauts Vision trotzdem einen möglichen Einblick in die langfristige Zukunft der Inselarchitektur.

récupérées dans un immense lagon immergé sous le niveau de la mer, situé au centre de l'île, et qui servirait de ballast à la structure.

La même coupe de verre immergée pourrait être utilisée pour créer des espaces commerciaux et de loisirs, tandis qu'au-dessus du niveau de la mer, des hébergements et des jardins suspendus croiseraient les rues et ruelles. Chaque île comporterait trois marinas, trois élévations et pourrait accueillir 50 000 personnes avec bureaux, résidences, boutiques et espaces de loisirs. La vision de Vincent Callebaut, tout droit sortie de la science-fiction, offre néanmoins un aperçu possible de l'architecture flottante dans un futur lointain.

Picture Credits/Bildnachweis/
Crédits photographiques

Images in the book are courtesy of the following:
Abbildungen in diesem Buch mit freundlicher Genehmigung von:
Les photographies présentes dans ce livre nous ont été fournies avec l'aimable autorisation de :

Aluminium Centrum 20-27
Willem Franken Architectuurfotografie: 20, 22, 23, 24bl, 25, 26, 27
Abbink x De Haas Architectures: 21, 24t

Benesse House Museum and Oval 72–77
© Tadao Ando Architect & Associates:
Mitsuo Matsuoka: 72, 74r, 75l, 75r.
Tadao Ando: 71t, 76–77
Tadao Ando Architect & Associates: 73, 74l

Bulgari Resort 236–245
Bulgari Hotel and Resorts: 215b, 236–245

Burj Al Arab 216–221
Getty Images/Robert Harding World Imagery/Amanda Hall: 217
Atkins/Jumeirah: 218, 219, 220, 221

Central Park Grin Grin 276–283
Hiroyasu Sakaguchi: 269b, 276–277, 278b, 280t, 281t, 281b 282
Toyo Ito & Associates Architects: 277t, 278t, 279, 283

Cruiseterminal 338–341
Waterstudio.NL and Dutch Docklands: 336, 338–341

Crystal Island 316–321
© Foster + Partners: 4–5, 302, 316–321

Dellis Cay 246–257
© Property Collection/dbox Inc: 212, 246–247, 248, 249, 250, 251, 257b
Hayes Davidson: 251, 252b, 254t, 255b, 256, 257t
Zaha Hadid Architects: 252t
Shigeru Ban Architects: 254b, 255t

Earth Spa 230–235
DWP: 215t, 230–235

Federation Island 298–301
© Erick van Egeraat associated architects: 298–301

Elbphilharmonie 120–123
© Herzog & de Meuron: 120–123

Floating House 174-181
Florian Holzherr: 151, 174–175, 176b, 178t, 178b, 179t, 179b, 180, 181
MOS: 175t, 176t, 177t

Guggenheim Abu Dhabi Museum 144–147
TDIC: 144–147

Hong Luo Club 190–197
MAD: 150, 190–197

Kansai International Airport 270–275
© John Edward Linden/arcaid.co.uk: 270, 274
© Renzo Piano Building Workshop:
Shinkenchi-hu-sha: 268, 271
Rpbw: 272
Sky Front's: 273t
Kawatetsu: 273b
Gianni Berengo Gardin: 275

Kastrup Sea Bath 42–49
Åke E:son Lindman: 19t, 43, 46–47, 48b, 49
Ole Haupt: 44t
White Arkitekter: 44b, 45, 48t

Lakeside Studio 182–189
© Mark Dziewulski Architect:
Keith Cronin: 148, 183, 184, 185, 186t, 188, 189
Mark Dziewulski: 185, 187b

Liangzhu Culture Museum 102–109
© Christian Richters: 70, 103, 104t, 106t, 106b, 107, 108–109
© David Chipperfield Architects: 104
© David Chipperfield: 105

Lilypad Project 350–355
© Vincent Callebaut Architectures: 337b, 350–355

Louvre Abu Dhabi 124–131
© Ateliers Jean Nouvel: 124–131

Maison Flottante 206–211
© Paul Tahon and R & E Bouroullec 206, 207, 209b, 210, 211
© Paul Tahon 209t

Maritime Museum 138–143
© Tadao Ando Architect & Associates: 138–143
Tomio Ohashi: 139, 140t, 141

Mur Island 36–41
© Nicholas Crane/arcaid.co.uk: 36
Acconci Studio: 37, 39, 40, 41
Harry Schiffer: 2, 38

Architects/Architekten/Architectes

Abbink X De Haas Architectures
Amsterdam, the Netherlands
www.abbinkdehaas.nl
Aluminium Centrum

Acconci Studio
Brooklyn, New York, USA
www.acconci.com
Mur Island; Performing Arts Center

A-cero Studio and Joaquín Torres & Rafael Llamazares architects
Madrid, Spain
www.a-cero.com
Wave Tower

Tadao Ando Architect & Associates
Osaka, Japan
Benesse House Museum and Oval; Maritime Museum

Paul Andreu
Paris, France
www.paul-andreu.com
National Center for Performing Arts

Atkins Design Studio
Epsom, Surrey, UK
www.atkinsdesign.com
Burj Al Arab; The Palm Jumeirah

AW2 (Architecture Workshop 2)
Issy-les-Moulineaux, France
www.aw2.net
Nurai Resort and Hotel

Shigeru Ban Architects
Tokyo, Japan
www.shigerubanarchitects.com
Dellis Cay

Ronan & Erwan Bouroullec
Paris, France
www.bouroullec.com
Maison Flottante

Vincent Callebaut Architectures
Paris, France
www.vincent.callebaut.org
Lilypad Project

C&C Studio (Carl Ettensperger)
Singapore, Singapore
www.ccstudiodesign.com
Dellis Cay

David Chipperfield Architects
London, UK
www.davidchipperfield.co.uk
Liangzhu Culture Museum; Dellis Cay

Antonio Citterio and Partners
Milan, Italy
www.antoniocitterioandpartners.it
Bulgari Resort

Denniston International Architects & Planners Ltd
Kuala Lumpur, Malaysia
www.denniston.com
Reethi Rah

DWP (Design Worldwide Partnership)
Bangkok, Thailand
www.dwp.com
Earth Spa

Mark Dziewulski Architect
San Francisco, USA
www.dzarchitect.com
Lakeside Studio

EEA (Erick van Egeraat associated architects)
Rotterdam, the Netherlands
www.eea-architects.com
Federation Island

Exposure Architects
Bergamo, Italy
www.exposurearchitects.com
Octospider

Foster + Partners
London, UK
www.fosterandpartners.com
New Holland Island; Crystal Island

Gehry Partners, LLP
Los Angeles, USA
www.gehrypartners.com
Guggenheim Abu Dhabi Museum

Architectuurstudio HH Architects and Urban Designers
Amsterdam, the Netherlands
www.hertzberger.nl
Watervilla (Middelburg)

Zaha Hadid Architects
London, UK
www.zaha-hadid.com
Performing Arts Center; Dellis Cay; Zorrozaurre

Herzog & de Meuron Architekten
Basel, Switzerland
Elbphilharmonie

Phu Hoang Office, llc
New York, USA
www.phuhoang.com
No Man's Land

Toyo Ito & Associates, Architects
Tokyo, Japan
www.toyo-ito.co.jp
Central Park Grin Grin

Kengo Kuma & Associates
Tokyo, Japan
www.kkaa.co.jp
Water/Glass Guest House; Dellis Cay

Lissoni Associati
Milan, Italy
www.lissoniassociati.it
Dellis Cay

Lundgaard & Tranberg Arkitekter A/S
Copenhagen, Denmark
www.ltarkitekter.dk
Royal Danish Playhouse

MAD
Beijing, China
www.i-mad.com
Hong Luo Club; Sanya Phoenx Island

MOS
www.mos-office.net
Floating House

Neutelings Riedijk Architects
Rotterdam, the Netherlands
www.neutelings-riedijk.com
Sphinxes Lake Side Housing

Vo Trong Nghia Co. Ltd
Ho Chi Minh City, Vietnam
www.votrongnghia.com
wNw Bar

Ateliers Jean Nouvel
Paris, France
www.jeannouvel.com
Louvre Abu Dhabi

OMA (Office for Metropolitan Architecture)
Rotterdam, the Netherlands
www.oma.nl
Waterfront City Island

Pei Cobb Freed & Partners Architects LLP
New York, USA
www.pcfandp.com
Museum of Islamic Art

Renzo Piano Building Workshop
Genoa, Italy
www.renzopiano.com
Kansai International Airport

Skidmore, Owings & Merrill LLP
San Francisco, USA
www.som.com
Treasure Island

Snøhetta AS
Oslo, Norway
www.snoarc.no
Oslo Opera House

Studio Dror
New York, USA
www.studiodror.com
Nurai Resort and Hotel

Studio Tamassociati
Venice, Italy
www.tamassociati.org
Prayer and Meditation Pavilion

Joke Vos Architecten
Rotterdam, the Netherlands
www.jokevos.nl
Periscope Houses

Waterstudio.NL
Rijswijk, the Netherlands
www.waterstudio.nl
Watervilla (Aalsmeer); *Cruiseterminal*

White Arkitekter AB
Gothenberg, Sweden
www.white.se
Kastrup Sea Bath

Wilmotte et Associés
Paris, France
www.wilmotte.fr
Museum of Islamic Art

Acknowledgments
Danksagung
Remerciements

© 2009 Tandem Verlag GmbH
h.f.ullmann is an imprint of Tandem Verlag GmbH

Book concept Dania D'Eramo, Mark Fletcher
Book and cover design John Round Design
Project coordination Dania D'Eramo

Coordination of the translations Textcase, Utrecht
Translation into German Daniela Gieseler-Higgs (for Textcase)
Translation into French Sophie Montigny (for Textcase)

Printed in China

ISBN 978-3-8331-5200-9

10 9 8 7 6 5 4 3 2 1
X IX VIII VII VI V IV III II I

If you like to be informed about forthcoming h.f.ullmann titles, you can request our newsletter by visiting our website (www.ullmann-publishing.com) or by emailing us at: newsletter@ullmann-publishing.com.
h.f.ullmann, Im Mühlenbruch 1, 53639 Königswinter, Germany
Fax: +49(0)2223-2780-708

The idea for this book came from my commissioning editor, Dania D'Eramo, who proved an excellent and patient editor. John Round produced a very intelligent and beautiful design. I would also like to thank all the architects, studios, photographers, and companies who cooperated in the making of this book by supplying invaluable information and pictures.

For special help in procuring material, I am indebted to Carmen Andrade, Yasmin Attallah, Dror Benshetrit, Dianne Beukema, Ronan & Erwan Bouroullec, Vincent Callebaut, Richard Davies, Eva de Bruijn, Micha de Haas, Mark Dziewulski, Willem Franken, Michael Freeman, Marina Garcia-Vasquez, Jean-Michel Gathy, Oliviero Godi, Phu Hoang, Katie Hodge, Florian Holzherr, Joann Hong, Charlotte Huisman, Tom James, Barbara Janssen, Alexandra Jenal, Ned Kihn, Eunice Kim, Eva Leoz, Sophie Levent, Jens Markus Lindhe, Dee McCourt, Jeroen Musch, Ann Nilsson, Jens Øblom, Hiroshi Okamoto, Laura Quickfall, Eva-Maria Rabini, Carole Rami, Pam Raymond, Christian Richters, Hiro Sakaguchi, Hilary Sample, Kelly Smith, Patcharalai Sripattanakul, Ankie Stam, Kathryn Tollervey, Miki Uono, Herman H. Van Doorn, Eveline van Engelen, Anette Vidnes, Masataka Yano, and Maria Zedler.

I have made every effort to trace and contact copyright holders of the illustrations reproduced in this book; I will be happy to correct in subsequent editions any errors or omissions that are brought to my attention. The images in this book are a mixture of photographs and computer renderings. In some cases the renderings will not appear as realistic as the actual photographs as they are intended to be representative of what the building will look like when finished.

And finally, I would like to dedicate this book to my late father, T.C. Fletcher, who sadly died while I was writing it. He would, in his own inimitable way, have been quietly pleased.